America's Japan and Japan's Performing Arts

America's Japan and Japan's Performing Arts

Cultural Mobility and Exchange in New York, 1952–2011

BARBARA E. THORNBURY

The University of Michigan Press
Ann Arbor

First paperback edition 2016

Published in the United States of America by
The University of Michigan Press
Manufactured in the United States of America
♾ Printed on acid-free paper

2019 2018 2017 2016 5 4 3 2

A CIP catalog record for this book is available from the British Library.

Library of Congress Cataloging-in-Publication Data

Thornbury, Barbara E.
America's Japan and Japan's performing arts : cultural mobility and exchange in New York, 1952–2011 / Barbara Thornbury.
pages cm
Includes bibliographical references.
ISBN 978-0-472-11885-4 (hardback) — ISBN 978-0-472-02928-0 (e-book)
1. Theater—United States—History—20th century. 2. Theater—United States—History—21st century. 3. Performing arts—Japan—Influence 4. Intercultural communication in the performing arts. I. Title.
PN2266.5.T48 2013
792.0973"0904—dc23 2013000017

ISBN 978-0-472-03678-3 (paper)

For Don

Acknowledgments

There are many I wish to thank.

For taking the time to answer my questions and for their assistance along the way: Yoshiko Chuma, Rachel Cooper, Ximena Garnica, John Gillespie, Beate Gordon, Paula Lawrence, Samuel Leiter, Carol Martin, Kenji Matsumoto, Naoyuki Miura, Aya Ogawa, Yukihiro Ohira, Mari Ono, Eiko Otake, Nigel Redden, J. Thomas Rimer, Ralph Samuelson, Somei Sato, Noriko Sengoku, Yoko Shioya, Bonnie Sue Stein, Kei Takei, Tadashi Uchino, John Weidman, John Wheeler, and Kumiko Yoshii.

For archival resources: Japan Society's C. V. Starr Library, Temple University Library, Princeton University Library, the New York Public Library for the Performing Arts, Waseda University Library, and the Tsubouchi Memorial Theatre Museum at Waseda University.

For permission granted by the following copyright holders and publishers to use material from previously published articles, in reworked and expanded form: the University of Hawai'i Press for "America's *Kabuki*-Japan, 1952–1960: Image-Building, Myth-Making, and Cultural Exchange," *Asian Theatre Journal* 25, no. 2 (2008), 193–230; VWB (Verlag für Wissenschaft und Bildung) for "Cultural Policy and Private Initiative: The Performing Arts at the Japan Society, New York," *World of Music* 46, no. 2 (2004): 123–36; and Johns Hopkins University Press for "Negotiating the Foreign: Language, American Audiences, and Theatre from Japan," *Theatre Journal* 61, no. 2 (2009), 249–69.

For feedback and stimulating conversations: fellow panelists and colleagues at meetings of the Modern Language Association, Mid-Atlantic Association for Asian Studies, Association for Asian Performance, and the Global Temple Conference.

For research funding: Temple University's College of Liberal Arts.

I would also like to express my gratitude to LeAnn Fields, Senior Executive Editor at the University of Michigan Press, for her interest in and support of my project, and to the readers of my work for all of their comments and suggestions.

Contents

Japanese Names and Terms

Scholars normally place family names before given names except in the case of people who reside or are professionally established outside of Japan. Because almost every artist to whom I refer in my study has presented his or her work in the United States, I have decided to apply that exception across the board. It will help avoid confusion and will mesh with the way names are rendered in the newspaper and magazine reviews and articles that form the bulk of my citations. Also for the sake of consistency, I have mostly dispensed with the use of macrons to mark long vowels in names and terms except when transcribing the Japanese titles of plays, books, and articles, as well as in cases where I quote other writers who use macrons. I have followed the convention of writing "noh" (instead of "no" for *nō*) and "butoh" (instead of "buto" for *butō*).

Introduction

It may not be *their*, but it is certainly *our* Japan.[1]

Q: Can you tell us a little more about what Americans perceive as Japan-ness?
A: For instance, it could be things like the stage set is extremely elaborately designed and constructed.
Q: Is it a kind of fetishism?
A: Well, you could say so.[2]

Eiko and Koma are quintessentially Japanese, and also longtime New York residents.[3]

This book is a study of the images and myths that have defined and shaped the reception of Japan-related theater, music, and dance in the United States since the postwar 1950s. In the mid-1980s, at the height of fierce trade tensions between the United States and Japan, Clyde Haberman reported in the *New York Times*, "Japanese contend that the trouble is not their lingering restrictions so much as American laziness in attempting to penetrate this country's markets. Learn our language, Prime Minister Yasuhiro Nakasone has said many times. Study our culture. 'Americans don't try hard enough' is a favorite catch phrase." Haberman contended, "The accusation infuriates many American executives, who feel that they could watch Kabuki plays all day and still get nowhere."[4]

The executives' angry sarcasm was rooted in a paradoxical fact. The American-led Occupation had targeted kabuki—especially its repertory of "feudal" plays such as *The Treasury of Loyal Retainers* (*Kanadehon chūshingura*)—as a cultural activity unsuited to a newly democratic Japan. But even before the Occupation ended in 1952, the art form was suddenly being put forward to the cold-war American public as a uniquely authentic example of Japanese culture. The kabuki boosters included a host of American theater professionals and writers—three Pulitzer Prize winners among them—eagerly intent on helping rehabilitate the image of Japan as a friend of the United States in a world where the Soviet Union had now become the foe. The effects linger: although the economic and political climate has greatly changed, kabuki is still a major element in American understanding of Japanese culture.

I look at how "Japan" and "Japanese culture" have been discursively constructed, reconstructed, and transformed in response to productions that have taken place in New York, the main entry point and defining cultural nexus in the United States for the global touring market in the performing arts. My research is based on published reviews and related articles—in short, the substantial archival record of public engagement with a broad array of issues related to performance and Japan. The principal source is the *New York Times,* which has the most comprehensive and influential coverage of theater, music, and dance events that take place in New York—and is the primary voice among mainstream publications in shaping and recording the multi-strand narrative of America's Japan. Examples also come from the "old-line general-interest print magazines," which, together with the *Times,* have a long track record of covering performing arts events on and off Broadway for a national readership. "For decades *Time* and *Newsweek* devoted more space to opera and art and theology than to Hollywood or health. You may never have visited New York City, but to be a respectable figure in your town . . . it was helpful to know what operas were playing or what people were reading in Paris"—as well as in New York itself.[5] I also include the *Village Voice,* "New York's most important alternative newspaper,"[6] for its in-depth treatment of the arts "downtown." My research is additionally based on interviews with artists and arts administrators in the United States and Japan, as well as my own experience attending presentations.

The title of my book refers to historian H. D. Harootunian's frequently cited essay "America's Japan/Japan's Japan." The America's Japan that Harootunian identified took shape during the Occupation era and continued to be developed by modernization theorists as an "appeal to fixed cultural values—consensuality—uninterrupted continuity, and an endless present derived from an exceptionalist experience."[7] The "America's Japan" that I analyze in connection with the performing arts is a complex chronicle of cultural mobility and exchange—one that often reduces Japanese culture to a worn-out set of Orientalist stereotypes, but one that also broadly engages in a dynamic, transnational conversation about artistic production and encounter. Through forms such as kabuki, Japan's culture is repeatedly depicted as a "timeless" one whose "enduring forms

[have] escaped mere history."[8] At the same time, the enormous volume of innovative and experimental work from Japan—introduced especially since the 1970s by downtown, avant-garde presenters such as La MaMa E.T.C. (Experimental Theatre Club)—has helped return "the realm of criticism," again to use Harootunian's words, "to the space of culture" by raising important questions regarding society and history.[9]

Two overlapping sets of Japan-focused performing arts events furnish a ready-made endpoint for this study. One is JapanNYC (Japan/New York City), a multi-genre, multi-site festival organized by Carnegie Hall that spanned eight months from fall 2010 until spring 2011. It encapsulates the America's Japan of this study, providing a distilled summing up of the six-decade history of Japan-related performing arts presentations on which I concentrate. JapanNYC festival programming, in the words of Carnegie Hall executive and artistic director Clive Gillinson, aimed at taking a close look at Japan's "fascinating culture . . . across the spectrum of its traditional and modern arts."[10] Performers from Japan included the Saito Kinen Orchestra, the Kashu-juku noh theater, the Kodo Drummers, the NHK Symphony Orchestra, the rock band Shonen Knife, a gagaku court music and dance ensemble, and individual artists ranging from shamisen, biwa, shakuhachi, and koto players to specialists in computer-generated sound. By also bringing together a roster of people with long and successful careers in the United States already behind them—including conductor Seiji Ozawa (artistic director of the festival), dancer-choreographers Eiko and Koma, and jazz musician Toshiko Akiyoshi—JapanNYC in effect paid tribute to key figures in America's postwar cultural relations with Japan while at the same time symbolically capping off that long chapter in history.

The other set of events was the benefit concerts organized by John Zorn to raise money for Japan Society's Japan Earthquake Relief Fund immediately following the magnitude 9 earthquake and ensuing tsunami that struck Japan in March 2011.[11] Zorn is a New York–based MacArthur "genius" award winner with a wide-ranging musical profile that welcomes frequent collaborations with fellow experimental musicians and composers from Japan—whose work he also produces in concert and markets on his own record label. The benefit concerts were based on "longstanding ties between what were (in the 1970s and '80s) known as New York's downtown improvisers and their Japanese counterparts and co-conspirators."[12] One held at Columbia University's Miller Theatre—which reportedly sold out in a couple of hours and was broadcast in Japan—featured Yoko Ono and her Plastic Ono Band, Yuka Honda and Miho Hatori of the rock duo

Cibo Matto, and rock and jazz singer Akiko Yano. A one-night double bill at the Abrons Arts Center brought together almost two dozen performers—singer-songwriter Norah Jones and the electronic experimentalists Miya Masaoka, Aya Nishina, and Ikue Mori among them. Participants in the marathon, thirteen-hour Concert for Japan held at Japan Society (which, along with Asia Society, refers to itself without the article *the*) included Ryuichi Sakamoto (piano and vocals), James Nyoraku Schlefer (shakuhachi), Mari Kimura (violin), and the rock quartet Hard Nips. All of the benefits were infused with the buoyant goodwill of audience members and performers drawn together in the face of crisis. Like Carnegie Hall's JapanNYC, they took place against the backdrop of regular, ongoing Japan-related programming that was also scheduled during the same period. Looked at as a whole, what occurred within the 2010–11 time frame represented both closure and counterpoint in the narrative of America's Japan through the performing arts.

Familiarizing and De-familiarizing America's Japan

Beginning in the 1950s, performing arts arriving on U.S. soil directly from Japan served the project of "educating Americans about their changing relationship to the world at large"—just as the American-made musicals and movies (such as *The King and I* and *South Pacific*) that have been the subject of Christina Klein's research did.[13] With travel "function[ing] as a cultural space in which Americans could be trained to imagine and practice the kinds of exchanges that would strengthen the nation's global ties,"[14] visits by performing artists *to* the United States were a significant category of exchanges aimed at strengthening those ties. The performing arts sometimes stood in interesting contrast to direct government-to-government diplomacy: in June 1960, at the very moment when President Dwight D. Eisenhower's planned trip to Japan was canceled because of angry rioting in Tokyo over renewal of the United States–Japan Security Treaty, the first fully professional kabuki troupe to perform in the United States was receiving wide and enthusiastic American media coverage—which in turn had positive reverberations in Japan.

Even before the 1960 visit, kabuki had come to represent postwar America's timeless Japan, the embodiment of an aestheticized exoticism that helped erase negative images of wartime Japan. James Michener, who won the Pulitzer Prize for fiction in 1948 for *Tales of the South Pacific,* was one of the earliest and most vocal proponents of a visit by kabuki to the

United States. He was, as Klein has pointed out, a chief public educator about the countries of Asia. The basic goal of the essays he wrote for publications such as *Life* magazine and *Reader's Digest* was "to supplant the old knowledge about Asia—that presented it as 'mute,' 'mysterious,' and 'remote'—with a new knowledge that renders it familiar, articulate, and approachable."[15] However, Michener and others eagerly promoted kabuki as a kind of safe harbor precisely because it revived "old knowledge" of a Japan unconnected to war. It was knowledge that had coalesced by the late nineteenth century around the image of "a secretive island with strange customs and impeccable taste."[16] Already in that era, American audiences had responded enthusiastically to the kabuki-esque dramas of the enterprising husband and wife team of Otojiro Kawakami and Sadayakko, who triumphantly toured the United States and Europe. For postwar America, Michener's kabuki—followed by other traditional arts from Japan—would be carefully authenticated and explicated by credentialed experts. Michener's vision took hold: grounded in periodic visits by troupes, kabuki in the United States continues to serve as a consummate symbol of an exoticized, ahistorical Japan.

In the summer and fall of 1970, productions directed by experimentalists Yutaka Higashi and Shuji Terayama at New York's La MaMa E.T.C. broke open new ways of talking and thinking about Japanese culture. They did so by bringing Japanese culture "downtown," into "the richly symbolic space claimed by the avant-garde,"[17] and thus de-familiarizing the Japan that in the two decades following the end of the war had become the stock-in-trade of well-funded and well-established "uptown" institutions such as Japan Society, Asia Society, Lincoln Center, the Metropolitan Opera, and Carnegie Hall. Uptown Japan largely meant the officially sanctioned, elite, cultural heritage canon; in addition to kabuki, this included forms such as gagaku, noh, kyogen, and bunraku puppet theater. By providing access to "unsanctioned," nonelite, contemporary, experimental, and even subversive work from Japan, La MaMa introduced Japan and its performing arts into new debates about artistic processes and practices in a self-consciously multicultural world while at the same time solidifying its own position as a prominent voice in those debates. The Brooklyn Academy of Music followed suit in 1973 with a presentation by Tsutomu Yamashita's multimedia Red Buddha Theatre. Even Japan Society signaled a notable shift in its programming by hosting the 1976 U.S. debut of Eiko and Koma, who took up residence in New York and went on to become leading figures in American contemporary dance.

A central question for postwar American society was "How can we transform our sense of ourselves from narrow provincials into cosmopolitan citizens of the world who possess a global consciousness?"[18] The question continues to be asked today by the presenting institutions whose mission includes bringing theater, dance, and music from Japan (and other parts of the world) to audiences in the United States. The answers—published and circulated in reviews and background and preview articles—form the ongoing narrative of America's Japan through the performing arts.

Why the Performing Arts?

In their real-time, visceral, in-person immediacy, the performing arts are unique sites of cultural production, encounter, and critique. They are, to use Stephen Greenblatt's descriptor, "mobile signifiers" of culture.[19] "The performing arts are my special concern," Sally Banes wrote in the introduction to *Greenwich Village, 1963: Avant-Garde Performance and the Effervescent Body,* "for the performing body is central to all the interconnecting arts of this period."[20] The same can be said for the more extended time frame of my study. Systematic examination of responses to theater, dance, and music from Japan also uncovers examples of what Paul J. Yoon has called the "Orientalist gaze upon Asian bodies."[21] And, as Deborah Wong has argued, performance (her particular reference is to taiko drumming) "highlights the meeting ground of transnational movement, gender and the insistence on being seen and heard."[22]

"[T]he security and economic issues of U.S.-Japan relations have attracted by far the most scholarly attention," Takeshi Matsuda has noted, "whereas the cultural dimension of that bilateral relationship has attracted relatively scant commentary."[23] As a body of knowledge, the performing arts merit more attention—if only because they are culturally, politically, and socially contextualized within some of the most highly acclaimed and accredited institutions in the United States. The actors, dancers, and musicians who are selected to appear on the stages of Lincoln Center, Carnegie Hall, the Brooklyn Academy of Music, La MaMa, the Joyce Theater, the Village Vanguard, The Stone, Japan Society, Asia Society, and other "spaces of authority" in the arts are those whose artistic credentials—and ethnic/national identities—are considered most definitively certified.[24] Their work has the greatest chance of being covered and reviewed by publications such as the *New York Times*—and, thus, of being documented in the archives of America's Japan.

Much has been said of Japan's "soft power," its cultural influence on a global scale, especially since the publication of Douglas McGray's "Japan's Gross National Cool" in 2002.[25] Although McGray was focusing on anime and computer games, the performing arts are a core element in the domestic cultural landscape that translates into cultural exchange—and soft power. "Living in Tokyo, especially in the last five years or so," Tadashi Uchino has written, "one does have an undeniable sense of the growing domain of the theatre industry, with theatre culture gradually recognized as an integral part of the social life of the urban middle class."[26] Uchino cites dance in particular as "a genre that quickly adapted and responded to the fast-changing sociocultural landscape of the post-9/11 post-political/ideological milieu."[27] Like the popular-culture products highlighted by David Leheny in his essay on Japan's soft power in East Asia, presentations in the United States of performing arts from Japan, to varying degrees over the past sixty years, have been espoused by producers, presenters, and funding agencies as a way for Americans to "get to know the Japanese" so that "they will realize that they are kind and decent, creative and curious, and not to be feared."[28]

The "performative," furthermore, is a defining element of intangible cultural heritage—the subject of global cultural policy making and dialogue, as reflected, for instance, in the Convention for the Safeguarding of Intangible Cultural Heritage enacted in 2003 by the United Nations Educational, Scientific and Cultural Organization (UNESCO) and the recent emergence of heritage studies as a field of scholarship.[29] The Japanese government enacted its own Cultural Properties Protection Law (Bunkazai Hogoho) decades earlier—in 1950.[30] In the 1950s and 1960s, visits to New York from Japan of gagaku, kabuki, noh, kyogen, and bunraku troupes firmly planted the expressions "national treasure" and "intangible cultural property" in America's vocabulary.[31] These became key terms in the narrative of America's Japan, helping build the image of Japan as a repository of cultural heritage.

It is worth noting, finally, that the reception of Japan's performing arts abroad has been a topic of considerable interest and concern in Japan. This was especially evident in the 1980s and early 1990s, when the traditional arts in particular were being endorsed by Japan as frontline cultural ambassadors to turn attention away from the international trade frictions that were roiling relations with the country's largest trading partners.[32] The August 1986 issue of *Gekkan bunkazai* (Cultural treasures monthly), a widely circulated journal published by Japan's governmental Agency for Cultural Affairs (Bunkacho), provides striking proof of the cultural-diplomatic role accorded the traditional performing arts: more than a dozen articles on the history of government-promoted and -financed overseas tours of kabuki, bunraku, noh (and kyogen), gagaku, and the folk performing arts followed one after the other.[33] Books on the subject have also come out, such as Kazuyoshi Nishi and Tamotsu Matsuda's *Nōgaku kaigai kōen shiyō* (A history of noh productions abroad).[34] Shochiku, the entertainment conglomerate that has most kabuki actors under contract, brought out a comprehensive history of overseas kabuki tours, complete with reproductions of worldwide newspaper reviews.[35] Individual actors have joined the conversation, perhaps the best known being Mansaku Nomura and his son, Mansai, who have performed kyogen outside of Japan on a number of occasions—and included lively accounts of their touring experiences in their autobiographical writings.[36] The potency of the performing arts as "mobile signifiers"—in this case, where the global stage feeds back on the local—is nowhere more apparent than in the renown attained in artistic and academic circles in Japan by a few "foreign"-born performers of the traditional arts, such as the noh actor and teacher Richard Emmert. It is a point made, for instance, by Hiroko Miura, who included material on practitioners like Emmert in a section titled "Gaikokujin to nō" (Foreigners and noh), in her introduction to the art form for Japanese readers.[37]

Why New York?

"No city in the world can offer a wider variety of such exotic musical alternatives than New York," critic John Rockwell once wrote.[38] For Japan-born playwright Chiori Miyagawa, New York is "[t]he city where I am allowed to be nothing and everything."[39] And, from the larger perspective of international history, New York more than anyplace else is where US postwar relations with Japan were reconfigured through cultural exchange—the setting, to give just one piece of evidence, for *Newsweek* magazine's proud declaration to its national readership in 1954 that the New York visit of the Azuma Kabuki Dancers and Musicians meant that "[f]or the first time in history, a major classical dance company from Japan performed in the Western world."[40] My focus on New York by no means denies the rich history of Japan-related theater, music, and dance presentations in Honolulu, Los Angeles, San Francisco, Chicago, Portland, Seattle, Washington, DC, Philadelphia, and Boston.[41] There are also the smaller locales where museums and universities take the lead in enabling audiences to experience "Japan" live onstage—among them, the Walker Art Center in Minneapolis, the Hopkins Center at Dartmouth College, the University of Pittsburgh, and the University of Michigan. But, since New York is the central arena of the performing arts in the United States—and many of the Japan-related events that unfold around the country are part of national tours that either originate or culminate there—critics and writers employed by what were long referred to as the New York media (a less meaningful term in the digital age) dominate the discourse of America's Japan in response to the performing arts.

Institutions such as the *Los Angeles Times, Washington Post, Boston Globe, Chicago Tribune,* and *San Francisco Chronicle* have long contributed to conversations about Japan, but the *New York Times,* the "most influential newspaper on earth,"[42] exemplifies what Christina Klein has called "a vast educational machinery designed to direct the attention of the American people to the world outside the nation's borders."[43] Attending the 2006 Contemporary Dance Showcase on a Saturday afternoon at Japan Society, I made my way past an easel holding a huge laminated enlargement of a *Times* article published the day before about the participants and their works.[44] That Monday morning the newspaper ran a detailed review of the multi-day program.[45] Both were by Rockwell, the paper's chief dance critic at the time. The extensive coverage indicated that the event was a noteworthy one for the *Times* in its mission to cover the arts as broadly as possible for as broad a readership as possible. And, the write-ups were significant for Japan Society: for arts professionals there is nothing more desirable and validating than recognition by the *Times.*

According to Eric Homberger, "By the end of the Second World War, the cultural dominance of New York was a fact of American life. In theater, television, publishing, magazines, popular music, the art world—in everything except movies—New York was the arbiter of America's cultural marketplace."[46] The New York press, not without a measure of self-interest, has frequently commented on expansions to—and occasional diminutions of—the city's perceived importance. "New York: Stage for All the World," a 1955 *Times* photo-essay, proclaimed: "New York is a mecca for virtually all the world's artists. Sooner or later they must seek the prestige that the applause of the critical, challenging New York audience brings." A photograph of the Azuma Kabuki Dancers and Musicians accompanied the piece, with the notation that the troupe was about to play again in New York after having "scored here last season."[47] Almost three decades later, in "City in Performing Arts: No. 1, with a Difference," the message was essentially the same: in dance "the city's dominance has increased, and New York is now recognized as the unrivaled world capital of dance—a title many would have denied it only 10 or 15 years ago." In music "New

York remains the center of the music world: the home of more orchestras than any other city and of the Metropolitan Opera, the titan in the world of opera; the major international crossroads for touring orchestras and musicians; the standard-setter for artists seeking to make their reputations, and the generator of artistic ferment." Although Broadway, which "continues to set the international standard for production professionalism," had become too expensive to allow for experimentation, the article noted, "As a showcase for the best of international theater, New York is incomparable. Virtually every important theatrical company passes through sooner or later, from England's Royal Shakespeare Company to Japanese Kabuki theater to outstanding avant-garde companies from Eastern Europe and Asia."[48]

The question "Why New York?" also points to the extraordinary attractiveness of the city for performing artists from Japan. Yuiko Fujita has used the term *cultural migrants* in her study of young people from Japan who move to New York and London for extended periods to engage in various types of cultural production. She cites statistics published by Japan's Ministry of Foreign Affairs in 2006 showing that New York had the largest number of resident Japanese nationals of any city outside of Japan.[49] A 1979 *Times* article, "Japanese Dancers in America: What Draws Them?,"[50] argued that the growing number of women from Japan trying to build careers in the arts in New York was attributable to their desire to escape the constraints (patriarchal and otherwise) of Japanese society, and their belief that New York was the most appealing alternative.[51] The point continued to be made (regarding both women and men) almost twenty years later: "Nearly all come to escape what they see as Japanese society's rigid dictates about what to study, where to work and even how to think. 'I was born with strong opinions, a tendency to reject rules, and I was rejected by a Japanese society which didn't allow that kind of woman,' said Chiori Miyagawa . . . who moved to New York as a teenager, [and] is one of the longer established and most successful of the expatriates."[52] Midori Yoshimoto has observed that New York "acquired a utopian image for Japanese avant-garde artists," noting, "After 1964, when the Japanese tourist visa to visit the United States became available, the number of artists who visited New York for a short time grew rapidly."[53]

Presentations on New York stages of Japan-related performance are situated within dense networks of border crossings and circulation, interactions, and collaborations. New York is a major node in those networks—a center in the not yet de-centered flow of cultural production. Reviewing Yukio Mishima's *Madame de Sade* (*Sado kōshaku fujin*), directed by Ingmar Bergman at the Brooklyn Academy of Music in 1995, Vincent Canby wrote,

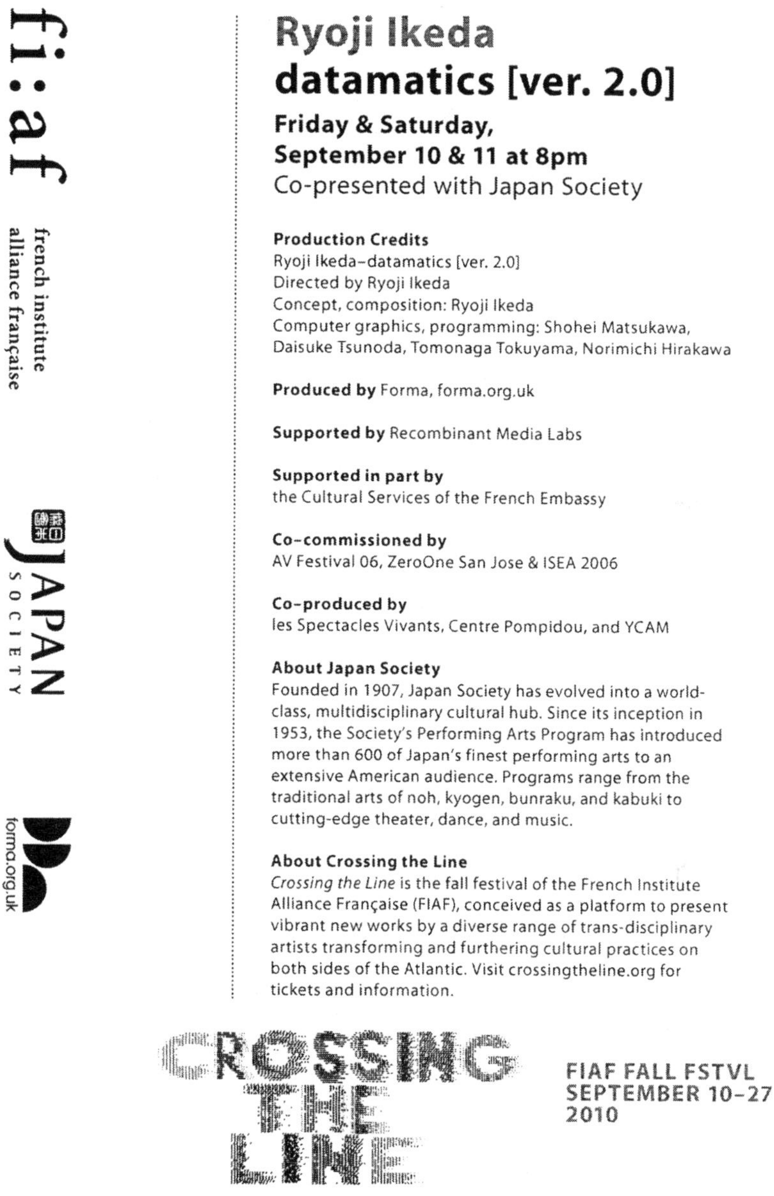
fi:af
french institute
alliance française

Ryoji Ikeda
datamatics [ver. 2.0]
Friday & Saturday,
September 10 & 11 at 8pm
Co-presented with Japan Society

Production Credits
Ryoji Ikeda–datamatics [ver. 2.0]
Directed by Ryoji Ikeda
Concept, composition: Ryoji Ikeda
Computer graphics, programming: Shohei Matsukawa, Daisuke Tsunoda, Tomonaga Tokuyama, Norimichi Hirakawa

Produced by Forma, forma.org.uk

Supported by Recombinant Media Labs

Supported in part by
the Cultural Services of the French Embassy

Co-commissioned by
AV Festival 06, ZeroOne San Jose & ISEA 2006

Co-produced by
les Spectacles Vivants, Centre Pompidou, and YCAM

About Japan Society
Founded in 1907, Japan Society has evolved into a world-class, multidisciplinary cultural hub. Since its inception in 1953, the Society's Performing Arts Program has introduced more than 600 of Japan's finest performing arts to an extensive American audience. Programs range from the traditional arts of noh, kyogen, bunraku, and kabuki to cutting-edge theater, dance, and music.

About Crossing the Line
Crossing the Line is the fall festival of the French Institute Alliance Française (FIAF), conceived as a platform to present vibrant new works by a diverse range of trans-disciplinary artists transforming and furthering cultural practices on both sides of the Atlantic. Visit crossingtheline.org for tickets and information.

JAPAN SOCIETY

forma.org.uk

CROSSING THE LINE

FIAF FALL FSTVL
SEPTEMBER 10–27
2010

Fig. 1. House program for Ryoji Ikeda's *datamatics [ver. 2.0]*, presented by the French Institute Alliance Française (FIAF)'s Crossing the Line Festival in 2010. (Courtesy of the French Institute Alliance Française (FIAF).)

"Here is a Japanese play about an 18th-century French writer and libertine, as staged for the Royal Dramatic Theater of Sweden, in Swedish, being presented in New York with Donald Keene's English translation heard via earphones. It could be utter confusion, but it's as clearly defined and as elegant as any production you're likely to see for a long time."[54] The performing arts networks are growing ever more complex, and New York was where, in September 2010, the French Institute Alliance Française (FIAF) hosted Ryoji Ikeda, a Paris-based experimental visual/sound artist and composer from Japan, as part of the organization's annual Crossing the Line Festival. Though "representing" France, he was simultaneously "reclaimed" by "Japan in New York" through cosponsorship of the event by Japan Society.

Performing Arts Databases: Japan's Japan in the Global Performing Arts Marketplace

America's Japan implies a concomitant Japan's Japan, which I locate in a set of databases assembled in Japan that define and demarcate the boundaries of theater, dance, and music originating there.[55] Japan's Japan is national culture for the global market, encompassing for the most part non-commercial performing artists—from those in traditional fields to experimentalists—whose stature and identification as representative Japanese artists have been "credentialed" by governmental, cultural, and scholarly entities in Japan. In contrast to America's Japan as a historical narrative of cultural mobility and exchange, Japan's Japan "brands" the concept of "Japaneseness" for the global performing arts marketplace. As Patrick Lonergan has observed, "[T]hrough the processes of branding . . . the authenticity of a cultural product is . . . grounded in the recognizability of its cultural sources."[56]

The Japan Foundation takes the lead here in its role as principal promoter and underwriter of Japan-initiated cultural exchange, which includes international performance tours by artists from Japan, as well as workshops and collaborative projects that bring together Japanese and non-Japanese performing artists. The foundation was formed in 1972 as a "special public institution" under the Ministry of Foreign Affairs and reorganized in 2003 as an "independent administrative institution" of the Japanese government. It compiles and publishes online performer and drama databases and disseminates material through publications that include *Theater in Japan: An Overview of Performing Arts and Artists* (2008) and its website, Performing Arts Network Japan (http://www.performingarts.jp), which is regularly updated with artist and presenter interviews and articles on developments in Japan's performing arts scene. The Japan Foundation also organizes and supports the annual weeklong Tokyo Performing Arts Market (TPAM), one of Japan's two main showcases—in a way "live databases"—for the performing arts. Like the yearly New York meeting of the Association of Performing Arts Presenters, TPAM, launched in 1995, offers performances, conference hall exhibit booths staffed by arts groups and presenting organizations, and programs of lectures and discussions, all of which provide meeting points for artists and presenters.[57] The other is the monthlong Festival Tokyo (F/T), which began in 2009: "In addition to presenting cutting-edge international co-productions without any 'time difference,' we produce works by renowned Japanese artists, transmitting them to the rest of the world."[58] The festival's organizers include individuals frequently cited by the Japan Foundation as seminal figures in Japan's performing arts: dancer-choreographer Ushio Amagatsu and directors Hideki Noda and Yukio Ninagawa.

Theater critic and University of Tokyo professor Tadashi Uchino has developed an original "cognitive map"—in effect a kind of database—of twenty-first-century Japan-based performance.[59] Uchino, a performing arts consultant to the Japan Foundation and a trustee of the Saison Foundation, which provides substantial funding to contemporary theater and dance groups in Japan, plots his map with forty theater and dance companies and individual artists. "Japan's theater culture is now so manifold and compartmentalized that nobody can really have a unified image of the field," he writes. "I was interested in the diversity of performance that we see every day in Tokyo, and 40 was the number required to give the map a certain degree of validity and reflect my understanding of Japan's contemporary theatre culture. In addition, I deliberately chose to highlight the younger generation of practitioners, most of whom were born after the 1970s."[60] Uchino arrayed groups such as the Condors, Nibroll, Kaitaisha, chelfitsch, Noda Map, and Seinendan (all of which have performed in the United States) on a grid under headings that include literary/text, performance/body, remnants of modernism, politics of the body, and politics of representation. The accompanying analysis speaks to two goals that Uchino set for himself: "one, to historicize Japan's theater culture, and the other, to encourage a younger generation of artists who I think have both artistic and intellectual potential."[61]

Membership Dance File is another major database, one that has been compiled by the Japanese Contemporary Dance Network (JCDN) mainly as a reference tool for presenting organizations and their artistic directors. The file supplies statistics on virtually every dance artist active in Japan. JCDN was inaugurated in 1998 by Norikazu Sato, whose résumé includes an internship at New York's Dance Theater Workshop, where he worked with the US-based National Performance Network to expand public knowledge of and access to the arts. Performance tours and showcases are organized by JCDN for artists in Japan, and it communicates information about them in print and online (http://www.jcdn.org). Also working in the field of dance, writer and critic Takao Norikoshi is the author of *Hyper: Kontenporarī dansu tettei gaido* (Hyper: Contemporary dance perfect guidebook), a one-volume "encyclopedia" of Japanese dancers and dance troupes.[62]

The Japan Foundation is among those bureaucratic apparatuses through which, as Aihwa Ong has written, "the nation-state . . . continues to define, discipline, control, and regulate all kinds of populations, whether in movement or in residence."[63] Inclusion in its databases—and the others that in effect supplement it—presupposes that in most cases the performing artist was born, educated, and professionally trained in Japan and established his or her career there. The databases are branding mechanisms that accord the status of global marketability to individuals who have already won recognition for their work from presenters, foundations, and other "accrediting" organizations within Japan. Recognition is tangibly measured in invitations to perform at important Japanese theater and arts festivals and in prizes that include, among others, the Toyota Choreography Award, the Asahi Performing Arts Award, the Kishida Drama Award, and the Kinokuniya Theater Award. The names of all those included in the databases of Japan's Japan potentially appear in the narrative of America's Japan, assuming that the artists participate in the flow of cultural exchange between Japan and the United States. The reverse, however, is not the case since America's Japan includes many artists who are neither based in Japan nor active as performers there.

America's Japan: A Taxonomy

"So what is authentic butoh, and who is entitled to do it?" The question was posed by Wendy Perron, dance writer, critic, teacher, and choreographer, in a 1999 *New York Times* essay previewing an upcoming series of performances by leading butoh troupes and individual artists from Japan, including Sankai Juku, Min Tanaka, and Kazuo Ono. Perron's interlocutor was Koosil-ja—an award-winning, New York–based dancer-choreographer and musician whose style reveals some affinities with the art form. She told Perron, "Butoh grows in Japan and needs the water, the entire cultural environment of Japan, for its authenticity."[64] Born and raised in Japan, Koosil-ja Hwang is ethnically Korean. She has lived in New York since 1981, when she came to study dance with Merce Cunningham. Until the mid-1990s she performed under her Japanese name, Kumiko Kimoto.[65] As her career was developing, so were ideas about multiculturalism and new ways of thinking about ethnic identity. Challenging monocultural understandings of Japan, she made the switch to her Korean name and began using her given name only. Today Koosil-ja heads her own troupe, which she calls koosilja/danceKUMIKO. Her work and teaching take her around the United States and to Europe and Japan. Given Koosil-ja's personal history of mobility and the wide-ranging theoretical grounding of her work (she "creates links between bodies and a digital environment" and cites the influence of philosophers Gilles Deleuze and Pierre-Félix Guattari),[66] her statement on butoh can be interpreted as an intentionally ironic commentary on attempts to draw fixed geographical boundaries around the performing arts.

Which artists "count," by virtue of being the subjects of reviews and articles, in the discursive construction, reconstruction, and transformation of "Japan" and "Japanese culture" through the performing arts? I propose a three-part taxonomy of America's Japan: cultural heritage artists, internationalist and flexible-citizen artists, and American artists influenced by Japanese culture.

Cultural Heritage Artists

Cultural heritage artists—an alternative, more anthropological-sounding term might be *cultural lineage artists*—populate the databases of Japan's Japan, presenting their work in New York as cultural exchange visitors. Almost without exception, they are Japanese by birth, education, and training and their careers are based in Japan. I subdivide them into two groups. The first is the "national treasures"—practitioners of kabuki and noh, among other arts, which are, in the aggregate, what Marilyn Ivy has referred to as "the traditional, immutable core of culture."[67] The second group is made up of all the other artists who represent modern and contemporary Japanese music, dance, and theater. Their work is often interpreted by American reviewers as embodying, in Steven C. Ridgely's succinct phrasing, "the enduring nature of Japanese cultural patterns," such as "group orientation, vertical society, minimalist aesthetics, and some hint of the samurai code."[68]

When philanthropist Lila Acheson Wallace donated a million dollars to Asia Society in 1971, her goal was to enable "a wide-ranging representation of the rich, ancient traditions of Asia's performing arts."[69] As already mentioned, the terms *national treasure* and *intangible cultural property* were introduced along with visiting troupes from Japan that included gagaku (in 1959), Grand Kabuki (in 1960), kyogen (in 1964), bunraku (in 1966), and noh (in 1966). The elaborately brocaded silk costumes, antiquated masks and patterns of makeup, and rich mix of unusual musical sounds and acting styles were irrefutable evidence of Japan's rich cultural heritage. Like the term *ritual,* which appears with a high degree of frequency in reviews of performing arts from Japan, *national treasure* and *intangible cultural property* remove a presentation from critical scrutiny. They indicate that audiences are being given the opportunity to learn about and experience the fully formed products of another culture. The values associated with heritage convey a "sense of gravitas."[70] Reviews and other articles are generally expected to respectfully introduce and help interpret such art—rather than critically evaluate it.

In Japan passage of the Cultural Properties Protection Law in 1950, which laid out a framework for identifying and designating "national treasures," was a crucial step in the country's postwar cultural rebuilding. It was not just a matter of trying to sustain practices that might succumb to the forces of modernization and Westernization but of producing a strong cultural identity for Japan. "The comprehension and valuing of different cultural expressions," Amanda Kearney has noted, "are at the very core of cultural heritage legislation worldwide."[71] Fifty years later Japan's cultural properties law became the model for a new set of cultural heritage designations intended to be applied globally. In 2001 UNESCO began identifying "Masterpieces of the Oral and Intangible Heritage of Humanity," with noh and kyogen among the first to be included. Bunraku was named in the second round of designations in 2003; kabuki was added in 2005. More recently, the organization has been compiling expanded lists under the heading "Intangible Cultural Heritage of Humanity." Kabuki, noh (and kyogen), and bunraku were inscribed—to use UNESCO's term—in 2008. Gagaku followed in 2009. Kumiodori (Okinawan dance drama) was added in 2010. The list also includes over a dozen examples of Japan's folk performing arts and traditional craftsmanship, including Ainu dance and a form of papermaking.[72]

The first visitors funded by Mrs. Wallace's gift were the Edo Festival Music and Pantomime troupe from Tokyo. In a production jointly arranged by Asia Society and Japan Society, they were booked into Lincoln Center—the apex of establishment performing arts venues—a site appropriately symbolic of American respect for Japan's cultural heritage. Since the major traditional forms had already been introduced, it became a goal of Asia Society and its sister organization, Japan Society, to bring to New York lesser-known "folk" arts. American audiences would quickly learn that practitioners of such arts—including the Edo troupe, "based on a tradition that goes back to the seventh century,"[73] and the Awaji Puppet Theatre (which had its US debut in 1971, helping celebrate the opening of Japan Society's new permanent home on East 47th Street)—also arrived with the imprimatur of national treasure. In the mid-1980s John Rockwell, then serving as a music critic for the *Times,* cited the "disparity [that] exists between classical, high-art musical traditions, folk music and commercial popular music," adding, "Now, however, more and more governments and private impresarios like Miss Gordon [Beate Gordon, head of performing arts at Asia Society and, previously, Japan Society] are seeking out the folk musicians, too." Rockwell's point was that "the more ancient folk forms, uncontaminated by Western influence, have been harder to bring here."[74]

Kabuki became emblematic of America's Japan not just because it was boldly exotic but also because it was perceived, to use Rockwell's term, as "uncontaminated," meaning that it was seen as untouched by globalized American culture. In contrast, troupes from the Takarazuka Revue, who have made several visits to the United States, have been dismissed by reviewers for their Radio City Music Hall–style proclivities. Unfamiliar, traditional arts from Japan appeal to seekers of distinction. "A work of art," Pierre Bourdieu has written, "has meaning and interest only for someone who possesses the cultural competence, that is, the code, into which it is encoded. . . . A beholder who lacks the specific code feels lost in a chaos of sounds and rhythms, colours and lines, without rhyme or reason."[75] Newspaper and magazine preview articles written by scholars and other experts help audiences attain a level of competence prior to a performance. And when people get to the theater they can solidify and expand their knowledge by studying the program notes, following the earphone commentary or reading the "supertitles"—translations projected above, or sometimes to the side of, the stage. *New Yorker* cartoons such Danny Shanahan's 1990 "Tuesday nights are Ed's Kabuki League bowl-offs" and Pat Byrnes's 2001"What part of Noh don't you understand?" provide proof of the strong impact on the American imagination of Japan-related cultural exchange efforts that give special prominence to the traditional arts.

"Tuesday nights are Ed's Kabuki League bowl-offs."

Fig. 2. Danny Shanahan's "Tuesday nights are Ed's Kabuki League bowl-offs," *New Yorker,* 10 December 1990. (© 1990 by The Cartoon Bank/Condé Nast Publications, Inc. Courtesy of The Cartoon Bank/Condé Nast Publications Inc.)

In the narrative of America's Japan, cultural heritage is rooted in the "traditional-arts-equal-national-treasures" equation but is not limited to it. It encompasses all artists understood as exemplifying "authentic" Japanese theater, dance, or musical practices—artists to whom the discourse of Japanese cultural continuity is often applied by critics in their reviews. A salient example is butoh. Along with Tatsumi Hijikata, Kazuo Ono originated the dance form in the mid–twentieth century—serving, until his death in 2010, as perhaps its most famous exponent within and outside of Japan. Ono's American debut at La MaMa in 1981 signified the formal introduction of butoh to New York audiences. Other now famous butoh artists who followed Ono on initial US visits in the 1980s include Sankai Juku, a troupe led by Ushio Amagatsu, and Dai Rakudakan, led by Akaji Maro. "What has happened in modern dance in Japan," readers of the *New York Times* were told in a 1982 essay previewing the appearance at that year's American Dance Festival of Dai Rakudakan and three other butoh

"What part of Noh don't you understand?"

Fig. 3. Pat Byrnes's "What part of Noh don't you understand?," *New Yorker,* 29 October 2001. (© 2001 by The Cartoon Bank/Condé Nast Publications, Inc. Courtesy of The Cartoon Bank/Condé Nast Publications Inc.)

ensembles from Japan, "is as diverse and confusing to the Western eye as the rest of Japanese culture may seem. However, a sense of proportion, or '*ma no kankaku,*' steeped in years of tradition, pervades choreography, as well as the other art forms."[76]

Butoh demonstrates the potency of labels as markers of cultural heritage. *Hogaku* is slowly becoming known as an umbrella term for "Japanese" music and musical instruments, although artists are commonly identified with the specific instrument they play: shamisen, koto, shakuhachi, and taiko drums, for example.[77] By the mid-1960s koto musician Kimio Eto was a well-known figure in American music circles, regularly appearing in recitals and concerts.[78] Other instrumentalists who have achieved renown in the United States include Kazue Sawai and Nanae Yoshimura (koto), Hiromitsu Agatsuma (shamisen), Kifu Mitsuhashi (shakuhachi), and the Ondeko-za and Kodo troupes (taiko).[79]

Contemporary theater from Japan is a segment of the cultural heritage/cultural lineage category in which language barriers and other sociocultural issues of translation sometimes seem even more daunting than in the case of the traditional genres. The most frequently staged works (in both English and Japanese productions) are Yukio Mishima's modern noh plays. Their appeal is attributable in part to Mishima's celebrity as a writer whose numerous novels- and plays-in-translation were released in the United States starting in the 1950s by Knopf, a major commercial publisher. Another reason is that, though "modern," the reference to noh plays readily reinforces images of Japanese cultural continuity.[80] Playwright-directors with a growing US reputation in the twenty-first century include Yoji Sakate and Toshiki Okada. Their work has been presented in Japanese (at Japan Society by their own Japan-based companies) and English (at other New York venues by American directors and actors).

Internationalist and Flexible-Citizen Artists

Mari Yoshihara has drawn attention to "audiences' inclination to assume that musical understanding and expression have a natural connection to the musician's geographical, historical, cultural—and by implication, racial and ethnic—background."[81] Such an assumption is articulated across performing arts genres in the narrative of America's Japan, where the dividing line is often blurred between the two groups I call "internationalists" and "flexible-citizen artists." Internationalists are those who work in what is typically regarded as a Western cultural idiom (as ballet dancers, for example). Flexible-citizen artists, a term I adapt from the work of Aihwa Ong,[82] form two subgroups. Both de-territorialize and re-territorialize Japanese cultural identity: one does so within the boundaries of what is typically regarded as a Japanese cultural idiom (such as butoh) while the other reconfigures those boundaries.

Internationalist and flexible-citizen artists are among those who "respond fluidly and opportunistically to changing political-economic conditions."[83] A number are the recipients of prestigious awards—such as the Grammy, MacArthur, and Guggenheim—which proclaim recognition of their status as established artists in the United States. They are Japanese by birth—and, sometimes, by education and training as well. Many internationalist and virtually all flexible-citizen artists base their careers outside of Japan. Some are no longer citizens of Japan. They include people who leave Japan having already developed professional ties to the arts world there or forge such ties later—and thus reinstantiate their Japanese identity. *Racialist conceptualizations,* a term E. Taylor Atkins has used in his study of Japanese jazz musicians,[84] link them and their work to Japan—manifested in offers of project-support grants from the Japan Foundation, invitations to perform at culture-specific venues (such as Japan Society) and events related to Japan, and, to a degree, attention from reviewers attracted to performance from Japan, loosely defined.

Across the performing arts spectrum—as directors of "Broadway" musicals, as ballet dancers, as classical "Western" and jazz musicians—internationalists contest racialist conceptualizations of artistic practices. They become part of the narrative of America's Japan in various ways—when they present their work at places such as Japan Society or in Japan-focused festivals, when they bring productions originating in Japan to New York, or simply by being identified as somehow representative of Japan. In 2002 Japan-based director Amon Miyamoto, whose résumé includes opera, musicals, and plays, brought his Japanese-language version of John Weidman and Stephen Sondheim's *Pacific Overtures* from the New National Theatre in Tokyo (where it ran in 2000) to the Lincoln Center Festival.[85] Two years later Miyamoto returned to New York to stage the same musical using the original English script, becoming the first director from Japan hired to work on Broadway. Director Yukio Ninagawa, who is also based in Japan, is particularly celebrated for his boldly conceived, Japanese-language interpretations of Shakespearean and classical Greek dramas, which he often presents abroad—especially in London. His first production in New York was *Medea* at Central Park's Delacorte Theater in 1986. He also brought *Macbeth* to the Brooklyn Academy of Music in 1990 and again in 2002. Other examples of internationalists are Yoko Morishita, "Japan's first ballerina of international importance,"[86] who made her New York debut in 1970. By the middle of that decade she was a star performer in productions such as the American Ballet Theater's *Sleeping Beauty* at Lincoln Center. Musicians form the largest cohort among the internationalists. Many of the names are well known: conductor Seiji Ozawa, classical pianist Mitsuko Uchida, violinists Midori (Midori Goto) and Mari Kimura, and jazz pianists Toshiko Akiyoshi and Hiromi (Hiromi Uehara). Although Midori's accolades include the 2001 Avery Fisher Prize—a major honor bestowed only on instrumentalists who are American citizens or permanent residents—she is regularly referred to as "the world's most prominent Japanese violinist."[87]

Flexible-citizen artists enter the narrative of America's Japan because they *and* their artistic practices are linked with and, by extension, considered representative of Japan. The East-meets-West trope has frequently been invoked in reaction to their work. "She has the dynamism of Western dance, the elegance and precision of Japanese dance," Philip Shenon wrote in 1984 about Junko Kikuchi. "Her style, it is said, was born in Japan,

[and] nurtured in the United States, where she spent several years in study. She tries to balance the best of the dance of the two lands: precision with energy, humility with freedom, restraint with daring."[88] East-meets-West has mostly given way to a more nuanced, "cultural studies" approach—and to concepts such as hybridity. Reviewing Akemi Takeya at Japan Society in 2005, John Rockwell quoted performing arts director Yoko Shioya in observing that the dancer, a resident of Vienna since 1991, is part of "'the diaspora of Japanese artists,' creating hybrid work caught between Japan and the host country." As if uneasy because there was no label that would readily place Takeya within a Japanese cultural matrix, Rockwell underscored her reputation as a "post-Butoh dancer."[89]

Dancer-choreographers are a particularly visible cohort of flexible-citizen artists, and the recipients of a large number of major awards—including the MacArthur "genius" award that went to Eiko and Koma (1996); the New York Dance and Performance (Bessie) Awards given to Yoshiko Chuma (1984 and 2007), Yasuko Yokoshi (2003 and 2006), Koosil-ja (2004), and Eiko and Koma (1984 and 1990); the Samuel H. Scripps American Dance Festival Award won by Eiko and Koma (2004); and Guggenheim awards that have gone to Kei Takei (1978), Eiko and Koma (1984), Yoshiko Chuma (1987), Koosil-ja (2007), and Yasuko Yokoshi (2009). The awards signify the individual achievements of the artists while also implicitly valorizing American ideals of multiculturalism. Eiko and Koma, who began their careers in Japan under butoh artists Hijikata and Ono, are a case in point.[90] Since their move to New York (from Japan, via Germany) and debut at Japan Society in the mid-1970s, they have been navigating the terrain of national, cultural, and ethnic identity. In a 1978 review Anna Kisselgoff described them as "[b]oth avant-garde and rooted in their own heritage," observing that they perform "the obligatory Japanese number for Westerners. The small pine of the Noh play has been replaced by a fat pine trunk that hangs from the ceiling. The sense of slow time of Japanese classical theater is also present. And yet there can be nothing but admiration for the brilliance with which Eiko and Koma develop their drama."[91] Despite a four-decade career of work that "subverts and transcends our everyday notions of time and space" in every conceivable way,[92] Roslyn Sulcas narrowly termed them a "Japanese-American duo" in a review of *Naked: A Living Installation,* given as part of Carnegie Hall's 2010–11 JapanNYC festival.[93]

Unlike Eiko and Koma, Chuma and Yokoshi have achieved renown in New York's avant-garde dance scene without extensive prior training in Japan—although both have cultivated connections there over the years.

Fig. 4. Advertising card, Eiko and Koma, Danspace Project, 2010. (Photo by Edwin Adhiputra, design by Takahiro Haneda. Courtesy of Eiko and Koma.)

Chuma moved to New York in 1978, four years after graduating from Kanazawa University. Shortly after arriving, she founded her School of Hard Knocks dance troupe, with which she has toured worldwide. Jowitt has written that Chuma "considers herself a citizen of the world, and she turns a penetrating and concerned eye on societies in turmoil and on the depredations of war. Some of her earlier pieces investigated the tensions between life in the U.S. and the postwar Japan she grew up in."[94] Chuma was the first performing artist not living in Japan and not doing "Japanese" work to receive a commission from Japan Society. The resulting piece was the 1984 *Eager Witness*—the success of which helped further Chuma's career in the New York dance scene and, at the same time, metaphorically "return" her to Japan within the institutional framework of Japan Society.

Yokoshi is an artist who has candidly suggested that her Japanese origin is one reason why American audiences pay attention to her.[95] Despite having come to the United States in 1981 to begin studying dance as an undergraduate at Hampshire College, and having built her career entirely on US soil, she has been mythologized as an artist "whom New York has been lucky enough to steal away from Japan."[96] After a trip to Japan led her to begin studying and working with kabuki dance master Masumi Seyama

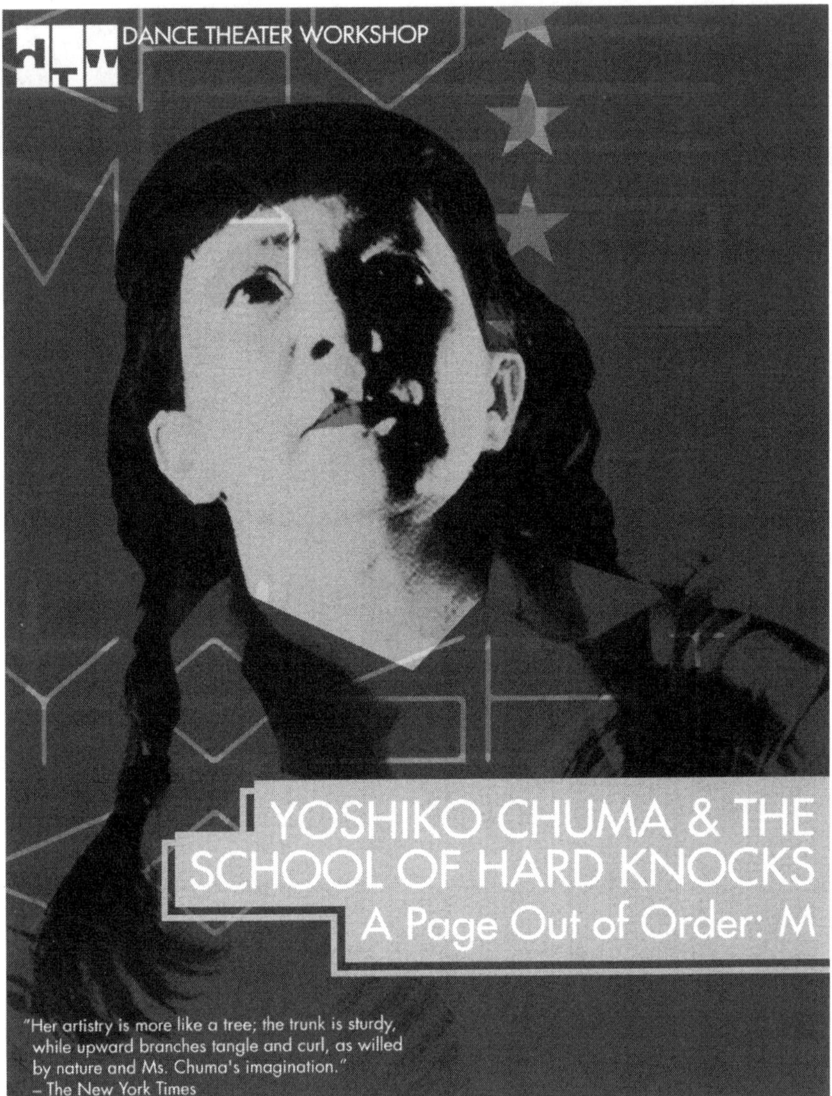

Fig. 5. Advertising card, Yoshiko Chuma and The School of Hard Knocks, Dance Theater Workshop, 2007. (Image by Hidetomo Mita. Courtesy of Yoshiko Chuma and The School of Hard Knocks.)

(who trained under "living national treasure" Kanjuro Fujima VI), Yokoshi choreographed the Bessie Award–winning *what we when we* (2006) and the critically acclaimed *Tyler Tyler* (2010), pieces that draw dance elements from kabuki. Yokoshi unhesitatingly describes kabuki as a purely serendipitous discovery: she had gone to Japan to accompany a boyfriend and just happened to start taking lessons from Seyama to pass the time. She had no prior interest in traditional Japanese dance. It was not an intentional career move.[97] Moreover, Yokoshi has expressed an unvarnished assessment of her identity as a "Japanese" dancer. In a roundtable discussion transcribed on the Movement Research website during the spring 2010 opening run of *Tyler Tyler* at Dance Theater Workshop, one of her company members remarked, "I feel I need to be extra familiar with the traditional Japanese form if I want to feel like I am coming close to doing it. A traditional Japanese dancer has trained and practiced for decades and this material comes out of them as if it was nature. It really becomes natural to them. We are faking that sense of being natural." Yokoshi said in response, "I must remind you that I am as fake as you are. I have been familiar with this form for only seven years, and I don't live in Japan. I only do periodical training with long absences. My familiarity with dance is closer to you rather than the Japanese dancers. If a well-trained dancer taught you, it would take triple the time. It's good they don't have to teach you. Their training is only mimicking. I teach you by remembering how I learned and struggled with it."[98]

Chiori Miyagawa is another forthright voice among flexible-citizen artists. "I am a Japanese-born American playwright," she states.[99] Professor and playwright in residence at Bard College and "one of the nation's foremost dramatists on Asian themes,"[100] Miyagawa came to New York as a teenager, having felt constrained in Japan, as already noted. Her work includes *Thousand Years Waiting*, "a contemporary ode to the 11th-century Japanese classic 'The Tale of Genji,'"[101] a play with "three simultaneous realities: present-day New York City, Japan circa 1000, and inside *The Tale of Genji*."[102] The 2006 production, directed by Sonoko Kawahara (who identifies herself as "a Japanese woman living in the United States"),[103] featured Osaka-based master puppeteer Masaya Kiritake in "the first collaboration between American theater artists and an Otome Bunraku puppeteer."[104] Another piece, *Woman Killer*, was adapted from a bunraku play. In *I Have Been to Hiroshima Mon Amour*, Miyagawa explores historical memory: "The suffering of Japanese citizens is something I didn't want to think about. It's always been in my blood, but I didn't think I was entitled to that memory," she has said. "When Jean [Wagner, artistic director of Voice & Vision theater company] asked me to write about it, it was like prying open a rusty door in my heart in a way."[105] Like other flexible-citizen artists, Miyagawa, who has been awarded grants from the Japan Foundation and the Asian Cultural Council, has extended the scope of her work to Japan. Her play *Stargazers,* which was commissioned by New York's Public Theater and presented in New York, was subsequently given a production in Japanese at the 2001 Asian Women and Theater Conference in Tokyo. "*Stargazers* was my first 'foreign' experience," Miyagawa has said. "I grew up as a theatre artist here, and I have always considered New York City my artistic home, even if in other ways I occasionally feel homeless."[106]

"American Artists Inspired By Japanese Culture"

When Japan Society celebrated its centennial in the fall of 2007, artistic director Yoko Shioya enumerated the Japan-related presentations that were concurrently taking place at the society and other locations in New York, declaring that the city was "witness[ing] one of the most exciting performing arts seasons in its history . . . with the most cutting-edge performing arts from Japan, as well as work from American artists inspired by Japanese culture."[107] The latter included Big Dance Theater's *The Other Here,* produced at Dance Theater Workshop. Codirected by Annie-B Parsons and Paul Lazar, Big Dance Theater already had a track record of interest in Japanese culture: in 2001, the company presented the critically praised *Shunkin,* an adaptation of the story with the same title by Junichiro Tanizaki. In it "Lazar and Parson layer and feather aspects of the contemporary American pop music scene into their tale of love and power in ancient Japan."[108] Funded by a Japan Society commission grant, *The Other Here* drew on stories by Masuji Ibuse, as well as Okinawan traditional dance and popular music. It premiered at Japan Society in February 2007.[109]

Within the narrative of America's Japan, "American artists inspired by Japanese culture," to use Shioya's phrasing, include people who are not "from" Japan but "perform" Japan. They encompass professionally trained and skilled players of Japanese musical instruments, practitioners of Japanese dance forms, directors of translated plays originally written in Japanese and dramas adapted from Japanese literary sources, and composers, dancer-choreographers, and other artists who create a range of Japan-related work—including pieces commissioned and presented by Japan Society.

American players of the shakuhachi and taiko are especially prominent. "[T]he dislocation and disjunctures brought on by cultural exchange have profoundly altered the demographics, ideologies, and cultural workings of musical practices," Yayoi Uno Everett has written, using the term *demographic 'inversion'* in reference to the large numbers of students from East Asia who train in classical music at conservatories in North America and Europe. "Another type of demographic 'inversion,'" she notes, "is observable in the practice of shakuhachi. In discussing the future of shakuhachi . . . at the 1997 World Shakuhachi Festival [held in Boulder, Colorado], the presiding masters expressed their concern over the waning number of shakuhachi practitioners within Japan: Katsuya Yokoyama half-jokingly predicted that 'the tradition will migrate to America' due to its popularity abroad."[110] New York–based shakuhachi musicians who appear on the concert stage include Ralph Samuelson, "an American expert,"[111] and a "virtuoso,"[112] who plays "hauntingly,"[113] and Ronnie Nyogetsu Reishin Seldin, whose artistry has been described as "mesmerizing."[114] There are also James Nyoraku Schlefer, "a master of the shakuhachi,"[115] and performer-composer Elizabeth Brown, who studied shakuhachi under Samuelson.[116]

Taiko drumming, as Paul J. Yoon observed in his analysis of the 1993 US film *Rising Sun*, is "a sonic synecdoche for 'Japan.' And sonically, the taiko is a menacing and thunderous icon for Japan, as opposed to the dulcet, almost tonal plucking of, for example, a *koto*."[117] Soh Daiko is a New York–based troupe that was founded in 1979, "attract[ing] those interested in and involved with Asian American political and artistic organizations in New York City."[118] While some of its members are ethnically Japanese, many have no ties to Japan. Nevertheless, Soh Daiko, which has been invited to perform at locations that include Lincoln Center and the Metropolitan Museum of Art, projects an image generally viewed as authentically "Japanese."[119] Appearances at Japan Society have helped sanction Soh Daiko as "Japanese"—especially following its joint concert in 1987 with the Japan-based Kodo troupe. "The issue of re-Orientalization," Yoon has written, "has concerned Soh Daiko for a long time. . . . The difficulty of presenting a 'traditional' Japanese musical form in the context of late-twentieth-century America highlights the discursive structures that embed identity formations. Also apparent are the difficulties in representing Asian American identities within a social context that frequently positions Asians in America as foreigners in their homeland, adopted or otherwise."[120] The inclusion of two Soh Daiko performances in the 2010–11 JapanNYC festival betokens the troupe's established presence in the narrative of America's Japan.

Other notable examples of American artists inspired by Japanese culture include Maureen Fleming, a longtime artist in residence at La MaMa, who is "perhaps the foremost American practitioner of Butoh."[121] The New York Butoh Festival, which was held every other year from 2003 until 2009, provided a well-publicized setting in which American butoh artists could present their work. Organized by Ximena Garnica and Shige Moriya, founding directors of the CAVE Organization (a center in Brooklyn, New York, for the study and performance of butoh), the event framed butoh as a transnational artistic practice by spotlighting American dancers and choreographers in a series of productions that also included recitals by artists from Japan.[122] In the field of theater, examples of plays translated from Japanese or adapted from Japanese literary sources and presented by American directors and performers include *Drum of the Waves of Horikawa,* based on a Chikamatsu play, which was directed in 2007 by Brooke O'Harra at the HERE Arts Center, and *Wind-up Bird Chronicle,* based on the novel by best-selling Japanese writer Haruki Murakami, which was directed in 2010 by Stephen Earnhart at the Ohio Theatre.

In 1963 New York City Ballet choreographer George Balanchine challenged American audiences to revise their assumptions about cultural identity in the performing arts. His ballet *Bugaku* was a stunning artistic experiment that had its inspirational genesis in the first visit to the United States of a troupe of gagaku musicians and bugaku dancers from Japan that was hosted four years earlier by the New York City Ballet itself. Balanchine asked Toshiro Mayuzumi, a pioneering Japanese composer of *musique concrète* who had already won worldwide acclaim for works such as the *Nirvana Symphony,* to compose the music. In the eyes of the *Times*'s music and dance critic at the time, *Bugaku* was a "stately mishmash,"[123] but with successive productions it gained many admirers—and now stands as a consummate example of work conceived by a (Russian-born) American artist inspired by Japanese culture. As Clive Barnes memorably wrote about the work later, "Whether the Japanese themselves know it, this is the Japan that any New York veteran of a few dozen Kurosawa movies would recognize. It may not be *their,* but it is certainly *our* Japan."[124]

Outline

In *America's Japan and Japan's Performing Arts,* I begin by looking at the period from January 1952, when the idea of bringing kabuki to America was initially aired in the pages of the *New York Times,* until the summer of 1960, when the first "authentic" (all-male, professional) troupe, dubbed Grand Kabuki, made its American debut in New York.[125] My purpose is to document and analyze the discourse that was shaped by prominent critics and "Japan hands" during this defining era for establishing a new relationship with Japan. Although represented by kabuki, it is a discourse that grows out of all of Japan's traditional theater arts. The 1959 gagaku visit referred to above, for example, marked a cultural exchange coup for the United States: the Imperial Household ensemble that traveled to New York had rarely performed publicly and never before outside Japan. I then track the expansion of America's kabuki-Japan from the 1960s through the first decade of the twenty-first century, beginning with the seminal introduction of kyogen, bunraku, and noh to American audiences between 1964 and 1968 and continuing through periodic return visits by kabuki and the other traditional forms. Held up early on as a model for the concept of "total theater," kabuki has now fully "arrived"—having entered the general American vocabulary as a richly suggestive (albeit somewhat negatively tinged) metaphor used by a range of commentators, journalists, and novelists. Over the span of sixty years, America's kabuki-Japan has been the product of and continues to reflect a complex mix of cultural and political issues and interests.

I next examine the ways in which four distinctive New York institutions—Japan Society, La MaMa, Music From Japan, and the Lincoln Center Festival—have structured and conveyed knowledge about Japan through the performing arts. How critics—and audiences in general—respond to Japan-related theater, music, and dance directly relates to where work is shown and how it is contextualized. Power resides with artistic directors and producers—"the filters through which . . . artists must pass to be seen by the public"[126]—who develop programming, select and recruit performers, schedule performance space, obtain financing, and generate publicity materials. Starting under the postwar stewardship of John D. Rockefeller III, Japan Society became—and continues to be—the foremost producer and presenter in the United States of Japan-related performing arts. It is also a leading granter of commissions to artists. The society has hosted scores of plays, dance events, and music programs; a rough count suggests more than six hundred, not even including the many workshops, lectures, and play readings that have also taken place. The other three institutions stand out among the substantial number of presenters and producers that have taken Japan-related performance outside of the walls of Japan Society and situated it within New York's competitive performing arts environment. Beginning in 1970, La MaMa, which epitomizes the avant-garde onstage in the United States, brought rock musicals and experimental theater and dance from Japan to its downtown space—and categorically de-familiarized a culture that audiences had come to think of chiefly in terms of the traditional arts. Founded in 1975, New York–based Music From Japan (the *F* is deliberately capitalized) has played a singular role in the arena of music-focused cultural exchange by serving as a conduit to US audiences of important new work by composers from Japan. With a roster of top-tier U.S.- and Japan-based musicians, it produces concerts every year, all of them taking place on the borrowed stages of well-known concert halls. Since the Lincoln Center Festival began in 1996, Japan-related productions have been integral to its lineup of international theater, music, and dance. One of New York's headline performing arts events, the three-week summer festival encapsulates the fluidity and contingency of cultural circulation and exchange on a global scale.

I then turn to a discussion of the critics, scholar/experts, and Japan-based correspondents whose writings construct America's Japan through the performing arts. They are "seeing-men" (and women), to borrow Mary Louise Pratt's terminology,[127] who function as cultural mediators and interpreters. Continually rendering judgments about what is authentically Japanese (and what is not), they help write "the histories through which the Orient, the East, and Asia have been configured through variegated practices of locating self against other."[128] Their output takes three basic forms: articles that preview forthcoming productions, reviews of presentations that have already occurred, and reportage intended to broaden and deepen American knowledge of the theater, music, and dance scenes in Japan. Preview essays, in effect, "soften the ground for nervous newcomers,"[129] alerting readers to upcoming productions and educating them about aspects of art forms with which they may be unfamiliar. The review that follows an event amplifies and contextualizes it for those who also attended and provides a kind of armchair theatergoing experience for those who did not. By the late 1990s the *Times* had launched an "Arts Abroad" column, giving space to pieces such as "Taking Taiko, Japan's Big Drum, into the Hip-Hop Age."[130] However, articles by correspondents and specialists with experience in Japan were being regularly and widely published long before that and are an important component of the archives of America's Japan. I consider how the terrain of language has been negotiated in US presentations of theater from Japan. Such presentations are sites of linguistic contestation and tension. Non-Japanese-speaking audiences rely on technologies of access to foreign words spoken—and cultures experienced—live onstage: supertitles, wireless earphone translation and commentary systems, and program notes. I begin by discussing what can be termed Japan's "theater of translation"—the ongoing, century-old project of translating plays from abroad into Japanese and bringing productions of them to the stage in Tokyo and other theater centers with Japanese casts. In contrast to the linguistic domestication of foreign theater that is the norm in Japan, language is a principal marker of foreignness when Japanese theater travels abroad. I go on to look at critical responses to a range of theater from Japan by way of proposing an analytical framework for what Susan Bassnett-McGuire has called the "intercultural transfer" that has taken place over the past sixty years.[131] I identify three principal discursive strategies: surrender, assuming universality, and resistance.

I conclude the study by focusing on Carnegie Hall's extended celebration of Japanese culture in 2010–11 and the concerts curated by John Zorn that stood out among the various benefits held in New York following the March 2011 earthquake and tsunami in Japan. Both sets of events took place alongside the regular flow of Japan-related programming that also occurred during the same general span of time. Taken together the presentations that unfolded from the late summer of 2010 to the summer of 2011 embody a period of closure and counterpoint in what Stephen Greenblatt has referred to as "the restless process through which texts, images, artifacts, and ideas are moved, disguised, translated, transformed, adapted, and reimagined in the ceaseless, resourceful work of culture."[132]

1

America's Kabuki-Japan

Many overseas visitors to Japan have the impression that Japanese theater is all about Kabuki. I would like to dispel that myth.[1]

Japanese art forms have always seemed about as distant as one could imagine.[2]

The Discourse Takes Shape, 1952–1960

Against the backdrop of a cold-war imperative to secure Japan as an American friend in Asia through projects of cultural diplomacy, three Pulitzer Prize winners—playwright-novelist Paul Green, producer-director-playwright Joshua Logan, and novelist-journalist James Michener—turned their individual enthusiasm for kabuki into a highly publicized campaign to bring American audiences into direct contact with the art form. What eventually followed was a series of celebrated tours of the United States by kabuki performers from Japan, starting with the female-led Azuma Kabuki Dancers and Musicians in 1954 and continuing to this day—with the most recent one occurring in 2007.

In labeling the discourse America's kabuki-Japan, I have in mind Masao Miyoshi and H. D. Harootunian's observation that following the war "Americans seized the initiative for constructing an image of Japan and portrayed the country as a model of peaceful modernization . . . based upon the presumed continuity of traditional values."[3] Periodic visits by kabuki—as well as gagaku, noh, kyogen, and bunraku—to the United States have reinforced (and continue to reinforce) images of a Japanese culture characterized by tradition and ahistorical continuity. Critics saw in the Azuma Kabuki Dancers and Musicians an art form that transcended theater; in Grand Kabuki they saw one that transcended history. In a 1960 review, Brooks Atkinson wrote that kabuki is "a rich, impersonal art that has no time or place," presented by actors who "move around the stage like gods in the style of their ancestors." Words articulating warm feelings toward Japanese culture in response to the successful kabuki visit formed a counternarrative to the "ugly and painful" situation arising on the political front over renewal of the United States–Japan Security Treaty. The actors left Japan in May 1960 amid massive anti-American protests. In June those protests turned into riots, causing Dwight D. Eisenhower, who was to have been the first American president in office to visit Japan, to cancel his trip. For kabuki in America, however, "Nothing intrudes on their world but grace, beauty and stateliness," as Atkinson declared.[4]

Kabuki was not simply introduced to America; it was promoted as part of a larger, postwar project focusing on American-initiated international reciprocity and exchange.[5] This was in stark contrast to the situation that prevailed during the war, when kabuki had been used to condemn Japanese culture: in 1943, as Marlene Mayo has pointed out, *Life* magazine published an article on kabuki in order "to expose the barbaric, feudal mentality of America's Japanese enemy in the Pacific War."[6] Following Japan's defeat and with the Occupation drawing to a close, however, spectacular, larger-than-life kabuki was seen as having the potential to reignite America's nearly hundred year old romance with exotic Japan. Green, Logan, and Michener took the lead in framing kabuki as a beckoning entry point for postwar American appreciation of Japan, an important part of the Asia that Americans were being urged to befriend.[7] By the mid-1950s, kabuki had become a symbolic prize in the cold-war struggle with the Soviet Union for an alliance with Japan—one that the United States captured by being the first to bring a professional troupe to its shores. (A visit to the Soviet Union took place in 1961.)[8]

One of the most sustained voices in the discourse of America's kabuki-Japan is that of Faubion Bowers, Occupation censor turned freelance writer. His books and articles, starting with *Japanese Theatre* (1952), were influential in shaping America's postwar understanding of Japanese culture.[9] While Bowers did much to educate Americans, his was in a number of respects an invented kabuki—portrayed as more central to postwar Japanese culture than it really was and as uniquely unchanged over time. The image resonated with American audiences, which came to applaud kabuki as the representative example of Japan's "ancient" arts.

American audiences also came to equate kabuki with Japanese culture as a whole. Especially before La MaMa's Ellen Stewart brought Japan "downtown" with productions by the Tokyo Kid Brothers and Shuji Terayama in the 1970s, this made it less likely that other performing arts from Japan, especially those that focus attention on issues of contemporary society and culture, would be given opportunities to be presented and attract serious critical attention in the United States. In the early 1950s alone, a great amount of innovative work was being done in Japanese theater by directors such as Koreya Senda, Sugisaku Aoyama, and Tetsuji Takechi; by playwrights such as Junji Kinoshita, Tsuneari Fukuda, and Yukio Mishima; and by companies such as the Bungaku-za (Literary Theatre) and Haiyu-za (Actors' Theatre). Out of this varied scene, little besides Mishima's modern noh plays has become known to American audiences. Over time, as the number of productions has slowly grown, theater from Japan has sparked new ways of thinking about Japanese culture—challenging, but by no means totally supplanting, America's kabuki-Japan.

"Wait Till You See the Kabuki Theatre"

The effort to bring kabuki to the United States got under way even before the Occupation ended in April 1952. On January 27 of that year, the *New York Times* simultaneously carried "Tribute to the Kabuki Theatre of Japan," by Paul Green, and an accompanying short piece by Joshua Logan titled "Mr. Logan Seconds Mr. Green." Green—a prolific writer of screenplays and works of nonfiction, in addition to dramas and novels—won the Pulitzer Prize in 1927 for the play *In Abraham's Bosom.* In 1950 Logan shared the prize with Richard Rodgers and Oscar Hammerstein for *South Pacific*—based on *Tales of the South Pacific,* for which James Michener won a Pulitzer in 1948. Identified in the author's note as having "recently returned from a 30,000-mile tour of the Orient," Green could barely contain his enthusiasm.

> Japan has in the main the finest theatre art in the world. . . . The Kabuki theatre is the true representational theatre art as I've yearned to see it. . . . What choreography! What color of costume and exquisite use of dance, pantomime and music! And the tremendous virtuosity and lyric reach of the acting—these take you like the rich outpouring of a great glowing flower. . . . In the Kabuki theatre I have found for the first time all the elements, all the materials of stagecraft, organic and inorganic, completely seized upon and possessed by mind.

Green's kabuki was totally removed from the present. In the sets he saw an architect's model come to life, replacing the war-ravaged landscape outside the doors of the theater with an idealized vision of a timeless Japan. He wrote, "The wide vast stage is bathed in a deluge of light. There before us stretches a fairyland of color, cherry trees, pagodas, an upland of pine trees, and in the distance the white mystic top of Mount Fuji." Instead of the defeated military officers of recent memory, there were "a dozen stylized lords, followers of the Mikado, their wide, rich robes billowing out and around them in waves of brocaded color. Motionless and Buddha-like they sit, and on a second level behind them another dozen of their fellows cross-legged, each in his own individualized and fabulous costume." Green assured readers that the Japanese people themselves viewed kabuki as central to their culture. When the curtain goes up, he said, a "huge sigh of pleasure, of anticipation rises from the crowded audience. . . . The audience in the theatre sits there breathless."

Green laid out one of the basic tenets of America's kabuki-Japan: that Japanese culture is firmly based in its traditional artistic forms. He dismissed "the modern young Japanese playwrights [who] are opposed to Kabuki. Their eyes are now turned toward the West where 'the land is bright.' New ideas, new ways and means must be brought in if the modern Japanese theatre is to flourish, they say. Kabuki must go, they declare." Green's verdict was that "if these young men in their mistaken zeal succeed in driving Kabuki out they will then, in my opinion, have destroyed the finest theatre existent today." His words echoing those of Occupation censors, Green criticized kabuki for being "too much taken up with dead ethics and empty loyalties." His solution for creating a modern repertory was consistent with his view of kabuki as a model of artistic classicism. Japanese playwrights "have a fabulously rich national heritage of folklore, music, and religion going back more than two thousand years to draw from," he wrote. He pointed to "the vital active challenge and opportunity of the present hour in the building of a new age for their country" and "the onward call of that new age toward freedom and spiritual greatness which is to be." For Green, kabuki perfectly represented a Japan from which unwanted elements of a smoothly flowing past could be eliminated. It was "the solution and the key for a new dramatic statement of all of this—of the nation's past, its present, and its future—a shining and inspiring statement. What more could any artist want! What Kabuki needs is not its destruction but its revising!"[10]

The thrust of Joshua Logan's accompanying article was that Americans need the chance to see kabuki. Logan outlined the events that brought him to that conclusion. He, too, had recently taken a round-the-globe journey to study theaters of the world. Meeting up with Green "on a sidewalk in Rangoon," he proceeded to head for Japan with the playwright's words, "Wait till you see the Kabuki Theatre," fresh in his mind. Were that not sufficient recommendation, he reported that while waiting at the airstrip in Okinawa, "I listened to our American pilot telling me about Japan. 'One thing you mustn't miss—the Kabuki Theatre. I'd love to be there right now.'" The next day, "in Tokyo, I sat from 4 o'clock until 9:30 in the evening watching a series of Kabuki plays. I felt that the American public must be given the opportunity of sharing my experience. The next morning I started making arrangements to bring the Kabuki to America for a tour."

Green's praise for kabuki was packaged with advice to Japanese playwrights; Logan's came with the avowed determination to bring about a US visit. Reporting that the State Department "has shown its willingness to help," he wrote, "Not only would it give the people of America a chance to see one of the most exciting theatre arts in the world, but in this way we could also make an outstanding gesture to the East, by applauding one of its greatest traditions." Appealing to the internationalist idealism of the times, he concluded, "I think it would be heartwarming for us to exchange something besides money with a foreign nation. Perhaps in this way we could see deeper into each other's minds and emotions and find sources of sympathy and similarity."[11]

"One More Vote for Kabuki Theatre"

Of all those who argued for a kabuki visit, no voice reverberated more authoritatively than that of James Michener. Best sellers like *Tales of the South Pacific* and a steady stream of widely read articles in popular magazines such as *Life* and *Reader's Digest* had already made him "America's foremost popular expert on Asia."[12] In "One More Vote for Kabuki Theatre," published in the 14 December 1952 issue of the *Times,* Michener sought to lay down a definitive statement on the importance of bringing kabuki to the United States. He wrote persuasively, basing his arguments on extensive firsthand experience.

> Recently in Tokyo, when I expressed continuing interest in Kabuki, the management of the theatre reserved for me without charge a private box for all performances, and I was free to come and go as I wished. For eight months I studied the bloody, tragic, highly comic and stately plays of this strange theatre. Like Logan and Green, from the first moment I saw the brocaded pageantry of Kabuki I loved it; but after I had seen nearly a hundred different plays, some of them four or five times, I began to appreciate the intellectual content of this rare art.

Michener praised Logan and Green as "two distinguished American theatrical experts [who] have extolled the Kabuki theatre of Japan in these columns." But his aim was not just to build on their accolades. He wanted to go further.

> [Logan and Green] have said that artistically Kabuki is the first theatre in the world today. But I am not sure that they have conveyed the more important fact that Kabuki is also emotionally and intellectually a major world theatre. For Kabuki is not only overpowering to look at. It is also spiritually satisfying to a unique degree if one is willing to accept certain conventions which have governed Japanese life and emotion for more than a thousand years. If Kabuki fails to visit the United States it will be a cultural tragedy. Today, more than ever, we need to understand the accomplishments of Asia.

The warning that "a cultural tragedy" would occur should a visit not take place underscored two points. One was that nothing better represents Japanese culture than kabuki. The other was that a kabuki visit would show the power of the United States—not just in its ability to export its culture but also in its capacity to open its doors to other cultures.

Like Green, Michener criticized the repertory, but only by way of cautioning American producers.

> I am not sure that American audiences would like Kabuki. Some of the plays are tedious. All of them are too long. (A complete play might contain eleven acts and last two days.) Some of the dancing scenes relished by Japanese are either coy or barren. Comedy is apt to be so local and idiomatic as to be incomprehensible to a foreigner. And the style of acting is at times so overpowering that I fear it might repel effete and sophisticated audiences. I would not care to guarantee that Kabuki would make money in New York or that it would even break even. I fear our critics might condemn it as too terrifying and exhausting.

Given his follow-up comment that "for America to wait any longer to see this supreme theatre is regrettable," Michener's caveats can be read as a clever dare to New Yorkers, who could be expected to respond with broad-minded enthusiasm to whatever challenges kabuki posed.

Michener's "vote" for kabuki revealed his impatience that a US visit had not yet taken place. "I understand there have been several attempts recently to bring Kabuki to New York," he wrote. "They have failed because of financial reasons on our part and obtuseness on the part of the Japanese." He urged "public-spirited agencies" in the two countries to "step in and get this venture organized." Time was of the essence, Michener argued, if only because several of the greatest actors were getting on in years. He concluded the essay with a direct appeal to New York pride: "It would be a shame if New York, the cultural center of the world, failed to see what I found to be the world's most satisfying theatre."[13]

Credentialing "The Man Who Saved Kabuki"

The publication in 1952 of Faubion Bowers's *Japanese Theatre* helped give needed weight to the assertion that kabuki was an important world art. Green and Logan had considerable stature as theater professionals, but they had seen kabuki only as tourists passing through Tokyo on their way around the world. Michener had stayed in Japan longer and had far broader exposure, but not enough to claim depth of knowledge. None of the three spoke Japanese. Bowers knew Japan, its culture, and language: he had traveled to Japan before the war, learning Japanese and developing a well-documented interest in kabuki and close personal ties with a number of actors. He joined the Occupation forces as an assistant military secretary to General Douglas MacArthur, eventually becoming a theater censor. Even if Green, Logan, and Michener had wanted to learn more about kabuki, there was very little published material available at the time in English.

Japanese Theatre also helped launch Bowers's career as a New York-based freelance writer specializing on Japan, Japanese theater, and the arts in general. Over the course of four decades—from the 1950s through the 1980s—Bowers published several more books and a long list of articles in publications such as the *Times, Saturday Review, Theatre Arts,* and the *Nation.* Bowers, who John Dower has called "an irrepressible aficionado of kabuki,"[14] is the subject of an engrossing biography by Shiro Okamoto, translated and adapted by Samuel L. Leiter under the title *The Man Who Saved* Kabuki: *Faubion Bowers and Theatre Censorship in Occupied Japan.*[15] The title refers to the contention fostered by Bowers himself that he championed kabuki at a time when others were seeking to repress or even eliminate it—a point challenged by James Brandon, who has persuasively shown that kabuki was not on the point of collapse during the Occupation and Bowers was not alone in thinking highly of the art form.[16] Even though, as Dower has written, relationships between Americans and Japanese during the Occupation "usually rested on the assumed superiority of American culture,"[17] a sense of superiority that Bowers may justifiably have wanted to counterbalance, he was portrayed by Okamoto as a singularly daring Occupation-era contrarian for his admiration of and familiarity with kabuki.

Logan's exuberant "Foreword" to *Japanese Theatre* and Green's laudatory review of it in the *Times* credentialed Bowers as a specialist on Japan and an authorized spokesperson on kabuki. Although *Japanese Theatre* was presented as an overview of Japanese theater history, its main focus was kabuki. "This book is a report on the theatre in all its forms in Japan. It is a survey of what theatre arts exist there today and how they arose," Bowers wrote at the beginning of his book, immediately adding, "Because Kabuki is the dominant type of drama in Japan today, and has been for some three centuries, I have given most attention to it."[18] The degree to which Bowers was emphatic that kabuki signified theater culture even in postwar, mid-twentieth-century Japan cannot be understated. Logan used the "Foreword" to praise Bowers and simultaneously press his case for a visit by kabuki to the United States.

> The Kabuki theatre of Japan is one of the few great living arts in the world today. It is a dazzling experience for the Western theatregoer to sit through a series of Kabuki plays at the splendid new Kabukiza Theatre in Tokyo. . . . The whole effect of Kabuki is so startling that I felt it would be a great theatrical experience for New York playgoers, and I set about trying to find a method of transporting one of these great troupes from Japan to the United States. The process is a complicated one, and in trying to find the answers to the many questions that arose I have met many people. The most helpful to me has been Faubion Bowers . . . a young American who has made a thorough study of the Japanese theatre, and although his work is a scholarly one it is full of entertainment.

Building on the platform erected by Bowers, Logan formulated a crucial element of America's kabuki-Japan: that kabuki itself would be a primary instrument of education about Japan. He wrote, "There are many walls between the East and the West: our languages, our music, our painting. It would take a great deal of care and study for us to penetrate these walls. Only the specialists have the patience. But the Kabuki theatre is so vivid, spontaneous and dynamic that it throws open a door and gives us a clear view of the Japanese people, customs and art." Employing the phrasing of popular postwar humanism, he added, "The Kabuki theatre is universal and timeless and reaches the core of man. If this great theatre ever arrives in America I believe it will be a great contribution to world understanding." Logan's words reached their crescendo when he observed, "The readers of Mr. Bowers' book will have an insight into the Japanese character that cannot be found in the newspapers."[19]

It was as if Bowers had brought forth a sequel to *The Chrysanthemum and the Sword* (1946), the controversial—and influential—study of the Japanese national character written by anthropologist Ruth Benedict for her employer, the US Office of War Information.[20] In fact statements by Bowers in the preface to his book suggest that he had this very goal in mind: "Since the theatre is one of the stronger forces and influences in Japan's civilization, it is hoped that the result of this book will be to help the Westerner to understand better the instincts and impulses of the Japanese people—if only by indirection and inference. . . . What makes a Japanese laugh or cry, what and where are the roots of how he thinks, seemed to have answers in his theatre."[21] And by theater he basically meant kabuki.

Like Logan, Green used his *Times* review to recommend Bowers to readers and to reiterate and build on his earlier argument about kabuki. He wrote that kabuki "from the point of view of production . . . is the finest theatre in the world today. It sums up in itself all the ingredients of the past forms of theatre theory and practice. Mr. Bowers rightly devotes the main part of his work to a study and interpretation of this wonderfully imaginative and colorful art." Although Bowers warned in his book that the popularity of kabuki in Japan might decline in competition with movies and contemporary theater forms, Green maintained that Japanese culture in large measure was synonymous with kabuki and other traditional forms: "I for one am willing to wager that it will continue to live. It is too much a part of the blood and bone and muscle of the people to perish. . . . Its very dynamic nature as an art form will guarantee its continuance." Anticipating the "total theater" movement and the esteem in which it held kabuki, Green wrote, "This is theatre as it some day may be in the United States. On no other stage of the world is there such color, spectacle, artistry of make-up, grace of motion, and such fusion of music with words, gesture and idea. We can all learn from Kabuki, and this work of Mr. Bowers is a necessary handbook for those who love the theatre and its wider reaches of inspiration and freedom."[22]

Bowers's reputation was further boosted, and at the same time kabuki captured "highbrow" attention, in a lengthy review of *Japanese Theatre* by Emerson Harris published in the *Nation*.

> In the welter of reports on Japanese culture which have been appearing in the slick-paper journals since it became permissible to speak kindly of Japan, there have been a few scattered accounts of the marvels of the Japanese theater. Here James Michener and Joshua Logan have taken the lead, preparing the way for the theatrical feast we hope is to come when Mr. Logan clears away State Department red tape and brings to Broadway a full-scale importation of Japan's fantastic dramatic form, *Kabuki.* Meanwhile many of us have felt the need for a new and definitive book on the Japanese theater, and the need has been at least partially filled by Faubion Bowers.

In a paragraph citing Bowers's "unusual linguistic gifts"—a reference to his knowledge of Japanese—Harris enumerated what were to become the oft-cited elements of Bowers's biography that attested to his position as an expert in the field of Japanese theater: his years in Japan before the war and his position as theater censor during the Occupation. Harris wrote that "it is a tribute to his compassion and his artistic understanding that he made many friends in the theatrical world. He also made the most of his opportunity to increase his knowledge of Japan's theater arts."[23]

With his broad knowledge of kabuki gained largely through repeated visits to the theater and his authority deployed in his ready use of Japanese words, Bowers normally contributed to publications that did not demand documentation for observations that few editors or readers would have reason to believe were in need of substantiation. The more books and articles he published, the more his reputation and credibility grew.[24] Mindful of the intellectual rigor expected of articles appearing in the *Nation,* Harris took care to note that *Japanese Theatre*

> cannot be put in the category of scholarly works. Whether by Mr. Bowers's intent or at the behest of the publishers, there is an almost complete lack of scholarly or critical apparatus. To the scholar, therefore, the book will be frustrating for its lack of footnotes and bibliography. For the interested non-specialist there will arise the problem of the many romanized Japanese names and terms, which, although necessary, frequently impede the reader's progress.[25]

Bowers's writings overall must be understood as a reflection of his deeply rooted self-image as the "savior" of kabuki. As Earle Ernst, an Occupation censor who became a professor at the University of Hawai'i, wrote in 1987, Bowers "has continued to advertise himself as the person who single-handedly 'saved *kabuki.*' . . . He has created the apparently accepted opinion that before he became chief censor, previous censors were engaged in willful destruction of *Kabuki.*"[26] Bowers's task of "saving" kabuki did not end with the Occupation: an underlying theme of his writing was that kabuki (the equivalent, by extension, of Japanese tradition in general) continually needs defense against its detractors. In America's kabuki-Japan, American audiences—by virtue of their appreciative response to the art form—share in its protection and support.[27]

Images of Exotic Femininity: The Azuma Kabuki Dancers and Musicians

Troupe leader Tokuho Azuma is "a lovely creature to look at and a beautiful artist," wrote John Martin in his opening night review of a performance by the Azuma Kabuki Dancers and Musicians.[28] Nine months earlier Louis Calta had reported in the *Times,* "A deal is on the verge of being made that will start activity for the importation of the centuries-old Kabuki theatre of Japan." Impresario Sol Hurok was to be Logan's partner in the venture. The details were complex. Takejiro Otani, who as president of the Shochiku corporation was the contact person for kabuki in Japan, had agreed to pay one-third of the costs associated with transportation and production. According to Logan, another third would come from "private individuals" and the rest from "an established foundation, not necessarily the Rockefeller Foundation, which has been mentioned as a potential 'angel.'" The target date was the spring of the following year, although Logan told the newspaper that the 1954–55 season might be a more realistic guess, given all the work that had yet to be done. The goal was to present a program of at least a half dozen works "possibly at the Metropolitan Opera House or at a large Broadway musical theatre." Calta reminded readers, "The project, intended to encourage cultural relations between this country and Japan, was conceived several years ago by Joshua Logan, who witnessed Kabuki presentations in Tokyo."[29]

The year 1954 did indeed see a visit of kabuki to the United States—but not exactly the one that Logan envisioned. Hurok struck out on his own, booking the Azuma Kabuki Dancers and Musicians into New York's Century Theatre for a monthlong run that began on 18 February. Hurok's involvement was significant. Between 1953 and 1963 he "rarely left the public eye while engineering an amazing string of 'firsts' . . . [and] the trademark 'S. Hurok Presents' had come to evoke an image of reliable luxury, pleasure, and status. Virtually guaranteeing sold-out houses, it had become synonymous with the very finest in classy entertainment, representing the epitome of glamour during one of the most glamorous eras in modern American history."[30] Among Hurok's "firsts," including the kabuki of the Azuma Kabuki Dancers and Musicians, were visits by many troupes from abroad. "In 1955, the editorial page of the *New York Times* praised [Hurok] as 'a goodwill ambassador of the first order as well as a shrewd judge of American taste' for bringing the Comédie Française, the Antonio Ballet Espagnol, the Scots Guards and the Japanese Kabuki dancers in a single extravagant season."[31]

The Azuma troupe's star performer and namesake was Tokuho Azuma IV, the entrepreneurial daughter of kabuki actor Uzaemon Ichimura XV and a highly ranked performer of Japanese dance, which draws much of its repertory from kabuki. "Although women are not accepted as professional *kabuki* performers," Eric C. Rath has noted, "they dominate *kabuki* dance as teachers and students in Japanese dance (*nihon buyō*) schools, which number more than 150."[32] Azuma "was and is a legitimate *nihon buyo* school of *kabuki* dance," Kevin Wetmore wrote in an article on the 1954 visit.[33] It was headed by Madame Azuma, as she was called by the American press, who assembled twenty-five performers for the trip. Among them were Azuma's son, the professional kabuki actor Tsurunosuke Bando IV, and her current husband, the troupe's head choreographer Masaya Fujima.[34] In a two-page photo spread, *Look* magazine proclaimed, "The legendary Kabuki dancers of Japan are touring the United States for the first time to display dance dramas that have spanned four centuries."[35] The overseas tour gave Azuma, around whom the show revolved, a starring role that would have been denied her in Japan. In coverage prior to her arrival, the *Times* told its readers, "Although steeped in Kabuki lore, Azuma has never appeared with the Grand Kabuki, since it bars women. However, her troupe includes several men from Grand Kabuki, as well as ten dance dramas which are associated with Grand Kabuki."[36]

The first major theatrical group from Japan to visit the United States in the postwar period,[37] the Azuma Kabuki Dancers and Musicians put a feminine face on Japanese culture. Newspaper and magazine photographs showed the kimono-costumed and carefully made up Azuma in demure, "feminine" poses—images that spoke to "the vision of a gentler, more innocent Japan" being promoted in the postwar period by the American media, which "highlight[ed] Japanese females and children."[38] The pictures of Azuma also suggested a "geishalike" allure and sexual exoticism that would be intensified with the introduction of *onnagata* (kabuki actors who specialize in female roles) to American audiences in 1960.

The Azuma troupe fully delivered on Logan, Green, and Michener's promise of kabuki-as-spectacle. Some twenty-four tons of scenery and props were shipped from Japan. The logistics were so complex that a delay in the arrival of the crates forced a two-day postponement of the show's opening. Once onstage the Azuma troupe set the pattern in American kabuki tours of presenting at least two or three different programs during a run—to increase the likelihood of return visits by audience members and as a hedge in case one program was not a box-office success. It also set the pattern of programs made up of a variety of best-of-kabuki scenes and dances chosen for their presumed appeal to American audiences. "The program has been arranged by Mme. Azuma with an eye to showing the Western world the various styles of Kabuki theatre dance and music," it was reported.[39] There were seven pieces during each segment of the run, including dance-drama staples such as *The Monstrous Spider* (*Tsuchigumo*) as well as made-for-America pieces like *Kabuki Dance* (*Kabuki odori*).

Patterns of "cultural exchange" press coverage were also established at this time: it became regular practice at the *Times,* especially, to publish preview articles aimed at teaching readers about Japanese performing arts prior to opening-night presentations. "The Dance: Kabuki—A Glimpse of Japan's Classic Theatre in Its Choreographic Aspects," for example, was published four days before the Azuma opening. Cognizant of the real-kabuki/not-real-kabuki ambiguity of the Azuma troupe, yet intent on asserting that America was at a watershed moment in its reception of arts from abroad, dance critic John Martin wrote that, thanks to the Azuma troupe, "New York will be getting its first authentic glimpse of the choreographic aspect of the great classical theatre of Japan." Putting the visit in historical context, he observed that Japanese performing arts companies had been to the United States only twice before: "One was a group called 'Players From Japan,' which had a short season in 1930, consisting of 'native dramas' which had been 'adapted and directed for the American stage' by Michio Ito, with Japanese performers assembled, it was said, in California. The other was a troupe of Takarazuka girls at the World's Fair, who came from Tokyo, all right, but occupied, it seems, something less than an exalted artistic position there."[40]

Martin might also have mentioned the husband-and-wife team of Otojiro Kawakami and Sadayakko, who in the late nineteenth and early twentieth centuries headed the first Japanese theater troupes to tour the United

States and Europe. It was a time, as Joseph L. Anderson has written, "when both [American and European] theatre and dance were undergoing revolutionary change. In the course of two lengthy and enormously challenging tours undertaken between 1899 and 1902, [Kawakami,] Sadayakko, and their small troupes began to exert a profound influence through their performances."[41] One of their most popular pieces was *The Geisha and the Knight,* a "pseudo-*kabuki* smash hit" that was an amalgam of parts of two kabuki works.[42] Nevertheless, Martin's point was clear: in postwar America, kabuki was to be seen as an admirable representative of Japanese culture and the Azuma troupe was to be viewed as admirably representing kabuki (at least in its "choreographic aspect").

The Azuma Kabuki Dancers and Musicians additionally helped imbue performing artists from Japan with the aura of official, government-sanctioned cultural-exchange visitors. In contrast to the previous productions Martin had cited, "The present company is in an entirely different category, and comes under the patronage of the Emperor's brother, Prince Takamatsu, and the Japanese Ministry of Foreign Affairs. That would seem to give it the highest official stamp of approval."[43] In time American audiences would become used to seeing the Agency for Cultural Affairs and the Japan Foundation credited in publicity materials and program booklets for their sponsorship roles. These government agencies validate the "Japan's Japan" authenticity of visiting performers.

For Faubion Bowers, the visit by the Azuma troupe opened opportunities for him to publish his writing—and to mythologize kabuki—in the mainstream press. "Concerning Kabuki," which appeared in the 27 February 1954 issue of *Saturday Review,* is a significant document in the early history of America's kabuki-Japan. Contributing to the magazine's mission to help educate Americans about Asia, Bowers's article received exceptional advertising in the form of an eye-catching, woodblock-print-like illustration of Tokuho Azuma (resplendent in her dance kimono, fan held aloft) adorning the cover of the periodical that week. Although a prefatory note to the article pointed out that "the Azuma Kabuki Dancers and Musicians have stimulated interest in the great Japanese theatrical art form," Bowers was not interested in the Azuma troupe per se. "Azuma Tokuho presents her own distillation of one of the oldest and most important theatrical art forms in the world," he wrote, effectively dismissing the female-led troupe to point out instead that kabuki should be compared "to full Shakespearian theatre at its height in Elizabethan times." But there was a difference, which, as Bowers saw it, put kabuki ahead of Shakespeare.

Fig. 6. The Azuma Kabuki Dancers and Musicians on the cover of *Saturday Review,* 27 February 1954.

Kabuki, he expansively wrote, "is still performed more or less as it originally developed in the seventeenth century. It is also popularly supported in Japan today as the country's most active and beloved theatre—a statement which, unfortunately, cannot be made about Shakespeare either in England or America. Kabuki remains the oldest classical theatre in the world still maintained by a ticket-buying public."

Bowers's mythologized kabuki was not just removed from history; it was also universally appreciated in Japan. "The theatrical attitude of the Japanese is different from that of the West," he averred. "It is an almost compulsory ritual for the family to go together once a year to Kabuki. . . . If the family is able to afford it, they may spend all day in the theatre." Writing that "the puppet theatre is now the taste of a rarefied few," he declared, "Kabuki is appreciated by everyone from the Imperial family to the charwoman, who saves her pennies in order to make her annual theatre visit."[44] Such statements fit Bowers's version of a kabuki that had been saved from collapse during the war, conveying the image of an art form extraordinarily beloved at home and waiting to be revered abroad. At the same time they exemplify a kabuki-Japan that severs Japanese culture from contemporary reality. Writing in the *Nation* a few years later that "not one Japanese in ten has ever seen the Kabuki, it is far too expensive," Donald Richie (who, the magazine noted, "lives in Tokyo and teaches there at a Japanese university") restored the connection in a way others at the time could or would not.[45] The comment was made in connection with observations about possible links between extreme poverty in 1950s Japan and the high rate of suicide there—and included a reference to the not uncommon depiction of suicide onstage and in film in Japan.[46]

Transcending Theatre: Critics' Responses

The Azuma troupe's performances transcended theater: critics saw in them the opening of a new chapter in the history of relations with Japan. "It would be hard to imagine a more completely captivating evening than the one supplied last night by the Azuma Kabuki Dancers and Musicians," wrote Martin in his opening night response, the first of three published reviews. "You need know absolutely nothing about Japanese art to enjoy it; all you need is eyes, ears and a delight in expert theatre performance."[47] Extensive coverage in the *Times* and other publications attested to the perceived newsworthiness of the event. Martin placed the Azuma visit within the larger framework of American theater history and engagement with performing arts from abroad. In an article that appeared ten days into the run under the title "The Dance: Japanese—The Azuma Kabuki Style Makes Alien Conquest," he wrote:

> There can be no doubt that the Azuma Kabuki Dancers and Musicians at the Century Theatre have conquered New York, and this must come as a surprise to a great many people. Advance warnings came from Tokyo that we would be bored to death; here at home experts in the better brands of show business prophesied that while it was artistic enough, the public would never pay its money to see it. Some of us, having boned up conscientiously, were fairly well resigned to being politely instructed and nothing more. But we could all scarcely have been more mistaken. After the curtain of the Century had been up for five minutes, the prophetic forebodings were forgotten and everybody settled down to a richly delightful evening of the pure art of the theatre. The word has got around; the box office is booming.

Martin viewed kabuki as above all "a vivid theatre experience . . . that elusive thing we call Theatre with a capital T." American theater suffered in comparison: "[Kabuki] does not give a thought to naturalistic nonsense and playing at credibility; it deals in symbols that are far larger than actuality, stripped of trivialities and deceptions, and not subject to disbelief." Perhaps signaling the influence of Bowers's *Japanese Theatre,* Martin wrote that if American theater puts a premium on the new, kabuki was refreshing precisely because "everything is based on long-proven traditions." Kabuki was not just a visitor to be listened to politely then sent on its way. It was a revelation: "If the present company is typical, there must be a tradition of great performers in the Japanese theatre."[48]

The visit by the Azuma troupe was a New York event judged worthy of wide attention, sparking reviews and articles in national magazines—*Newsweek, Saturday Review,* the *New Yorker,* and the *Nation.*[49] The 1 March 1954 issue of *Newsweek* declared, "For the first time in history, a major classical dance company from Japan performed in the Western world." The article seemed intent on giving permission to Americans to praise Japanese culture: "The visitors had it all. The songs and rhythms were surprisingly pleasing to Western ears. The movement of the dancers was poetry in motion—slow motion."[50]

Saturday Review music critic Irving Kolodin commented that the Azuma troupe introduced New York to "the traditional art of Japan—colors that delighted the eye, sounds that engaged the ear, movement that fascinated both senses." In communicating a sense of frustration with the "otherness" of the presentation, Kolodin's review may have struck readers as a more clear-eyed appraisal than Bowers's "Concerning Kabuki," which had been published in the same magazine a week earlier. Kolodin wrote, "As tends to be the case with such adaptations of Oriental art for Western display, the program varied folk dances with more formal dance dramas. I had some fear beforehand that the latter might be drawn out too long, but such was not the case. . . . My feeling, however, was that for all the artistry they contained nothing, very much, really happened." He was generous in his praise, however, even while finding himself adrift: "The musical portion . . . was executed with absorbing precision by the dozen or so players of plucked, patted, and beaten instruments. In the purely musical numbers . . . a considerable but orderly din was set up. More than this I couldn't possibly say."[51]

Winthrop Sargeant, music critic for the *New Yorker,* echoed Bowers in describing the Azuma presentation as "a charming distillation in which elements of the famous Kabuki drama are combined with more popular types of entertainment. Only one item, called 'Tsuchigumo,' has the atmosphere of formality and austere dedication that characterizes Kabuki theatre in Japan." In a statement well illustrating the essentialist exoticism of America's kabuki-Japan, Sargeant wrote that "the show is authentically Japanese in its quaint symbolic pantomime, its solemnly exaggerated, crooning dialogue, its striking ritualistic dancing, and its music, and the costumes and scenery are enchanting examples of the artful simplicity so often found in Japanese art."[52] For Sargeant the Azuma troupe may not have been real kabuki, but it was "real" Japanese culture.

The *Nation* also gave the Azuma assignment to its music critic, B. H. Haggin, who unceremoniously rejected the appeal of "Japanese music" while lauding the attractiveness of other aspects of Japanese culture. He piquantly wrote, "Most of us get nothing out of Japanese music; but Japanese painting and sculpture make exciting sense to us, even if not the sense they must make to the Japanese; and this is true also of the highly formalized and ritualized dances presented by the Azuma Kabuki Dancers."[53] Even his dismissive remarks on music from Japan were a contribution to the exoticist discourse of America's kabuki-Japan. Several months later, reviewing a recording of musical numbers from the Azuma troupe's tour issued by Columbia Records, Haggin commented, "I find again that Japanese music and I are not for each other." This was immediately followed by "On the other hand I have had great pleasure from the recordings of American bird songs issued by Cornell University Records."[54]

A Program Statement for America's Kabuki-Japan

The virtual equation of kabuki with Japanese culture reached a defining moment in the March 1954 issue of *Theatre Arts,* "America's most influential theatre periodical,"[55] which appeared on newsstands and in subscribers' mailboxes while the Azuma troupe was still performing in New York. The monthly magazine's primary audience was New York theater and arts professionals and aficionados. Opening the publication, readers found a special section titled "Theatre in Japan," which, in retrospect, constituted a program statement for America's kabuki-Japan.[56]

The section was produced "with the assistance of" Beate Gordon, who was just beginning a career at Japan Society (and later Asia Society) that would make her New York's—and America's—leading presenter of performing arts from across Asia. She had already made her mark in history as one of the writers of Japan's postwar constitution. To validate America's embrace of Japan's performing arts, Gordon opened "Theatre in Japan" with "An Appreciation" written by Hisanaga Shimadzu [*sic*], consul general of Japan. Thanking the magazine "[o]n behalf of the people of Japan, for the enthusiastic interest and scholarship that has gone into this colorful and informative supplement on Japan's theatre arts," the consul wrote that the Japanese people "have cherished and supported [their theater arts] with devotion and patronage since the dawn of our history." Politely playing along with the section's overwhelming emphasis on kabuki, he observed that it "is among the most honored of our traditional stage arts." He expressed admiration for American knowledge of the art form, noting that the essence of kabuki "lies deep in the aesthetics and sacred symbolism of antiquity. Yet, these articles on Kabuki—all written by non-Japanese—strike me as remarkably lucid and perceptive; they manage somehow to convey the intrinsic qualities and beauty of this unique and peculiarly Japanese art form."[57]

The articles to which the ambassador was referring begin with Green's "East Meets West." Green, pressing his case for kabuki as a key to good US-Japan cultural relations, lauded the decision of *Theatre Arts* to focus the issue on Japan, writing that it depicted the "universal urge to cut across language and ideological barriers and enjoy the best of man's common heritage. The editors are to be congratulated on this fine service to theatre-lovers in America—in giving us these samplings of Japan's ancient and profound art." Referring to the trip two years previously that took him to "Hawaii, Japan, the Philippine Islands, Malaya, Thailand, Burma and

India" to learn about, experience, and talk about theater, he concluded, "There was no question about it—the theatre of Japan far excelled that of all the others. I found an abundance of dramatic activity in that dynamic little country"—going through a list that extended from noh to television. "And of these," he continued, "Kabuki was my special love. For here at last I found the lyric theatre I had yearned for so long. Here was the theatre in which finally were interwoven in their proper proportions the various elements of dramatic imagination—music, dance, pantomime and the fervent, soaring word, all clothed in colorful costume and the habiliment of the poet's dream."[58]

Bowers used his essay, "Backstage at the Kabuki," to help solidify his credentials as America's kabuki expert. He explained that he had been "a regular patron at the all-day performances of the huge Kabuki-Za theatre in Tokyo" since before the war, becoming friends with the actors and being welcome backstage. Furthermore, he wrote that during the Occupation he spent all of the time he could at the Tokyo Gekijo theater, where kabuki was temporarily presented before the war-damaged Kabuki-za was rebuilt. Proud of not being confined to his assigned seat in the theater because of his acquaintance with the actors, he had been able to experience the "ancient atmosphere of the greenroom . . . and the mystery of seeing my friends turn from ordinary human beings into personages. . . . The vivid impression of so many people gathered in concerted action has somehow left me with a sense of community and harmony that perhaps no other theatre in the world could have given."

Bowers intensified his mythologizing of kabuki, the core of America's kabuki-Japan—describing the art form as not only ancient but also sacred. The consul general's article contained a vague reference to the "sacred symbolism of antiquity," but Bowers stated outright that "theatre is still sacred in Asia"—noting that kabuki actors "must" bow to a shrine set up backstage.[59] Kabuki does have many ritualistic and religious elements. Its very origins four centuries ago are traced to a woman named Okuni who, it has been claimed, was a priestess from the Izumo Grand Shrine. Numerous plays are set within shrines or temples. However, kabuki is not ritual performance, although readers unfamiliar with the art form might have concluded otherwise.

Michener's impassioned "Kabuki Is a Must for America" injected new life into the project to bring a Grand Kabuki troupe on a visit to the United States. "For America to delay bringing the Japanese Kabuki theatre to New York any longer is intolerable," he declared. "We are depriving ourselves of one of the greatest artistic and dramatic treats the world has to offer." With his own reputation as an early champion of a cultural-exchange tour by kabuki artists on the line, he wrote, "Since almost every American visitor to Japan has reported that Kabuki is a staggering experience, I shall not belabor the point insofar as staging, costumes and vitality are concerned. Instead I should like to review briefly what Americans have done to get this amazing theatre to New York and to make some recommendations about what ought to be done next."

Michener offered a detailed prospectus in terms he believed left no room for error: "It would take about sixty Japanese men—there being no women connected with the theatre—to put on a first-rate performance. This would include not less than twenty musicians, for much of Kabuki is what we call opera and much of the rest, ballet." A practical man of the theater, he noted that the hosting venue would have to be modified to accommodate construction of the *hanamichi* ramp that is essential to kabuki productions—"the result would be the loss of some seats." Characterizing kabuki as Japan's "national theatre," Michener observed:

> Logan and his associates have from time to time felt that they could finance a Kabuki visit in which no one would lose money and nobody make very much. . . . At the height of negotiations Billy Rose generously offered his Ziegfeld theatre to the venture free of charge. The tour seemed set. In Japan, however, the Shochiku Company, which controls Kabuki, reviewed certain facts in its history. A tour to Russia some years ago [in 1928] had not been a success. Americans before Logan had made foolish and confusing promises. And other Japanese theatrical ventures in America had been robbed by unscrupulous agents. There ensued that heartbreak period which seems to characterize any Japanese-American business negotiations. The former grow suspicious and wary. The latter grow impatient. Nothing happens. So everybody on each side of the Pacific says, 'To hell with it.' . . . If we can bring trivial acts across various oceans to America and if we can import other national theatres to New York, some way ought to be found to bring in Kabuki.

Michener's contention that kabuki actors would have a "shattering effect" on US audiences neatly summarized the points made in the *Theatre Arts* articles by Green, Bowers, and Michener himself. "Americans are going to gasp," Michener wrote. "And that's what the best of Shakespeare and Molière and Ibsen and O'Neill make us do."[60]

Azuma Returns: More Kabuki but Still Not the Real Thing

The metamorphosis of kabuki into a symbolic cold-war prize occurred by early 1955. On 2 February of that year, the *Times* announced, "Japan was invited today to send a troupe of sixty Kabuki players—classical dramatists, dancers and singers—to Russia as state guests for a month's tour. The invitation from the unrecognized Soviet Union Mission in Tokyo was sent to Kunizo Matsuo, president of the Matsuo Entertainment Company. The company is studying the request."[61] Similarly, the 14 February issue of *Newsweek* contained an article titled "Japan: Invitation to Dance." It reported that the Soviet Union, which did not sign the treaty at San Francisco in 1951 that formally ended the war with Japan, was seeking to normalize Soviet-Japanese relations. An invitation to Japan to send a kabuki troupe to the Soviet Union was coupled with these efforts. Referring to the Azuma troupe, the article noted, "Last year a troupe of 24 Japanese Kabuki dancers and musicians staged a smash-hit tour of the United States. Last week Moscow invited Tokyo to send a troupe of 60 Kabuki (literally 'sing-dance-act') performers on a month's tour of the Soviet Union. It was one sign of the thoroughness with which the Communist world has begun to woo Japan."[62]

Newsweek also pointed out that China was making overtures to Japan—and, as it turned out, the first postwar tour by Grand Kabuki outside of Japan was to China in 1955. Meanwhile, Sol Hurok brought the Azuma Kabuki Dancers and Musicians back to New York for a three-week run at the Broadway Theatre starting on 26 December 1955. As before, Hurok presented the show "with the cooperation of Prince Takamatsu, brother of the Emperor of Japan, and the Japanese Ministry of Foreign Affairs."[63]

John Martin was almost as effusive in his praise for the second tour as he was for the first. "They made it quite clear that the success of their first visit last year was neither an illusion nor an accident," he wrote in his opening night review.[64] "Those who liked them before (and that includes this department) could scarcely fail to like them again," he wrote in a second review a week and a half later, "and those who found them originally to be slow, dull and altogether alien undoubtedly found new recruits to their point of view. The truth is that art is probably the least exportable of all commodities, in spite of the popular belief to the contrary." Martin regretted that the show appeared "less spectacular" than before, although he took pains to praise the music, which he described as "enchanting, even to Western ears that do not truly grasp its substance."[65]

By this time audiences were aware that Azuma Kabuki was not necessarily the "real" thing. Press coverage was ambiguous: in a preview article, the *Times* reported that the Azuma troupe "will introduce two traditional phases of the Japanese Kabuki theatre art"—one being "the playing of female roles by male actor-dancers" and the other being "the form of stage acrobatics called 'tombo.'"[66] Bowers, in part, turned a review of A. C. Scott's newly published *The Kabuki Theatre of Japan* into his own commentary on the Azuma visit, labeling the presentations "kabuki-style." The piece was illustrated with three photographs of the performers, including one somewhat confusingly captioned "Tokuho Azuma, A Kabuki star." Bowers joined Green and Michener in calling for a visit by an authentic kabuki troupe. The Azuma tour, he wrote, showed that "the pleasures of Japanese theatre are eminently exportable and, despite their exoticisms and unfamiliarity, are a genuine theatrical delight even for Westerners." Alluding to the role of kabuki as an instrument for building friendly relations between the United States and Japan, Bowers observed: "Japanese theatre has shown itself to have far broader implications than at first imagined. Its importance as one of the keys to bridging that troublesome gap between East and West is at last pretty well established."[67]

The Run-Up to Grand Kabuki: A Gagaku Coup and the Much-Maligned Takarazuka Dance Theatre

Perhaps kabuki was taking too long. In 1959, a full twelve months before the Grand Kabuki actors would step off of the plane, Lincoln Kirstein, director of the New York City Ballet, and Mitsuo Tanaka, Japan's consul general in New York, called a press conference to announce that gagaku musicians and accompanying bugaku dancers from Japan's Imperial Household would perform in New York that spring. It was a cultural-exchange masterstroke, the first time such a troupe had ever traveled abroad. "Few Japanese outside the imperial household have seen them," the *Times* reported. "Their coming performances outside Japan are unprecedented in the history of the group, which dates back to the year 703." On a diplomatic level, the visit was framed as "a celebration of the coming marriage of the Crown Prince Akihito to Miss Michiko Shoda and is also to be considered as returning the visit made by the New York Ballet to Japan last year."[68]

Kirstein guaranteed a ready-made and sophisticated New York audience by putting the gagaku performers on the same bill with ballet. In retrospect the bold, if rather ad hoc, arrangement made the gagaku visit a kind of warm-up for American audiences in advance of Grand Kabuki, which would appear on its own. The first half of each evening's performance was devoted to gagaku. An intermission followed, and then viewers watched resident company dancers in works of ballet. Combinations of different works made up four separate programs over a period of three weeks during which ballet acted as a host in sharing its stage with the visitors from Japan. The initiative was a success. "The New York City Ballet last night introduced to us an art as remote from its own as it could possibly be and still remain within the broad definition of dancing," wrote Martin. "It is supremely calm, exquisitely poised, as unhastenable as the rising sun and almost hypnotically beautiful."[69]

Coverage in the national newsweeklies uniformly communicated the image of an exoticized, ahistorical Japan. "Gagaku mirrors the serenity, classic beauty, and disciplined order of a culture more than a thousand years old," commented *Newsweek* in a review titled "Oddest and the Oldest." An accompanying photo depicted a performer whose face was covered with a hoodlike mask, his bare hands raised chest high, the caption dryly noting, "Gagaku musician: He dances, too." There was a reference to gagaku as an art in decline: "Regrettably, few young Japanese of today care to spend the ten years it takes to learn [gagaku's] delicate subtleties . . . [and] it is entirely possible that more of this dying art form will be seen by Americans in its performances in seven United States cities than has ever been seen by the Japanese themselves."[70] The idea that American admiration of Japan's traditional arts encourages their continuation is a salient component in the discourse of America's kabuki-Japan.

In sharp contrast to the gagaku visitors, the forty-two-member Takarazuka troupe, which arrived in New York three months later, was derided for not transmitting the image of authentic Japanese culture. Although the all-female dance theater had been respectfully introduced in Michener's best-selling novel *Sayonara* (1954) and the eponymous 1957 film directed by Logan and starring Marlon Brando, critics quickly expressed disbelief that such a troupe was actually booked into the Metropolitan Opera House, Manhattan's most opulent and prestigious performance space, for a lengthy eighteen-day run.

The tour, covering thirty-two cities in the United States and Canada, was arranged by veteran New York music, opera, and ballet impresario Albert B. Gins, who, as he wrote in the program booklet distributed to New York audiences, "first heard of Takarazuka early in 1956 through a friend newly returned from Japan." In 1957 Gins "visited Japan and promptly fell in love with the country and the people," spending two weeks in the town of Takarazuka (the troupe's home base near Osaka) "in constant attendance at the theatre, learning with each new visit the better to appreciate the subtlety of performance and the exquisite refinement of every phase of production." Gins—like Logan, Kirstein, and Hurok—was a theater man with a diplomatic mission. He expressed the "hope that the appearance of this magnificent company on our continent will help to strengthen the bonds of friendship between America and Japan and contribute in some small measure to the understanding that is so desperately needed in our world today." Gins's enthusiasm for the Takarazuka undertaking seems to have been reciprocated on Japan's side: the first page of the program booklet contained a message from Japan's foreign minister, Aiichiro Fujiyama: "The Takarazuka with its shining history of 40 years is sending across the Pacific Ocean a troupe composed of its best talents with a unique repertory of its own. The artistic and competent performance by these well-trained players is sure to be accorded a warm reception on the part of American audiences in every city they visit. Thus, they will not only win laurels for themselves but also contribute handsomely to the furtherance of Japan's international relations of friendship and goodwill with Canada and the United States."[71]

Despite the high-minded intentions of those involved in the tour, the Takarazuka was already a magnet for cultural mockery. In a 1953 "Special Report" from Japan, *Newsweek* had characterized it as "the most brilliant spectacle and bizarre institution in the Japanese theater."[72] Two years later a Japan-based correspondent for *Time* reported on its "rare, sukiyaki-like mixture of the Folies Bergères, Radio City Music Hall, the Metropolitan Opera and native Kabuki. It is the Japanese teenager's most popular musical entertainment," reproducing for readers some of the "mispronounced" (i.e., Japanese-inflected) English-language lyrics of "Jinguru berru" (*Jingle Bells*) sung during a Christmas season show.[73] In a *Times* Sunday magazine preview article published just before the show's opening in 1959, Japan-based correspondent Robert Trumbull wrote, "One of Japan's living legends—forty-two living dolls—will be seen in New York in the lovely living flesh when the girls of the renowned Takarazuka Dance Theatre open a two-and-a-half-week run at the Metropolitan Opera House on Sept. 16." It was, Trumbull sarcastically hyped, "a type of musical show that has been enchanting Japanese audiences for nearly half a century." The tour "will offer a variety of classical and folk dances, comedy routines and songs and dances, some of them derived from the classic *kabuki* drama, and all of them done with the lavish staging typical of Takarazuka." However, as Trumbull also pointed out, in Japan it is only the first half of Takarazuka shows that is "Japanese." The second half "is completely Western in style—usually a singing-dancing revue with up to 100 girls on the stage at one time, in a Radio City type of spectacle." Trumbull remarked that it was the Western type of show—which Takarazuka had been doing since the 1920s—for which the "girls are most admired at home."[74]

Martin's own preview piece—subtitled "All-Girl Spectacle from Takarazuka Designed to Entertain the Tourist"—averred that the troupe would have difficulty winning accolades in New York. Takarazuka, Martin reminded readers, would be "the third type of Japanese dance company to visit this country since the war." However, in contrast to the Azuma company, "from the Kabuki Theatre in Tokyo in that time-honored and traditional theatrical style," and gagaku, which "showed excerpts from fascinating court ceremonials of even more ancient origin," Takarazuka "will take us now into the modern and commercial field." Within the discourse of America's kabuki-Japan that was quickly taking shape, it was the traditional performing arts that were held in high regard. They wore the patina of age—and did not date only from 1914, like Takarazuka did.

The Takarazuka troupe already had another strike against it: Martin (who started writing dance criticism in 1927) recalled that it had "appeared twice nightly at the New York World's Fair in 1939 (and also on tour) under the title of 'Cherry Blossom Ballet,' and was not well received. Naturally every effort will be made to see that this does not happen again." For the upcoming visit, "The Western portion of the repertory [jazz, Rockette routines, and sometimes operetta] will be omitted here [in the United States], no doubt because of characteristic Japanese delicacy. The decision was made, it seems, by the Japanese themselves without any dictation by their American impresario."[75] Martin's information turned out to be incorrect, however, and his review was extremely negative. What the Takarazuka "is doing at the [Metropolitan] Opera House is hard to determine," he said. "In its home theatre . . . where it is surrounded by Ferris wheels, roller coasters and swimming pools, it undoubtedly has an authentic form and feeling, for it has endured there for forty-five years and has even spread to other cities. At the Met, however, it is an unclassifiable hodgepodge." Audiences witnessed, in Martin's words, "a long series of what can perhaps best be described as revue numbers—jazz-textured dancing, singing and acting, sometimes in English—while a Western orchestra discourses tunes in old-fashioned Tin Pan Alley style, with hints of the later Caribbean rhythms, and a great deal of fox-trotting. The result is neither art, show business nor even first-class Radio City Music Hall."[76] *Time* facetiously referred to the "thinly disguised Broadway and Paris turns, together with jazzed-up versions of Japanese fairy and folk tales, all held together in a sukiyaki-like mixture of muted native music and brassy show tunes."[77]

When Martin had reviewed the gagaku visit, he called attention to the fact that all of the performers were men—a distinguishing feature, as Americans were learning, of Japan's traditional performing arts. While he had warmly welcomed the Azuma Kabuki Dancers and Musicians, a troupe that included both women and men, he found an ensemble comprising only women a different matter entirely: "Why the performance should be given by an all-female troupe is not clear. They may be the most charming of creatures off stage, but on stage nothing at all is made of their femininity. It is about as sexless an evening as can be imagined. In the dramatic roles, and elsewhere, men would obviously have more force and conviction. The all-girl angle appears to be purely a stunt." The critic was so displeased that even the costumes, which in previous shows from Japan were cited for their beauty, were subject to derision: they "upholster the cast as if they were so many larvae in cocoons."

The unfavorable response to the Takarazuka visit in 1959 helped clarify and inscribe the discourse of America's kabuki-Japan in the months leading up to the arrival of Grand Kabuki. "[T]he show as a whole," Martin wrote, "is a long, thin and sterile crossing of East and West, and not the best aspects of either. Happily, we are all aware of the rich and artistic and theatrical heritage of the Japanese, and will not be deceived." Takarazuka, well appreciated by thousands of fans in Japan who reveled in the loud, brash, and sentimental kitsch that provided a vehicle for their stars, did not match Americans' expectations of an aestheticized Japan either in 1939 or twenty years later. Because authentic Japanese culture was being defined in terms of the "untouched" remoteness of arts such as kabuki and gagaku, Martin could write in the conclusion to his Takarazuka review, "We may be a little shocked, however, by our own responsibility for putting into foreign circulation such libels on our culture as are here brought home to us."[78] America's Japan in the 1950s rejected anything that did not pass the smell test of tradition equals authenticity—to the extent that Americans, as victors in the war with Japan, might, with a slightly self-satisfied air, blame themselves for corrupting that authenticity with "libels on our culture," such as (to use Martin's examples) Tin Pan Alley and the foxtrot. In contrast, gagaku, as a *Times* headline had earlier proclaimed, was "1,000 Years from Broadway."[79]

1960: The First US Visit by Grand Kabuki

The first Grand Kabuki tour of the United States came about as a result of determined, internationalist enthusiasm on the American side and reciprocal cooperation on the Japanese side. After the Azuma Kabuki Dancers and Musicians completed its second New York run in January 1956, there was no further word about plans for more kabuki visits until the news four years later that the Japanese government would help finance a first-time trip by a Grand Kabuki troupe to the United States. Japanese officials gave the upcoming tour a diplomatic spin, announcing that it would "commemorate the centennial of the signing of the first agreement for trade and commerce between the United States and Japan in 1860."[80]

If the 1960 kabuki visit were to be a singular event, like nothing that had ever occurred previously in the United States, it was important to distinguish it from the earlier tours by the Azuma troupe. Following Michener's lead in referring to kabuki as opera, the *Times* reported that "Japan's traditional operas" would be seen for the first time in the United States. In contrast to "the full operas" of Grand Kabuki, the Azuma ensemble was retrospectively categorized as only dance—performed by a "new" group that included women. The performers slated to travel to the United States were identified as a "top group" and all male. Productions were initially and, as it turned out, too ambitiously envisioned for six cities—New York, Washington, DC, Boston, Chicago, Los Angeles, and San Francisco. In the end, these were reduced to three: New York, Los Angeles, and San Francisco.[81]

Kabuki in 1960 acquired a new set of negotiators. In Japan, instead of Prince Takamatsu and the Japanese Ministry of Foreign Affairs, there were the Shochiku corporation and the Kokusai Bunka Shinkokai (Society for Promoting International Cultural Relations, forerunner of the Japan Foundation). On the American side, Hurok was replaced by Kirstein, who built on his success in bringing gagaku to the United States, aided by Bowers. Administrative assistance was also provided by New York's Society for International Cultural Relations and Japan Society, as well as by the Greek Theatre Association of Los Angeles. Logan's name was not mentioned.[82] Seven works—a selection of visually attractive dance pieces and showcase scenes from popular dramas—were rotated over the course of the tour: *The Subscription List* (*Kanjinchō*), *The Miracles of Tsubosaka Temple* (*Tsubosaka reigenki*), *The Sword, Kagotsurube* (*Kagotsurube*), *The Maiden at Dojo Temple* (*Musume dōjōji*), *The Treasury of Loyal Retainers* (*Kanadehon chūshingura*),

The Zen Substitute (*Migawari zazen*), and *The Sake-Cup Stand* (*Takatsuki*). American producers were concerned that "Americans would not like what they saw"; Japanese producers likewise were concerned that "foreigners would not understand."[83] As it turned out, audience response to all of the works was positive, even to *Chūshingura,* a particular focus of Occupation censorship—a clear sign of the postwar rehabilitation of the image of Japan as a friend of the United States.[84]

Extensive pre-event press coverage generated a sense of excitement for the spectacle to come. The *Times* reported, for example, that a curtain for the stage was being shipped from Japan, containing "73,000 small sheets of gold foil" especially woven for the occasion in Kyoto.[85] However, the most important article was saved for the week before the opening: "Classic Spectacular from Japan: New Yorkers Are About to Witness Kabuki, the Dramatic Excitement That Has Fascinated Japanese Audiences for Over 350 Years" was the *Times*'s marquee introductory essay on kabuki, published in the paper's influential Sunday magazine section on 22 May. The author was Donald Keene, then associate professor of Japanese at Columbia University, who would become recognized as the twentieth century's foremost Western scholar of Japanese literature. Keene's task was to educate all readers (whether or not they would actually attend a performance) about to be given "their first opportunity to discover the Grand Kabuki, one of the world's great theatres."

The March 1954 issue of *Theatre Arts* had in effect served as a program statement for America's kabuki-Japan. Keene's article, published six years later on the eve of a Grand Kabuki visit—symbolically a crucial juncture in the postwar history of US-Japan relations—was a far more significant document in the development of the kabuki-Japan discourse. It put the imprimatur of *New York Times* prestige (not to mention Ivy League scholarship) on the exoticization of kabuki as representative of Japanese culture. Despite mentioning that a simultaneous-translation earphone system would be available, Keene wrote that audiences could enjoy the "flowing movements of the dances, the bold gestures, and the sharp notes of the music . . . even when not one word is understood." Though already known as a translator of Japanese literature and drama, Keene suggested that understanding the dialogue "enhances enjoyment" rather than being necessary to it, implying that American audiences were not expected to penetrate the words of kabuki even in translation. He described kabuki as a kind of colorful anomaly: "Nothing could be farther removed from the normal Japanese preference for the muted and understated, but even the most devoted believer in astringency of color and line will be seduced by the brilliance of a Kabuki performance."

The article tried to address the nervousness of those who worried that Americans might somehow be repelled by kabuki and would project their distaste onto Japan as a whole. Anticipating an adverse reaction to the content of some plays, Keene attempted to separate kabuki from the very culture it was said to represent. He wrote, "It should not be supposed that these Kabuki plays present an accurate picture of the Japan of their day. . . . Men studying severed heads and children sacrificing themselves were hardly more common than they are today in the United States." He reported that "Japanese critics, always concerned with what foreigners will think about their country, at first opposed the inclusion of a *seppuku* scene in the repertory to be presented in America. They feared that Americans might conclude from such a scene that the Japanese were an uncivilized people." Keene's defense was an appeal to "universal" values: "[T]he reactions of American audiences are unlikely to differ greatly from those of Japanese audiences. The terrible confrontation with death rises above national cultures, and the solemn beauty of the suicide surely can reflect no discredit on the Japanese level of civilization."

The article was a lost opportunity to bring balance to conversations about kabuki—a massively complex form with a massively complex four-hundred-year history—that were already being skewed, by Bowers especially, and to start a richer and less reductive dialogue with and about Japan. Not given any contextual information about theater in Japan, readers of the article could easily assume that all theater there is kabuki and the average Japanese theatergoer is well versed in the art form. Despite the long-standing popularity of opera in Japan, Keene structured Japan and "the West" as a kabuki-opera binary: "Kabuki audiences, like Western opera audiences, know the famous plays by heart and wait for the great moments with anticipation," he wrote. Even though Keene concluded by arguing that the "appeal of Kabuki for Americans will not be merely that of an exotic spectacle," the art form was conveyed in exactly that way.[86]

Transcending History: Critics' Responses

Kabuki opened at New York's City Center during a Broadway strike. "Amid the inky darkness of the theatre district there is one bright gleam—the 'Grand Kabuki,'" Brooks Atkinson wrote. "Since they have done us the honor of trekking all the way from Japan, it is fortunate that the blackout does not include them." Following Bowers's and Keene's lead, he observed with simplistic certainty that kabuki exists in, but is not of, the present: "Imagine a theatre not interested in today. Imagine a theatre that has withdrawn from the world as austerely as a religious order. That is the Kabuki, which is a style of theatrical presentation that derives from ancient Japan and has not abandoned its origins."[87]

As the leading theater critic for America's most influential newspaper at the point of America's first encounter with "authentic" kabuki, Atkinson published four pieces in all—three reviews and an essay. "Visit by Kabuki," the title of that essay, is another foundational document in the discourse of America's kabuki-Japan. "Although realism is no longer the sacred goal of theatrical ambition, realism is an Occidental concept that underlies our approach to the stage," he wrote. "But the closer Kabuki comes to realism the further it departs from its nature." Atkinson suggested that "the play with relatively realistic characterizations ('Tsubosaka Reigenki') seemed insipid in comparison with the controlled fury and the gargantuan humor of 'Kinjincho' [*sic*]." The critic was attracted to the "fantastic costumes," "stylized movement," and "fabulous make-up" in *The Subscription List* (*Kanjinchō*). Kabuki had to be spectacular and "unreal" or it was not kabuki: "Nothing could be more unlike our theatre; and nothing could be more elegant and bravura, two qualities seldom blended in a single work of art."

Atkinson professed some insider knowledge of Japan by mentioning that he had been there before the war and had experienced kabuki. He saw the art form as an icon of extreme cultural difference. "After World War II," he wrote in the same essay, "Kabuki was discovered by hundreds of Americans stationed in Japan. No doubt, it visualized the enormous difference between the Orient and the Occident and curbed any foolish notions that Japan could be or should be Americanized." He ended the piece with a statement that set the tone for future reviewers: "None of us is able to understand the nuances of [kabuki] acting. But now we have a brief opportunity to study a mature art that stands at the opposite extreme from our own."[88]

With the publication of Atkinson's final review during the 1960 visit the discourse of America's kabuki-Japan fully took shape. Referring to the onstage musicians and singers as "Buddha-like," by way of describing their solemn expressions during a comic routine, the critic segued from theatrical to political events: "Strange that the Kabuki should conquer New York so spontaneously at a time when our political relations with Japan are ugly and painful. The stories and pictures in the news columns convey violence and hatred. The passions are personal, focused on the present moment." He then pronounced kabuki unconnected to history or even individual action, calling it, as mentioned earlier, an "impersonal art that has no time or place."[89] Kabuki was from Japan but not *of* the Japan that had been America's wartime enemy and now was convulsed by treaty protests directed against the United States.

The Grand Kabuki tour elicited broad national coverage. Henry Hewes of *Saturday Review* praised "Kabuki's superb theatricality" while occasionally admitting to being stumped by its "symbolic complexity."[90] *Time* found "theatrical vividness" and "esthetic purity."[91] *Newsweek* reported that the "rich costumes and the gorgeous sets are the East that the West cannot imitate; the controlled gestures and ceremonial ritual on stage are from a past that is ever present."[92] Louis Calta of the *New York Times* tried to put a human face on the actors, writing that they "were indescribably happy" with the welcome they had received in New York. They went sightseeing, saw Broadway shows, and were guests of Lee and Paula Strasberg at the Actors Studio. He reported that when the kabuki actors were asked if they had ever heard of the Stanislavsky Method, their answer was that it had been introduced to Japan some forty years earlier and "many modern directors and actors" were "experimenting with it."[93] Left unsaid was that, unlike the call for kabuki to come to the United States, there was as yet relatively little call for Japan's modern theater to visit.

After the New York critics had their last word on Grand Kabuki's US debut, the 9 July 1960 issue of the *Nation* published a wrap-up article by Bowers. Buoyed by the enthusiasm with which kabuki had been received, Bowers claimed a place for kabuki and himself at the center of New York theater circles, writing that many of the actors in the visiting troupe had been his friends "for some twenty years." While they were in New York, he said, "I had occasion to see them a good deal here, and almost every day I was called upon to interpret for one reason or another." The kabuki actors received many messages of thanks, "particularly from theatre people I do know," citing luminaries such as Anne Bancroft, Henry Fonda, and Greta Garbo—who "went backstage, for the first time in her life, to watch [Utaemon Nakamura VI] at close hand."[94] During the next kabuki visit, nine years later, Bowers would invoke Garbo's name in an article illustrated by Al Hirschfeld titled "Even Garbo Wasn't Allowed Backstage."[95] In 1960 Bowers's purpose was to make it clear that he was not merely allowed backstage but had a welcome place there.

In the *Nation* article and one in *Dance* magazine, Bowers put forth his mythologized kabuki. "Those in the rear of the auditorium *felt* the power that has been Kabuki's heritage for more than three centuries," he wrote, "and those in the front seats saw the tears, the real tears that welled up through the composed, concentrated, seemingly artificial formulae of stylization. Even the hard-hearted critic of *Variety* acknowledged the universality of humanity when he witnessed the *harakiri* scene performed in the controlled, mannered formality of ritualism."[96] He commented in *Dance* that kabuki "has been an easy beacon light" for Japanese in Westernized Japan in "their struggle to rediscover the values of the history within their blood." But kabuki is not for Japan alone, Bowers asserted, writing that "what the 20th-Century spectator sees in Kabuki is the past within the present. And through it all courses the unchanging warmth and humanity or coldness and cruelty of human beings. When history is transmuted by art and suffused with emotion, as it is in Kabuki, you have a moving and important achievement. And this attracts both foreigner and Japanese alike.[97]

In 1952, the same year that Bowers's *Japanese Theatre* was published in the United States, Koreya Senda's important and provocative work *Engeki to wa nani ka* (What is theater?) was released in Japan. Senda, who had been repeatedly jailed for his antimilitarist stands, had become founding director of the modernist Haiyu-za theater troupe in 1944, the year before the war's end. In the book he criticized kabuki, writing that it "is totally incompatible with the spirit of the new age. Some people defend *kabuki* saying it is an art of common people of the Tokugawa period and shows the townsman's spirit of resistance to feudal samurai rule . . . but such an extremely roundabout form of resistance and sentiments from the past have no hope of nourishing our souls today."[98] As James Brandon has pointed out, one reason that "*kabuki* did not modernize is that American theatre officials [during the Occupation] were quick to embrace traditional *kabuki* and call it a great theatre art." On its side the Shochiku corporation did not want to remake kabuki with a contemporary repertory—its mission being "to preserve *kabuki*'s traditional form." Suggesting that the art form might have become far different had Occupation officials not "in the end accepted *kabuki* on Shōchiku's terms," Brandon observed: "The adulation that Bowers [and other Occupation censors] developed for *kabuki* found expression when the Occupation was over. Soon there were translations of classic plays, and books, university classes, and television specials that highlighted traditions of continuity. This reification of the traditional mode of *kabuki* by highly regarded foreigners strongly contributed to classicizing (*koten-ka*) and aestheticizing (*bijustsu-ka*) the art in the decades that followed the Occupation."[99]

Green, Logan, and Michener took the censors' lead further by promoting kabuki as the preeminent example of a Japanese culture that could be presented with no reference to the Japan that was America's wartime enemy. As the Occupation drew to a close, and as it became increasingly desirable to the United States to build good relations with Japan as a cold-war ally by demonstrating appreciation of and admiration for Japanese culture, efforts to bring kabuki to the United States got under way. Those efforts resulted in the tours by the Azuma Kabuki Dancers and Musicians in the mid-1950s and Grand Kabuki in 1960. The project to introduce kabuki to the United States, and all of the visits by Japanese traditional theater troupes that have subsequently taken place are the raw material from which the discourse I have called America's kabuki-Japan was and continues to be constructed.

Kabuki as Metaphor

By the mid-1960s, as Japan's postwar economy steadily grew stronger, there were an estimated four thousand employees of Japanese corporations and their families living in the New York metropolitan area—"the largest colony of foreign businessmen" in the city, as journalist Gay Talese wrote in a 1964 article titled "Japanese Enjoy Bit of Tokyo Here." Their careers may be in international trade and finance, but Japanese residents of New York, according to Talese, "are deeply involved with the older Asian tradition and have little inclination toward abandoning it. In fact, it is now possible for a Japanese businessman to fly from Tokyo to New York and to carry on in full ritual, hardly missing a step, the same sort of daily routine he followed 7,000 miles away."[100] There was accompanying photographic evidence: snapshots of kimono-attired women at a New Year's party held at the executives-only Nippon Club in Manhattan, a banker posing with an abacus in hand, and a cluster of customers' shoes outside the tatami-matted dining room of a Japanese restaurant in the city. Talese might have more convincingly written that at that moment in time it was in fact Americans who had little inclination to abandon their belief in the steadfastness of "the older Asian tradition" when faced with reimagining the defeated enemy turned cold-war ally now transitioning to powerful economic rival.

My purpose in the remainder of this chapter is to give a brief overview of the expansion of America's kabuki-Japan following the first Grand Kabuki visit in 1960. The outline I trace begins with the seminal introduction of kyogen, bunraku, and noh to American audiences between 1964 and 1968 and extends right up to the present in the periodic return appearances by troupes performing kabuki and the other traditional forms. Held up as a model for the concept of "total theater" in the 1960s, kabuki continues a half century later both to attract and confound American audiences. It has now fully "arrived"—insofar as the word *kabuki* has entered the general American vocabulary as a richly suggestive metaphor (though one with occasionally amusing yet somewhat negative overtones) used by a range of writers.

Introducing Kyogen, Bunraku, and Noh

America's kabuki-Japan was progressively fed by the arrival of the other major Japanese traditional theater forms within the decade following Grand Kabuki. A kyogen troupe headed by Manzo Nomura made a two-part debut. There was a low-key "educational" tour in February 1964 "to demonstrate an ancient theatre art."[101] The show, at New York's Institute for Advanced Studies in the Theatre Arts, was co-sponsored by Japan Society and the Center for Asian Arts at the University of Washington in Seattle (where presentations also took place). The troupe then returned to New York in 1968 for a higher-profile visit produced by Japan Society at the 92nd Street Y. Kyogen, Richard Shepard wrote in response, "destroyed the stereotype of Japanese art so carefully built up over decades." Whereas "[t]o judge from opera, films and novels, Japanese are sad, tragic, fantastically arty and, in newsreels, angry," the critic discovered in the theater form the kind of readily accessible comedy "that unmasks human conceit."[102]

New Yorkers' initial encounter with bunraku came in 1966, arranged by impresario Paul Szilard. The *Times* Sunday magazine ran a detailed preview article by John Nathan, who had published another Sunday magazine piece three months earlier about his experiences as the first foreigner to appear in Japan on the *shinpa* stage—*shinpa* being a type of often melodramatic, modern-style Japanese drama that was still quite popular in the 1960s. Part of a new generation of Americans in Japan—foundation-funded students of Japanese language and culture with invitations to study at prestigious Japanese universities—Nathan was intent on putting some cracks in the bedrock assumptions of America's Japan. A graduate of Harvard, where he was active in campus theater productions, he was enrolled at the University of Tokyo when he suddenly found himself cast in the role of the historical figure Townsend Harris—in the nineteenth century, America's chief trade negotiator with Japan and the first US consul general there—on the Tokyo stage opposite Yaeko Mizutani, one of the country's most famous actresses.[103] If Americans assumed that Japanese theater was entirely traditional—and mostly kabuki—Nathan's firsthand account of his experience onstage revealed the existence of a thriving popular theater. His *Times* article on bunraku, despite its mission to elucidate the form, also attempted to contest preconceptions about Japanese culture. He wrote that the bunraku players "have prepared for the trip with enormous pride, and with a certain quiet desperation, too, for they are convinced—perhaps not so naively, it would seem—that Bunraku's future in Japan depends on winning recognition in the West. It is another of the traditional arts threatened by the new Japan, too esoteric now to appeal widely to the general public."[104] In contrast to Bowers, who tenaciously clung to the position that Americans needed to appreciate what "all" Japanese people already loved, Nathan presented a more nuanced view of the challenges faced by practitioners of the traditional arts in Japan.

"Japan's classic puppet theater Bunraku, which last night opened its first New York season at the City Center," Clive Barnes remarked in the first of two reviews, "is a theater of fantasy, a theater of disbelief, a theater of high seriousness where dolls take a time-honored place as classic actors in a heroic theater dating back to the 18th century."[105] A second evening's performance intensified his appreciation of the art form: "[T]his nearly 300-year-old puppet theater is clearly one of the artistic wonders of the world. . . . You watch the skillfully manipulated puppets and their urbane, almost uninterested keepers, flitting deftly around them, and somehow the whole performance takes on the quality of a metaphor for human life and tragic destiny. The puppets are reality, and their manipulators nothing more than the impersonal slings and arrows of outrageous fortune."[106]

The year 1966 also saw a tour by the Hosho noh troupe, "the first full Noh group ever to appear in the U.S.,"[107] which reached audiences in thirty locations—mostly university campuses. The planning was carried out by Prof. Donald Keene of Columbia University, with Japan Society handling the logistics. In contrast to bunraku, the critical reaction was subdued—little more than a report that the event had taken place. The *Times*'s Emerson Chapin let composer and New York Philharmonic conductor Leonard Bernstein speak for New York audiences. "It was marvelous. I'm crazy about it," he was quoted as saying.[108]

Total Theatre—and Grand Kabuki Returns in 1969

The inaugural tours of kyogen, bunraku, and noh completed the process of introducing Americans to all of the major genres of traditional performing arts from Japan. At the same time, new strands in the narrative of America's Japan began to emerge. One offered Japan's traditional, "authentic" arts in general—and kabuki in particular—as primary examples of "total theater" at a pivotal point in the history of the American stage. Samuel L. Leiter's observation, "Theatre artists everywhere were searching for new forms, new ways of expression, new ways to escape the dead ends of fourth-wall realism,"[109] could especially be applied to the United States in the 1960s. In his groundbreaking 1967 work *Theater East and West: Perspectives toward a Total Theater,* Leonard Cabell Pronko argued that Americans should open themselves up to "the many unexplored theatrical forms of the East," writing that "there is confusion and misunderstanding regarding Oriental theater, even by those who are theater specialists. Or rather, there is no misunderstanding, for there is no understanding at all, but total ignorance."[110] The task of learning was taken up with alacrity. "No form of theater is more exotic to Western audiences," Clive Barnes wrote in 1969, when the second Grand Kabuki tour took place. He praised kabuki as an "an early manifestation of what we now call 'total theater'" in which "the actors can express humanity with all of the richness of their Western colleagues."[111] Echoing these statements, Harold Clurman commented, "We talk a great deal about 'total theatre.' It is an ancient thing. Kabuki is one of its most brilliant forms."[112] Focusing on the same visit, Brendan Gill wrote, "[W]hat held me at once and made the exceptional length of the evening rush by unmeasured was the fierceness of the passion that the actors conveyed—and were enabled to convey—by conventions of speech and gesture that have been preserved largely unaltered from generation to generation." He expressed admiration for kabuki in contrast to what is "sometimes so unnerving in our contemporary theatre—that an actor has got up a role by ransacking his private life for mood-creating snippets of past miseries and joys."[113]

The 1970s and 1980s

By the late 1960s cultural exchange between the United States and Japan was undergoing a major shift in response to Japan's rapidly growing economy. Motivated to foster better relations with the United States, its most important trading partner, Japan increasingly sought opportunities to build on the goodwill generated by US tours of kabuki and the other traditional art forms. Government and corporate entities in Japan—from the Agency for Cultural Affairs to the *Asahi* newspapers—eagerly backed Japanese artists on an expanding number of trips abroad. Among notable visits from that time are a joint production of noh and kyogen at Carnegie Hall in 1971, bunraku at City Center in 1973, the Awaji Puppet Theatre at Carnegie Hall in 1974, and kyogen at Carnegie Hall in 1975. In 1976 the Felt Forum was the setting for a folk dance extravaganza. "From the land of the Honda, the Minolta and the Toyota," Anna Kisselgoff wrote, "comes the Odori Festival of Japan, a dance company that deals with a folk tradition that the classical groups such as Noh and Kabuki dance theater have not shown us."[114] There were three kabuki visits in the decade. *The Martial Arts of Kabuki* at Carnegie Hall in 1976 showcased young kabuki performers-in-training from Japan's National Theatre. In 1977 Grand Kabuki was presented at the Beacon Theatre on a tour organized by Kazuko Hillyer, a Japanese-born, New York–based impresario. Breaking the pattern of eight or nine years between visits, kabuki reappeared a scant year and a half later, in 1979, again at the Beacon Theatre in a Hillyer production.

The 1979 kabuki run highlighted a new assertiveness on the part of an economically powerful Japan that played out against the backdrop of a recessionary and somewhat self-consciously diminished United States. The tour included a stop at the Kennedy Center, a national cultural showplace in Washington, DC, that was deliberately timed to coincide with the opening of the center's Terrace Theater—calling attention in a not so subtle way to the fact that construction money for the new facility had been donated by the Japanese government. The title of a *Times* preview article demanded "Can Our Theater Learn from Kabuki?," with director Andrei Serban quoted as saying that kabuki "is living proof of what theater was like hundreds of years ago, when it was something much, much stronger than it is today . . . [and by] seeing the Kabuki, we must question why we work in theater and why our theater is so much less complete than the Kabuki and Noh. And our actors must ask again, when they see a Kabuki actor, who does everything, 'What does it mean to be an actor?'"[115] The implication was that Americans were falling short not just economically but culturally as well.

The 1980s marked the climax of the US anger over trade friction with Japan that was so graphically captured in an illustration that appeared on the cover of the 9 October 1989 issue of *Newsweek*. The kimono-wearing, geisha-like figure with her right arm dramatically held aloft, her hand grasping a torch with rays emanating from it, was an obvious parody of the "Western" lady in a loosely flowing garment, also holding a torch in her raised right hand, in the Columbia Pictures logo. It was a biting reference to the recent announcement that Sony Corporation of Japan had embarked on a multi-billion-dollar deal to buy the American movie company.[116] Cultural diplomacy went into overdrive, with kabuki tours in 1982, 1984 (a solo visit by Tamasaburo Bando V), 1985, and 1989. The 1982 visit, which celebrated the seventy-fifth anniversary of Japan Society, New York, was kabuki's first booking at the Metropolitan Opera House. Funding for that tour came from Matsushita Electric, the Japan Foundation, and a special grant from "the people and Government of Japan" to Japan Society. No expense was spared. A company of fifty-six actors and musicians—plus a crew of twenty—traveled to New York, and a full-sized *hanamichi* walkway, the sine qua non stage element in a kabuki theater, was constructed at the Metropolitan, necessitating the removal of over 130 orchestra seats.[117] Thirty-two-year-old Tamasaburo, "Kabuki's brightest young star," performed for the first time outside Japan—and was the subject of a *Times* Sunday magazine cover article. Shown relaxing in Japan in front of his silver-gray Cadillac, a potently conciliatory image for trade-war times, the actor was described as a "superstar 'onnagata'" who "has brought fresh excitement and a new young audience to the traditional art form."[118] Reaction was predictably positive, though there was a sense of weariness, as if critics' vocabulary had been exhausted. Citing the "brilliantly colorful costumes and makeup, elaborate sets and ingenious stage devices," Jennifer Dunning wrote in her opening night review, "The message of the Grand Kabuki is a simple one, readily transmittable across the years and continents—enjoy, enjoy."[119]

Before Tamasaburo came back to New York in 1984 for solo dance performances at both the Metropolitan Opera House and Japan Society, bunraku—an art that "alters one's perception of the uses of puppetry in drama"—returned to New York in 1983 to perform at Japan Society.[120] The year after that kyogen leapt forward in popularity with a free presentation of "torchlight kyogen" at Lincoln Center: "The setting was magical. A platform was built out over part of the reflecting pool in front of the Vivian Beaumont Theater. The pool's sculptures by Henry Moore and the façade of Avery Fisher Hall served as backdrops. Illumination was provided by torches, as well as by electric lights, and the waters of the pool reflected the stage action with a beautiful serenity."[121] Noh was still on the radar but less as theater than as cultural demonstration: in 1982 Asia Society presented excerpts from two plays in conjunction with a meeting of the International Symposium on Theater and Ritual sponsored by the Wenner-Gren Foundation for anthropological research.[122]

The remaining two Grand Kabuki visits of the 1980s were also the last ones of the twentieth century. In 1985 "the largest Kabuki contingent to appear outside of Japan"[123]—comprising over ninety performers and support staff—arrived at the Metropolitan Opera House for a run that would incorporate the first name-taking ceremony ever to be held outside of Japan. Since many people already had a basic acquaintance with kabuki, the standard preview article introducing the art form was no longer deemed necessary. Information conveyed before the 1985 production began included the fact that Essex House on Central Park South, the hotel where the performers were staying, had just been bought by Japan Air Lines and that the visit was being underwritten by Japan's Mazda Corporation.[124] The name-taking ceremony was a well-timed bit of theatrical business that seemed to strike a perfect note at a particularly uneasy juncture in postwar US-Japan relations. Kisselgoff followed the expected script in her review, making note of "the spectacular values of an ancient theatrical tradition that has sought to entertain its public for centuries." Lowering himself to bow almost prostrate before the audience, the former Ebizo Ichikawa X—who had recently ascended to the venerable stage name Danjuro Ichikawa XII—declared that he was "unripe" and promised to improve. "No American actor could possibly carry off such a public confessional," Kisselgoff wrote, "much less on his knees with head to the floor." It was not really a confessional, of course, but a well-established way that kabuki actors bond with audiences and win their affection. Kisselgoff solemnly added that "this initiation ritual places informality within formality very naturally."[125]

By the time the final Grand Kabuki visit of the twentieth century took place, American audiences were firmly wedded to the kabuki-Japan discourse but had seemingly had enough actual kabuki for the time being. It was also being reported that the art form was becoming less popular even in Japan: "For young people, classical theater (Kabuki, Noh and Kyogen) has lost its appeal," and audiences for kabuki "now tend to consist mainly of elderly people (mostly women), foreign tourists and groups whose tickets are paid for by corporations."[126] Ennosuke Ichikawa III, who had led the 1977 tour, styled himself as an energizing force—an individual who wanted to bring kabuki "back to the people" using techniques that used to be common when it was a popular art rather than the elitist refined art it became after the Meiji Restoration in the late nineteenth century. Ennosuke headed the troupe in 1989, again at the Metropolitan Opera House. Japanese producers surely hoped that New York audiences would respond with enthusiasm to Ennosuke's theatrics, but such feeling was not evident in the reviews. One remarked, "While Japanese movies have been popular here for many years and Japanese food has conquered New York astonishingly in the last decade, Japanese theater is still essentially foreign and remote."[127] Another griped that the show was more than three hours long and the pace at times "maddeningly slow."[128] Yet another was impressed with little more than Ennosuke's rapid costume changes.[129] No one seemed to regret the troupe's departure at the end of the run.

Perhaps nothing better represents Japan's emboldened confidence on the world stage in the 1980s than the reappearance of the Takarazuka, this time at Radio City Music Hall. Derided thirty years earlier as being a poor copy of American entertainment culture—a kind of anti-(authentic)-kabuki from Japan—it now rode the wave of Japan's economic might. In a preview article for the *Times,* Faubion Bowers suddenly sounded like a public relations agent for the Takarazuka organization. "[F]or the very first time," he wrote, "New Yorkers will see Takarazuka's distinctive concept of show-biz razzmatazz," referring to the show that took place in 1959 at the Metropolitan Opera House as a mere "fragment."

Bowers still called Takarazuka the "antithesis of Kabuki,"[130] but the word *antithesis* now had a new meaning. Takarazuka's popularity on its home turf is due in part to the fact that it serves up Japan's make-believe America. Historically, on the Takarazuka stage, as Jennifer Robertson has noted, "the concatenated fragments of cultural data often amounted to a fantastical vision of us-ness and (Japanese-inscribed) otherness."[131] The 1989 Takarazuka visit made a profound statement in the arena of cultural exchange: at the pinnacle of its twentieth-century economic might, Japan now had the leverage to show Americans what it wanted them to see. As Bowers recounted with a tone of surprise, the five-day run that year cost a massive three million dollars—covered by the powerful Mitsubishi corporate conglomerate.[132] It was money spent on, in effect, giving back to America the equivalent of America's Orientalist-fantasy-Japan. Stephen Holden described "the sight of rows of showgirls decked out like floats" when "the glitz and pomp [of the sixty-one-member Takarazuka Revue Company] momentarily matched anything that has been seen on a stage specifically designed for such extravaganzas." But Holden completely missed the point in his disapproving references to "the performers' phonetic pronunciations of American lyrics," the revue's "odd, sometimes monotonous cross-cultural hybrid," and the "relentless, overbearing hodgepodge" of music. All of those things went over well in Japan—just as all of the Gilbert and Sullivan–inflected Japan fakery in the long history of America's Japan went (and, to a considerable degree, still goes) over well with American audiences. "Perhaps the show's most amusing number, 'Flower Fantasy,' finds the cast costumed as garish Southern belles," Holden wrote, "creating an expressionistic parody of the picnic scene from 'Gone with the Wind.' Its least effective moments are those that try too hard for a specifically New York feel—a production number danced to a cheesy pastiche of 'Rhapsody in Blue' and a chirpy all-cast-member version of 'Manhattan.'"[133] Holden may have seen parody in the *Gone with the Wind* number, but it was arguably Japan's "straight" fantasy.

The 1990s and into the Next Century

There was a foreshadowing of sorts that the era of big productions from Japan—exemplified by Grand Kabuki at the Metropolitan Opera House and Takarazuka at Radio City Music Hall—was over. It was symbolized by the arrival in 1989 of a small company of performers demonstrating the string-operated mechanical puppets (*karakuri ningyo*) that have long entertained festivalgoers in some parts of Japan. The show was a return to a smaller-scale, quietly exotic Japan that was "unusual and delightful . . . remarkably agile. . . . One puppet performed acrobatic balancing tricks on a pedestal. . . . Still another dipped a pen into an inkwell and wrote calligraphic characters on a small banner."[134] It was also a segue to a new decade in which economic factors—the bursting of the real estate/stock market bubble in Japan in the early 1990s and the advent soon after of the dot.com/stock market bubble in the United States—underlay yet another significant realignment in the US-Japan relationship. Grand Kabuki would not be back for a decade and a half. A 1993 production of noh in front of the Metropolitan Museum of Art's two-thousand-year-old Temple of Dendur—one of New York's most splendid global treasures and one of the most unpredictable settings for a production of traditional theater from Japan—counts as the last "big" show of the century. "In a stunning collaboration between theater and architecture and between diverse cultures over a period of centuries," wrote Mel Gussow, "the Temple of Dendur is being used as an environment for the presentation of Noh drama. . . . [It] is a remarkable event for both the Metropolitan Museum of Art and the Japanese theater." In Japan the 1990s saw a push by specialists in the traditional arts to invigorate presentations and attract new audiences by taking performances out of their familiar contexts and moving them into unexpected settings, such as public parks. Although an acceptable substitute for a traditional noh stage had never been found in New York, the Temple of Dendur at the Met proved to be precisely the kind of setting artists in Japan were searching for to intensify the impact of their work. It was as if all of a sudden noh made sense in New York—not just as a remote cultural exchange project but as a meaningful artistic experience. "Throughout the performance, the Temple of Dendur is a silent sentinel. This is the ultimate in site-specific spaces. With the Kanze company in residence, time stands still and theater is transporting."[135] The Public Theater presentation of noh outdoors, lit by bonfires at the Delacorte Theater in Central Park in the late summer of 1995, was a well-received extension of the same experiment, also by performers from the Kanze school of noh.

The kabuki-Japan discourse has continued to expand in the twenty-first century. Large-scale kabuki productions returned to New York at the 2004 and 2007 Lincoln Center Festivals (discussed in chapter 5). The productions' troupe leader, Kanzaburo Nakamura XVIII, like Ennosuke, is intent on reinvigorating kabuki for a new era. Development of the discourse is also notably in the hands of Japan Society, where programming since 2000 has incorporated noh, kyogen, the Awaji Puppet Theatre, and rakugo (comic monologues and other routines). For a 2004 production titled "The First Noh and Kyogen Program Witnessed by Americans," a cast of actors from Japan reproduced the program of plays given in 1879 to an audience that famously included former US President Ulysses S. Grant, who was visiting Japan at the time. Like Kanzaburo and Ennosuke's kabuki, the event was a kind of "going back" in order to "go forward," a historical reenactment in the service of cultural exchange.

Kabuki, Metaphorically Speaking

On the evening of 1 July 2011, viewers of the weeknight Public Broadcasting Service (PBS) *Newshour* heard Joshua Rosner, coauthor of a newly published book on the mortgage crisis, speak of troubled assets still hidden on the balance sheets of US banks. "Which means," Rosner told *Newshour* reporter Paul Solman, "that we have a Kabuki theater, where some future administration, future legislators, and future regulators are going to have to resolve a crisis which hasn't fully been dealt with yet." In immediately picking up where Rosner left off—and ending the segment—Solman said it was a "metaphor that may be unfair to Kabuki theater, but suggests the obscurity in which the funding of housing in America and Fannie Mae came so disastrously to operate."[136]

There is perhaps no more definitive indicator of the expansion—not to mention the thorough rootedness—of the kabuki-Japan discourse than the emergence of "kabuki" as a metaphor of choice used by individuals prominent in the American media—commentators, journalists, and even novelists. The performing arts overall provide a rich trove of metaphors in English—words such as *drama, melodrama, tragedy, comedy, symphony, ballet, jazz,* and *opera.* Most noticeably within the past decade, *kabuki* has joined that list. In his book *Kabuki Democracy: The System vs. Barack Obama,* Eric Alterman, Distinguished Professor of English and Journalism at Brooklyn College and the City University of New York Graduate School of Journalism (in other words, a man who chooses his words carefully), wrote, "For if our politicians cannot keep the promises they make as candidates, then our commitment to political democracy becomes a kind of Kabuki exercise; it resembles a democratic process at great distance but mocks its genuine intentions in substance."[137] Unlike a "well-choreographed" ballet or a symphony "in perfect harmony," the word *kabuki* is applied to situations that are excessively complex and difficult to fathom or in cases in which there is a lot of show but little substance. As in Alterman's lexicon, it may even imply outright dysfunction.

The context can be Japan-related, as when the drawn-out bidding war won by the Boston Red Sox in 2006 for pitcher Daisuke Matsuzaka was described as a "kabuki auction."[138] Often, however, there is no connection with Japan. A period of debate in 2001 on the issue of Social Security was described as "sort of like Kabuki theater. . . . They pretend to be listening. We pretend that they're listening. But the fact is . . . they're going to ignore the testimony."[139] A 2004 essay reflecting on recent cases in the annals of US financial crimes noted that "once the scandal begins, there's a Kabuki-like quality to the drama. Every person enveloped by the scandal seems to assume an almost ritualized role. . . . As to the story line, the public knows it can tune in at any random point."[140] In 2007 the lengthy back-and-forth with the media leading up to Hillary Clinton's decision that she would be a candidate for president was referred to as "the Clinton presidential kabuki."[141] The examples are wide-ranging and continue to accumulate rapidly: "Richard looks around the boardroom, at the polite but impatient faces," Helen Schulman wrote in her novel *This Beautiful Life,* "—busy, important people, all of them—turning away from him now and toward each other in a Kabuki-like effort to offer him some false modicum of privacy."[142] An article on changing US attitudes toward divorce remarked, "These days, divorce doesn't sob and drink to excess; it dons a joyful Kabuki mask to obscure the anguish of marital bliss gone sour."[143] Even though no fact checker seemed to mind that masks, while occasionally used, are not generally associated with the art form, all of these quotes provide evidence in a way that Logan, Green, and Michener could never have envisioned that kabuki has indeed arrived in America.

2

"America's Japan," the Performing Arts, and Japan Society, New York

Decisions about how cultures are presented reflect deeper judgments of power and authority and can, indeed, resolve themselves into claims about what a nation is or ought to be as well as how citizens should relate to one another.[1]

"In this modern era, where boundaries—national, cultural and conceptual—are constantly bent and traversed, Japanese culture is no longer confined to the geographical borders of Japan," Japan Society told readers of its brochure for Japan Transatlantic: Tokio-Berlin, its fall 2009 performing arts season. The three "Japan-themed performances . . . were developed in Berlin by international artists in collaboration with Japanese artists based outside of Japan."[2] These were *Heavenly BENTO,* by post theater, identified on its website as an "interdisciplinary performing arts unit"[3] based in New York, Berlin, and Tokyo, founded by media artist Hiroko Tanahashi and director Max Schumacher; *Ame to Ame,* by inkBoat, a dance project of Shinichi Iova-Koga based in San Francisco and Berlin, and cokaseki, the Berlin-based butoh artists Yuko Kaseki and Marc Ates; and *there is no end to more,* by Berlin-based choreographer Jeremy Wade in collaboration with, among others, New York-based manga artist Hiroki Otsuka and Berlin-based video artist Veith Michel.

This chapter looks at Japan Society, New York, in its role as the leading producer and presenter in the United States of Japan-related performing arts. As illustrated by Japan Transatlantic: Tokio-Berlin, twenty-first-century arts programming at Japan Society directly engages with complex issues of identity—an approach that reflects the administrative voices now in place. In 2003 Yoko Shioya became the society's first director of the performing arts who was born and educated in Japan.[4] An expert on arts management and funding who regularly publishes articles on those topics in Japanese newspapers and magazines, Shioya started working at Japan Society in 1997. Her title since 2006 has been artistic director, with oversight responsibility for both the performing arts and film programs. For Shioya, grappling with the ambivalent nature of "performing arts from Japan" is central to her project as director. In his analysis of museums, Ivan Karp has shown that exhibitions—a category that can arguably include performing arts presentations at Japan Society, where they function as a kind of ethnographic display—"are privileged arenas for presenting images of self and 'other.'"[5] Shioya is both self and other within the context of an entity that, since the 1950s when a performing arts department was inaugurated, has sought to negotiate the terrain of "us" and "them" through theater, music, and dance.

Shioya is the seventh director of the performing arts in an institution with a long history of structuring and conveying knowledge about Japan. In March 1952 newly elected president John D. Rockefeller III and chairman of the board John Foster Dulles took on the task of reconfiguring the image of Japan in the American popular imagination. Rockefeller, who made the performing arts one of Japan Society's core enterprises, set forth his agenda: "The society's long-range objective is to help bring the people of the United States and of Japan closer together in their appreciation and understanding of each other and each other's way of life. It is our hope that a vigorous Japan Society can be of real benefit by functioning as a private, non-political organization interested in serving as a medium through which both our peoples can learn from the experiences and the accomplishments of the other."[6]

As an influential adviser to cold-war-era American policy makers, Rockefeller did much to ensure that the development of cultural relations with Japan would be a national priority. With Japan Society becoming "the outstanding example of a successful bilateral organization in the United States,"[7] no single cultural entity has occupied a more powerful position in American reception of theater, dance, and music from Japan. Its highly developed network of government, corporate, and private financial sponsors in the United States and Japan allowed it to emerge quickly as a prominent presenter within the New York performing arts scene and a producer of events at touring locations around the country. Identifying itself as "a world-class, multidisciplinary hub for global leaders, artists, scholars, educators, and English and Japanese-speaking audiences,"[8] the society also hosts a steady stream of lectures, workshops, and symposiums on a wide range of topics. Fellowships and exchanges, corporate and policy programs, and language instruction and educational outreach are part of its mission, too.

Fig. 7. Present-day exterior of Japan Society, New York. (© 2012 by Japan Society, New York. Courtesy of Japan Society, New York.)

Japan Society dates from 1907—although it was not until 1971 that it got its own building. Japan House, located in midtown New York near the United Nations, was constructed on land donated by Rockefeller.[9] Designed by architects Junzo Yoshimura and George G. Shimamoto, it now includes a 262-seat auditorium, an art gallery, a library, a language center, conference areas, and office space, as well as indoor gardens and a waterfall. Exemplifying cultural bodies as "arenas of discourse and negotiation,"[10] Japan Society is part-theatre-and-multi-use-performance-space, part-art-and-anthropology-museum, part-think-tank, and part-cultural-exchange-institute.

Early History: Images of an Aestheticized Japan

"Japan Society of New York was one of the pioneers of cultural exchange in the early 20th century," Michael Auslin has written. "Begun in a time when few Americans knew anything about Japan, it swiftly reached a wider audience than the few learned societies that focused on Asia at the time."[11] In 1907 a group of business, professional, and social leaders in New York decided that America needed to know more about Japan and that they were the ones to accomplish, or at least oversee, that task. It was not the first Japan Society in the United States—there has been one in Boston since 1904—but it had a particularly large number of people among its founders who stood to profit financially or professionally from stronger relations with Japan.[12] In his history of the society, commissioned to mark its seventy-fifth anniversary, former ambassador to Japan Edwin O. Reischauer wrote that most of the original members "had business ties with Japan, primarily through banking and finance and trade in silk, which was then Japan's major export. They were joined by some of the leading Japanese residents of the city, who were eager for stronger ties between the two countries. Most of the founding group were to remain active in the Society for many years, shaping the policies that guided it until its temporary suspension during World War II."[13]

So renowned were its founders that press coverage of the birth of the society was immediate. However, not everyone in New York believed that an institution dedicated to "the cultivation of friendly relations" with Japan was necessary or even desirable.[14] On 21 May 1907, a day after the *New York Times* published a page-one article reporting on the formation of the society, the newspaper ran an editorial expressing its bewilderment.

> But really, when one comes to ask what the Japan Society is to be about, or for, the answer is not obvious. . . . To form a "Japan Society" for the purpose of vaguely "whooping it up" with Japan and entwining the Rising Sun with the Star-Spangled Banner is an operation the like of which we have undertaken with no other Power or people. We have no French or German or Italian Society, although these nations are every one of them much nearer to us than Japan in traditions, in culture, and in mutual understanding. In

> the absence of a clearer explanation than has thus far been vouchsafed us the reason of being of the Japan Society is not plain.[15]

As Reischauer wrote, "International relations in those days did not seem important enough for associations of this sort. American contacts with the countries of Western Europe were already close enough not to require them and with non-Western lands too distant and amorphous to merit them." He added, however, that Japan was growing in commercial importance as "America's largest trans-Pacific trading partner [and] was starting to loom as America's chief rival in the Pacific."[16]

Japan Society attracted a membership of wealthy and educated people at a time when there was still "a tremendous vogue in the United States for all things Japanese—Japanese prints and porcelain, judo and Buddhism, geisha and samurai."[17] In 1912 the society launched an in-house travel service and sponsored tours to Japan, a trip only a person of means could have afforded. Society members also had a taste for aristocratic Japan and took it upon themselves "to see to it that distinguished Japanese visitors to this country are entertained."[18] For the marriage and December 1926 "coronation" of the Showa emperor "a great deal of time [was devoted] in executive meetings to discussing appropriate messages and gifts to be sent."[19] In 1953 "[t]he big social event of the year . . . was the dinner held at the Waldorf on September 17 in honor of the eighteen-year-old Crown Prince Akihito of Japan, on his way home after representing his country at the coronation of Elizabeth II of England in June."[20] Akihito was again a Japan Society guest shortly after his marriage in 1960. When Japan House opened in 1971, guests of honor at the ceremony included Prince Hitachi, son of Emperor Hirohito. Four years later the emperor himself visited.[21]

Japan Society declared from the outset that it would not take political stands—that it was solely dedicated to helping America and Japan get to know each other better. Nevertheless it provided an important forum for high-profile politicians, businesspeople, and others to come together and express their views. The Japan that was not politicized was carefully aestheticized—itself a kind of political statement. Within three years of its founding, the society had a Committee on Arts and Literature charged with organizing art exhibitions, holding lectures, and producing publications on cultural topics. The first major project was the construction of a Japanese garden and teahouse on the roof of the Astor, a large, fashionable hotel in midtown Manhattan. Hotel roof gardens were a popular location for entertainments—especially the "stunning" one at the Astor,[22] and for over two weeks in March 1912 visitors could observe tea ceremonies and noh presentations and attend lectures on flower arranging and Japanese gardens.[23]

"The undertaking was a smashing cultural success,"[24] Reischauer has written, but it was more than just exotic fare for New Yorkers. In an article covering a Japan Society lunch for Viscount Chinda, the new Japanese ambassador to the United States, the *Times* reported that "on the roof of the Astor this week Japan Society has created a perfect, though miniature, Japanese tea garden, built by Japanese, manned by Japanese, and with as exact and true an assembling of detail and as Oriental an atmosphere as could ever be obtained in the pine woods of Nikko or the suburbs of Osaka." At the invitation of Japan Society, the luncheon guests visited the garden, having just heard speeches and participated in discussions related to the request by American and European bankers that Japan join them in providing financial aid to China, "which needs to be done in the restoration of peace, which is so essential to the cause of civilization." The purpose of the garden visit was to impress Viscount Chinda with the sincerity of America's respect for Japan, as well as to show Americans a Japan that was beautiful and refined—and therefore not threatening to the security of the United States and its global interests. The *Times* continued, "In miniature ponds miniature gold fish swim about in miniature submerged castles, while the tiniest of Japanese ladies and kimona-bedecked [*sic*]-Japanese gentlemen solemnly contemplate the scene."[25]

The wealth of the society's elite membership allowed the organization, which was still many years away from having its own auditorium, to book events in prestigious locations. In turn, association with the Hotel Astor and other prominent venues—such as the Metropolitan Museum of Art for society-sponsored exhibitions—helped bring notice to the society. While the press reported growing public fears that Japan might assert itself militarily against the United States, Japan Society programs on flower arranging, gardens, the tea ceremony, and noh were an early "appeal to a premodern endowment as an irreducible essence."[26] The sophistication of these arts well captured the aestheticized image of Japan that the society wished to convey. Such a Japan was far from bellicose. It was a home of high art: worth knowing, worthy of admiration, and, for those so inclined, a worthy business partner.

Postwar Performing Arts and Cultural Exchange

Japan Society's goal of fostering mutual understanding between the

United States and Japan aligned with Rockefeller's role as adviser to the US government in formulating cultural policy with Japan after the war. John Dower has written that Rockefeller, who helped craft the peace treaty with Japan as a member of the mission led by John Foster Dulles, "took care to emphasize that future interchange between the erstwhile victors and the vanquished must be a 'two-way street' that avoided 'the problem of cultural imperialism.'"[27] Japan Society would play an important role in the US-Japan interchange Rockefeller envisioned—as would Asia Society and Lincoln Center, two institutions that he helped establish in the mid-1950s. By the early 1960s, Rockefeller was simultaneously chairman of the board of his family's philanthropic Rockefeller Foundation, president of Japan Society, chairman of Asia Society, and president of Lincoln Center. He was treated seriously and respectfully by the press for his civic leadership and his expertise on Asia.[28]

War and the enormous expense and sheer difficulty of travel in the first half of the twentieth century had made visits by Japanese performers to the United States a rarity.[29] The postwar resumption of Japan Society activities and the election of Rockefeller as its president marked the start of a new era for the performing arts as a programmatic cornerstone of the organization. In 1953 Beate Gordon, who had been hired by the society as a part-time employee to help with student programs, organized a Festival of Japanese Theatre at Columbia University featuring arts students from Japan who were already in New York furthering their training at Juilliard and other institutions. The event's success led to the creation at the society of a performing arts department with Gordon as its full-time director. One of the writers of Japan's postwar constitution whose family had emigrated from Austria to Japan when she was a child, Gordon transformed what began as a way to help Japanese students in New York make ends meet into one of the most influential impresario careers of the twentieth century. She eventually presided over the performing arts programs at both Japan Society and Asia Society. When she announced her retirement in 1991, *Times* critic John Rockwell said that the news "came as a shock." He wrote that "for about as long as the toothiest of us can remember, she has been the primary provider of exotic Asian music, dance, theater and film" to New York audiences.[30]

Rockefeller regarded educational exchange as crucial to building friendly relations with Japan. In addition to its grant-in-aid program for students from Japan, the society tried to find them supplemental work to bolster their finances. "In the fifties and sixties," Gordon wrote in her memoir, "what Japanese students in America had most in common was a shortage of cash. One young violinist I knew whose name is now internationally known was washing dishes. . . . So, with the help of a small endowment and a title—Director of the Performing Arts Program—I put together teams of young performers who went around to various schools presenting dance and music programs, accompanied by a narrator to explain things."[31] Arranging school presentations became a regular part of the society's day-to-day functions, linking the performing arts to its core goal of helping Americans broaden their knowledge of Japan: "A typical 'package' consisted of three performers who would demonstrate three different Japanese arts in a forty-minute program. The performers were singers, musicians, dancers, and masters of the tea ceremony, calligraphy, ink painting, and *origami* or paper folding. In one academic year, these programs reached 12,000 students in the New York area, many of whom had never before been exposed to Japan or Japanese culture."[32]

Kabuki already dominated American images of Japanese culture by the time Japan Society emerged as a sponsor and producer of performing arts presentations. Such images were reinforced by the society itself: the cover of a set of classroom materials prepared by Gordon and her staff for distribution to schoolteachers was decorated with a drawing of the twelfth-century warrior-monk Benkei—a popular character in kabuki plays—in a billowing costume. Crests of kabuki acting families were arrayed along the lower edge of the cover, and the word *Japan* was written in "old Edo" brushstroke-style lettering at the top.[33] Although the visits by the Azuma Kabuki Dancers and Musicians in the mid-1950s and Grand Kabuki in 1960 had been beyond the scope of its producing capability at the time, the society took an increasingly visible role in New York's Japan-related performing arts projects. With high-level connections in the US and Japanese governments, Japan Society had, for instance, helped coordinate arrangements when the gagaku troupe visited the city in 1959.

As a producer in its own right, Japan Society built on its school-focused programs. In the early 1960s Gordon began arranging recitals by Japanese musicians and dancers at major venues in New York. Some doubled as fund-raising events for Japan Society scholarship programs. Special travel arrangements generally did not have to be made, since most of the individuals were already spending extended periods of time in the city studying and developing their careers. Violinist Kenji Kobayashi, for example, who went on to become a renowned performer and teacher in Japan, was a Juilliard student in the 1950s. He made his Japan Society-sponsored American debut at Town Hall in 1961. Dancer-choreographer Suzushi Hanayagi was introduced to New York audiences in 1962 in a society-sponsored

Fig. 8. Japan Society general brochure cover, 1999–2000. (© 1999 by Japan Society, New York. Courtesy of Japan Society, New York.)

program at Hunter Playhouse. A collaborator with avant-garde director and playwright Robert Wilson in the 1980s and 1990s, Hanayagi, who was trained in Japan in both classical Japanese and modern dance, had come to New York to study with Martha Graham. She was a popular kabuki-dance performer in Japan Society school programs.[34] Appearing frequently in society-sponsored recitals, she carved out a reputation in the United States as both a principal exponent of Japanese classical dance and a profound contemporary dance experimentalist.

"Japan Society Presents," the Opening of Japan House, and Wallace's Donation

Persuasive, resourceful, and with Rockefeller's backing, Gordon turned Japan Society into a significant producer of the performing arts in New York. She was guided by her own outlook and tastes, which meshed well with those of the organization's leadership.[35] In the half decade leading up to the opening of Japan House, the phrase "Japan Society Presents" was affixed to a series of professional-level productions hosted by Gordon and her staff at various borrowed locations. The Theresa Kaufmann Concert Hall at the 92nd Street Y, well known for the high quality of its cultural and educational programs, became one of the regular venues. Mime artist Yass Hakoshima, who performed with the Yokohama Ballet before leaving Japan to study dance with Erick Hawkins and mime with Étienne Decroux, appeared there in 1966. Dancers Ayako Uchiyama and Rankei Fujima, whose work combined aspects of both classical and contemporary dance, followed in separate recitals the next year. Manzo Nomura led his kyogen troupe on a US visit that brought them to the "Y" in 1968.

The expanding performing arts program and overall growth at Japan Society in large measure mirrored developments in Japan. By 1960, as Thomas R. H. Havens has noted in his study of postwar movements in Japanese dance, music, painting, and sculpture, artists from Japan could far more easily step out into the world: Japan Air Lines had jet planes in its fleet, and "[f]or outbound Japanese travelers, restrictions on taking currency out of the country were eased in stages and had largely disappeared by the Tokyo Olympics of October 1964." The 1964 Olympics indeed marked a turning point, along with "the opening of the Shinkansen bullet train the same year, Japan's first postwar trade surplus with both the United States and multilateral partners in 1965, and the unexpected speed of income doubling."[36]

Change was also occurring in New York. An announcement was made in May 1967 that Rockefeller had bought property on New York's East Side with the intention of donating it to Japan Society. Finally, the society would have its own building, one that would convey its cultural status and function as a symbol of Japan in Manhattan.[37] Japan House would be tangible proof that Japan was important to the United States. Groundbreaking ceremonies took place in September 1969, celebrated with a dance performed by Hanayagi. The planned structure would be "the first building of contemporary Japanese design" in New York City, reflecting "[c]ontemporary interpretations of traditional Japanese architectural and design forms."[38] Having its own home and its own stage gave the society more control and wider public recognition. It was no longer forced to use facilities belonging to others—including those of Asia Society, with which Japan Society had been sharing office space and occasional use of the Asia House auditorium.[39] Reischauer glowingly noted, "The Japan Society began to become one of New York's major cultural institutions, and its offerings were regularly reviewed in the local press and in national news magazines such as *Time* and *Newsweek*." The society was on its way to becoming "a truly national organization."[40]

By the time Japan House opened in 1971 Gordon was serving as director of the performing arts at both Japan Society and Asia Society. In that same year the High Winds Fund, run by philanthropist Lila Acheson Wallace, donated a million dollars (earmarked for Asia Society, but Japan Society was also a beneficiary) to endow a five-year program "designed to introduce Asian music and dance forms that have never been presented here before." The gift gave Gordon considerably more visibility and, at the same time, opened a new chapter in the presentation in New York of performing arts from Japan, as well as from other countries of Asia. The first program, "Edo Festival Music and Pantomime," clearly demonstrated that "Asian music and dance forms" under the terms of the gift meant the traditional arts: "So now after the court music, the drama of the kabuki, noh and kyogen plays of Japan, we are presented with an older form."[41] With the receipt of the grant, Gordon began traveling abroad extensively to select artists and make arrangements for them to appear in the United States. Because the grant stipulated that troupes coming to the United States were to perform not just in New York but for as many audiences as possible around the country, she began the touring program (focusing mainly on university campuses), which is integral to the work of Japan Society today.

With substantial new resources now at her disposal, Gordon was in an even stronger position to shape the image of Japan through the performing arts. She received the greatest possible encouragement for her endeavors from the individuals and institutions that generously funded and unreservedly supported her work, from the audiences that enthusiastically attended her productions, and from the critics and writers who publicized and, more often than not, praised her productions. She became a celebrity impresario, both for the variety of programs she presented and for their aura of authenticity as direct representations of cultures previously unfamiliar to Americans.[42] Among the tributes paid to Gordon when she eventually retired, Robert Oxnam, president of Asia Society, said, "It's hard to think of anybody who's had a greater influence in opening American eyes to Asian cultures and values. She almost single-handedly began bringing the greatest dancers, musicians and actors from cultures across Asia to American audiences who had never seen or appreciated them."[43]

Gordon famously set out to show New Yorkers the "unchanged version," and yet she herself was an agent of change.

> Mrs. Gordon has sometimes seized upon a traditional dance glimpsed between proud performances of more homogenized stuff. "You like *that*?" is often the response from the stunned performers. Then the work begins of paring down programs that might seem interminable to Western sensibilities. The aim is to preserve the essence of the dance. "I prefer to present units of a complete work rather than a potpourri, reproducing as much as possible the rituals and atmosphere of the whole, although it can't be done entirely."[44]

The presupposition was that the true cultures of Asia are traditional and what America should see must be free of the "taint" of modernization.

Looking back over her career in later years, Gordon told an interviewer that the key element in selecting performers was their ability to communicate: "[O]nly the best performers can communicate to an audience that doesn't know their art. That is why I have traveled so extensively and been so careful to bring only what is very close to the well. It is like drinking from the well, getting the very pure things. Although I did bring over such 'modern' amalgamations as Butoh, I am mainly interested in bringing the originals." In defense of her emphasis on the traditional arts, Gordon said that she "realized a lot were museum pieces. But we do go to museums to see art that is very old and to learn from it. We don't know what Egyptian dance was like, but in Japan we do know what was present 1,000 years ago in the Imperial courts and the shrines. What a glorious thing to present to American composers and dancers, and to see what has held for generations."[45] Gordon, like Faubion Bowers, advocated that the performing arts were Japan's past-alive-in-the-present. Moreover, the quality of the product was thoroughly validated by scholarly opinion and the "cultural property" designations conferred by the Japanese government.

Japan Society's Contemporary Turn

The Wallace donation was pivotal, but so were events occurring under Ellen Stewart at La MaMa beginning in 1970. In this changed environment, Gordon's department began a quiet move toward more innovative and experimental Japan-related work. New York–based dancer-choreographers Saeko Ichinohe and Kazuko Hirabayashi began performing frequently at the society. Like Hanayagi, they cultivated repertories drawn from traditional Japanese and "Western" contemporary dance styles. Whereas Japanese performers of Western classical music had long been familiar to Gordon's audiences, in 1975 she agreed to host the first concert produced by Music From Japan (then called the Society for Contemporary Music From Japan) featuring new works by Japanese composers.

In retrospect the emblematic event that marked a programmatic shift at the society was the American debut in May 1976 of Eiko and Koma—as a result of which the society has been able to lay claim to "the discovery" of artists who would become two of the most important figures in contemporary American dance. The historical significance of that occasion for Japan Society was well articulated by performing arts director Paula Lawrence in connection with a recital by the dancer-choreographers marking the twentieth anniversary of that first US performance.

> Eiko and Koma hold a special place as Japanese artists who have chosen to make their careers in the United States. We are proud to present these performances celebrating their American debut at the Japan Society and subsequent 20 years of visionary artistry. We are also proud to see them frequently in our audience. Last year, Eiko and Koma and their two children joined other audience members to receive blessings from the sacred Gongen during the Yamabushi Kagura performances. It is gratifying that the Japan Society not only launched Eiko and Koma's American career, but remains a meaningful connection to Japan for them, and now for their children.[46]

Lawrence's statement reflects the fact that the society contextualizes artists within a framework of "Japan"—even when the practices of those artists, as in the case of Eiko and Koma, may not in any obvious way be related to Japan.

For Eiko and Koma, Japan Society in 1976 provided a crucial path to getting seen—and in a major venue at that—just after they arrived for the first time in New York, the city where they soon decided to reside permanently. Having their American debut at Japan Society was paradoxical, though, for artists who had left Japan to study dance in Germany and did not consider their art "Japanese." Nevertheless, their ethnicity—not to mention their education and early artistic training in Japan—"qualified" them to appear on the Japan Society stage. "Nobody knew us, of course," Eiko has said about the couple's US debut. "The tickets had to be given away. But it was a wonderful way to start."[47] Graciously appreciative of the chance afforded by Beate Gordon, Eiko told William Harris, who wrote the twentieth-anniversary article for the society's *Newsletter*, that she and Koma "owe a lot to the Japan Society."[48] The society's ongoing celebration of its connection with Eiko and Koma, validated by the artists' public acknowledgment of benefits they have derived there, helps to reinforce its own identity as a major performing arts presenter.

The society's contemporary turn under Gordon peaked in 1979 with the three-month, nationwide Japan Today festival. A project of the National Endowment for the Humanities, which began operations in 1965, it was one of five international cultural symposiums to take place. The others focused on Belgium, Egypt, Mexico, and Scandinavia. Described as "the most comprehensive and far-reaching program on Japan ever undertaken anywhere outside that country,"[49] the program grew out of and stimulated a demand for presentations of the contemporary arts. Japan Today helped establish Japan Society, the program's coordinator, as capable of identifying and giving American audiences on a national scale access to innovative work from Japan.

With policies at the time in both the United States and Japan encouraging development of their cultural infrastructures and with new sources of money available to underwrite the arts, Japan Today attracted funding that included grants of $250,000 each from the National Endowment for the Humanities and the National Endowment for the Arts (which also dates from 1965). Matsushita Electric contributed $400,000. The Japan Foundation, formed in 1972, gave $100,000, and the Japan-US Friendship Commission, which was founded in 1977, put in $50,000. Another $1 million "in the form of services" was also collected.[50] Japan Society worked with the Resident Associate Program of the Smithsonian Institution and Meridian International of Washington, DC, in organizing the program. Events took place in New York, Washington, Chicago, Denver, Los Angeles, Boston, and Miami.

In the performing arts, the keywords of Japan Today were *modern, new, experimental,* and *avant-garde.* The demand for knowledge about contemporary Japan was not merely the product of cultural curiosity: Japan Today took place against the backdrop of intensifying US-Japan trade friction, which Reischauer characterized as "potentially very dangerous."[51] Productions included a one-week run of *The Little Elephant Is Dead: An Exhibition of Images* (*Kozō wa shinda*), performed by the Kobo Abe Theater Troupe at La MaMa. There was also a modern noh play written and directed by Shin Higuchi, which had its world premiere at New York's Open Space Theater Experiment. The Japan Society name was now beginning to be connected with cutting-edge, "downtown" artists and locations. The entity that laid claim to being the preeminent authority in matters related to the presentation in the United States of Japanese culture in general had thereby opened its doors much wider to contemporary voices in the performing arts.

In 1981 Gordon resigned from Japan Society to work full time at Asia Society. It was difficult to fill her shoes. After she left, Rand Castile, director of the society's art gallery, took over her responsibilities. He soon passed them on to Peter Grilli, founder of the society's film program, whose title became director of education, film, and the performing arts. With all programs growing in size, in 1986 the performing arts again became an independent unit headed by John Gillespie. In 1989 Cora Mirikitani came onboard as the new performing arts director. Paula Lawrence, who had been working under Gordon at Asia Society since 1980, took over the position in early 1992. She was succeeded in 2003 by Yoko Shioya.

There were indications that Japan Society planned to carry on the theme of the Japan Today festival by taking steps to become a center for contemporary theater from Japan. In the spring of 1982, for example, the society co-sponsored with La MaMa a New York tour by the experimental troupe Waseda Shogekijo and its director, Tadashi Suzuki. There were two productions, dubbed "interpretive rearrangements,"[52] of *The Trojan Women* (performed at Japan Society in Japanese) and *The Bacchae* (given at La MaMa, with lines delivered in English by American guest actors and in Japanese by the members of Suzuki's company). Several weeks prior to Suzuki's arrival, Japan Society's *Newsletter* carried what amounted to a "call to arms" for the society's new direction in programming in the form of a lengthy and strongly worded article by scholar-playwright-translator Roger Pulvers.

> Cocteau sat through fifteen minutes of Noh and became an expert. Meyerhold saw a phony traveling Kabuki troupe in Moscow and it changed his life. In fact, most Western theater people who have gone to Japan to seek its demonic theatricality have, in a sense, docked with the wrong craft; they have connected themselves with the mother-ship of traditional Japanese theater. The modern writers and directors and actors of Japan have long ago taken off in other, more exciting directions. It's curious that Europeans, Australians and Americans fail to form the connection with the people in Japan who actually share their aspirations for a relevant, effective and contemporary theater.

There was no doubt that America's leading resource on Japan had a great deal of catching up to do. As Pulvers pointed out, "In the early 1960s, a genuine and original modern Japanese theater began to emerge. In one sense, the Japanese were tiring of European naturalism as had the Europeans in the immediately preceding years. But, more deeply, they were truly responding to the social and political upheavals that came out of the security treaty crisis and the radical student movement." In 1963, for instance, Suzuki had produced Minoru Betsuyaku's play *Elephant* (*Zō*) "about the aftereffects of the bomb on Japanese society, about social discrimination against radiation victims and about the Japanese custom of taking frightful pains to hide whatever is seamy and unpleasant from public view."[53] Although Suzuki was beginning to attract worldwide interest for his innovative directing style and approach to training actors, Betsuyaku, who by the early 1980s had had over forty of his plays produced in Japan, remained unknown in the United States.

It was not just Betsuyaku. With the exception of productions beginning to unfold at La MaMa, American audiences had little access to contemporary Japanese theater up to that point. Under the new performing arts directors who followed Gordon, however, the society began moving in the direction of showcasing such work. John Gillespie, who came to the society with a background as a scholar of Japanese theater and a translator of Japanese plays into English, was especially committed to the task. One of his projects was a 1987 production of the play *Make-Up* (*Keshō*) given by the Chijinkai troupe from Japan. The work, written by Hisashi Inoue, is a nostalgic look at an actress in a small acting company whose theater is

Fig. 9. Flyer advertising *Make-Up,* a play by Hisashi Inoue, Japan Society, November 1987. (© 1987 by Japan Society, New York. Courtesy of Japan Society, New York.)

about to be torn down. A preview article cautioned, "Japanese audiences have a weakness for melodrama that many New York theatergoers may find they cannot abide," but added that the presentation at Japan Society "provides an uncommon opportunity for an American audience to see modern Japanese theater." American "cultural imports" from Japan, as the article hardly needed to point out, "lean toward the traditional—Kabuki, bunraku puppets, Noh drama, Kyogen comedy. It is not so routine to see something that is less than 300 years old."[54] Unfortunately, readers may have had reason to be somewhat confused, since the title of the article was "Presenting Kabuki for the Common Man," and the main character of the play was an actress whose job is to play a male actor in a kabuki play about a mother who abandoned her son.

The following year Gillespie took advantage of the opportunity afforded by the monthlong First New York International Festival of the Arts to draw significant new attention to Japan Society's developing role as a presenter of contemporary drama from Japan.[55] The society hosted the festival production of *The Water Station* (*Mizu no eki*), written and directed Shogo Ota. The performers were members of Ota's company, Tenkei Gekijo. Gratifyingly, the work—two hours long, without intermission—sold out its scheduled three-night run, and another performance was added to accommodate eager ticket buyers. Critic Mel Gussow was expansive in his praise for the play, in which "no words are spoken and no sound is heard, except for occasional soothing passages of music in the background and the constant trickle of water at a fountain in the center of the stage." He wrote that *The Water Station* "is an evocative antidote to our daily cacophony, offering quietude as a way of theater. . . . Returning to fast-paced New York life after the performance, one undergoes nothing short of a cultural shock."[56]

The 1990s and 2000s: Seasons, Series, and Scholars

The big kabuki tours that had been taking place in rapid succession, and even the Takarazuka extravaganzas, had already come to an end by the time Japan's economy began slipping in and out of recession in the 1990s. At the same time, however, there was an upsurge of interest in Japanese popular culture—anime, "Harajuku" fashion, and J-pop music. At Japan Society an expansion of the endowment during the buoyant "tech era" in the United States allowed the performing arts department under Lawrence and then Shioya to enlarge substantially the number and scope of activities that would provide a much more detailed and nuanced picture of Japan-related performing arts. Even during intervening spells of budgetary contraction, the 1990s and the first decade of the 2000s were a dynamic period for performing arts at the organization.

Seasons and Series

Starting in the 1990s, Lawrence took the important step of dividing performing arts productions into formal fall and spring seasons. The aim was to boost recognition by critics and the public of Japan Society as a "regular" performing arts venue and, at the same time, to encourage ticket sales for multiple events. The society also noticeably put increased emphasis on organizing seasons thematically in order to promote new ways of thinking about Japan through theater, dance, and music.[57] There was Japan Transatlantic: Tokio-Berlin, the fall 2009 season mentioned at the beginning of this chapter. Another example comprises the fall 2008 and spring 2009 seasons, which were linked under the title Beyond Boundaries: Genre-Bending Mavericks. As the accompanying brochure noted, "This year Performing Arts celebrates the Japanese artists whose works have reached beyond conventional categorizations to define parameters on their own terms."[58] The productions included *Kiosk* by the ARICA Performance Company; *Gagaku Revolution: New Sounds of Ancient Bamboo,* a presentation by the Reigakusha ensemble; and *True* by the multimedia performance troupe dumb type.

The society also developed a number of multi-year, genre-based series that have helped foster the organization's identity as a live-arts presenter. Examples include Jazz from Japan, which ran for a decade beginning in 1993. The music recitals that were formerly a significant part of programming at the society had basically come to an end with the departure of Beate Gordon. Whereas the focus was previously on artists from Japan specializing in classical Western and Japanese music, only a handful of jazz musicians had ever performed at Japan Society: Teruo Nakamura and the Rising Sun (in 1976), the Mas Yajima Trio (in 1977), and Ryo Kawasaki and the Golden Dragon (in 1980). By starting its series in the 1990s, a period of surging international interest in jazz, the society's performing arts program under Lawrence was acknowledging the accomplishments of Japanese artists in a genre that, though extraordinarily popular in Japan, occupied an uncertain status there. As E. Taylor Atkins has written in his study of jazz in Japan:

> Because the essentially American character of jazz is regarded as so incon-

> testable, aesthetic distinctions between authentic and inauthentic practitioners are made to seem natural, even by Japan's own culture industry: the commercial marketing and presentation of jazz performance by the indigenous entertainment industry reinscribes Japan's artistic and cultural subordination. . . . For most of the twentieth century . . . jazz folk were singled out as inimical to the national project of nurturing and preserving Japan's cultural "essence," even if that essence was subject to constant reformulation as circumstances dictated.[59]

Jazz musicians who appeared in Japan Society series included pianists Junko Onishi, Aki Takase, Toshiko Akiyoshi, and Yosuke Yamashita; shakuhachi artist Akikazu Nakamura; trumpeter Terumasa Hino; and saxophonist Sadao Watanabe.

The society's goal was to introduce New York audiences to jazz musicians from Japan (several of whom were already longtime New York residents or frequent visitors), as well as to enable new "international" collaborations among musicians. Hino, who headlined the first concert, appeared onstage with fellow trumpeter Freddie Hubbard. Yamashita shared a program with the Turtle Island String Quartet. While the series was an affirmation of Japan's place in the jazz world, it was also important as a way for the society to newly position itself as a site of contemporary musical performance. It has also done so more recently in the realm of experimental music—with projects such as John Zorn's Tzadik Label Music Series, discussed below.

Contemporary Dance Showcase, a series that began in 1998, quickly became the society's marquee annual event.[60] First called Emerging Dance from Japan: A New Generation from Japan,"[61] the name was changed in 2001 to Contemporary Dance Showcase. It took place over a weekend in January, always scheduled to coincide with the Global Performing Arts Marketplace and Conference, the annual meeting in New York of the Association of Performing Arts Presenters (APAP). By holding special pre-performance information sessions to introduce the visiting artists to meeting participants attending the showcase, Japan Society took on a new role—not just as a presenter in New York and a producer of US tours but also as a promoter of performers from Japan to presenters throughout the world.

The showcase became known for inviting audiences to "[s]pend a breathtaking evening on the cutting edge of Japan's contemporary dance scene!,"[62] an annual reaffirmation that "the experimental dance scene in Japan spawns surprise and creativity."[63] The series also provided a flexible

Fig. 10. Advertising card, 2010 Contemporary Dance Showcase, Japan Society. (© 2010 by Japan Society, New York. Courtesy of Japan Society, New York.)

framework for cultural programming at Japan Society. For instance, all ticket holders attending the 2003 showcase—with performers Dance Company Nibroll, Dance Theatre Ludens, Strange Kinoko Dance Company, and Akemi Takeya—were invited to a supplementary show that began an hour before the main event. The added segment, which was titled "Dancing in the Diaspora: Japanese Dancers in New York," featured individual performances by Yasuko Yokoshi, Satoshi Haga, and Tsuyoshi Kaseda. The back-to-back presentation of the two groups of artists—one Japan-based, the other New York-based—revealed the complexities and contradictions inherent in attempting to view culture in terms of fixed geographic boundaries. Whereas Dance Theatre Ludens did not have any recognizably specific Japan references in its presentation, Haga "mixes ballet, drama, mime, butoh and traditional Japanese theater."[64]

In 2006 the showcase moved in a new direction altogether, with the addition of a two-day program of contemporary dance from Taiwan that the society co-presented with the Taipei Cultural Center. Two years later, in 2008, the showcase was renamed the Contemporary Dance Showcase, Japan + East Asia and reframed to include dancers from South Korea and Taiwan: "The Annual Contemporary Dance Showcase is back with a bang! Continuing to offer the most outstanding cutting-edge dance, the Showcase for the first time expands to present a broader range from Japan and East Asian countries."[65] In that first year the Japan-based artists were Makotocluv, Kingyo, and Yun Myung Fee. The Korea-based artist was Yong-In Lee of the UBIN Dance troupe, and the Taiwan-based participant was the Sun-Shier Dance Theatre. "This year, in a first, the showcase also includes contenders from Korea and Taiwan, as well as Japan," the *Times* review noted. "It used to be that a person could go, take in a few new Japanese works and feel only slightly sheepish about pronouncing on the state of that nation's dance. Now all bets are off."[66] The pattern continued to be followed, illustrating a larger move at Japan Society away from an almost exclusive emphasis on the US-Japan bilateral relationship to a focus on the ties between Japan and its geopolitical neighbors. Korea and Taiwan represent Japan's expanding cultural sphere—places where J-pop and J-drama especially are being eagerly consumed by a new generation not particularly interested in the difficult history with Japan their parents or grandparents may remember.

With the dawn of the twenty-first century quickly approaching, the society won the support of the Japan-based Saison Foundation for a new series, Japanese Theatre NOW. For Japan Society it was a coveted chance to expand its role as a presenter of new drama from Japan, work that—as the deliberate capitalization of the word *now* so emphatically indicates—would potentially open up for American audiences fresh ways of looking at and thinking about contemporary Japan.[67] One of the first plays in the series was the October 2000 production of *Tokyo Notes* (*Tōkyō nōto*), written and directed by Oriza Hirata. The work was performed by Hirata's troupe, Seinendan. A *Times* preview article introduced Hirata as a playwright "known in Japan for pioneering 'quiet theater,' the name critics gave to a style of naturalistic and analytic theater that forms the cornerstone of the most influential Japanese movement of the 1990's." As if to assure readers that they were on firm ground, Hirata's work was compared to that of the film director Yasujiro Ozu for its "delicately wrought realism like in Tokyo Story."[68] However, what stands out in the article is its apparent comprehension that a "postmodern" shift in programming had taken place at Japan Society—a comprehension conveyed through a comment attributed to playwright Minoru Betsuyaku: "Hirata doesn't have the same consciousness of borders that the previous generation had. He sees the world very much in terms of a network, and communication as possible. That's what he stands for."[69]

Satoshi Miyagi's *The Castle Tower* (*Tenshu Monogatari*), performed by

Miyagi's Ku Na'uka Theatre Company in 2003, was another play in the series. The *Times* preview article quoted Paula Lawrence: "Western audiences are ready to be introduced to theater inspired by Japanese themes and to Japanese literature. They can appreciate the universal in works of other cultures, not only Western classics. This is a rare opportunity to see a Japanese production of a modern Japanese play."[70] Despite Lawrence's optimistic statement, newspaper coverage of productions in the series has consistently taken the form of preview articles only, rather than preview articles *and* reviews written by theater critics. This has also applied to, for example, Yoji Sakate's *The Attic* (*Yaneura*), presented in 2005 by Sakate's Rinko-gun Theater Company, and Toshiki Okada's *Five Days in March* (*Sangatsu no itsukakan*), presented in 2009 by Okada's chelfitsch Theater Company. With preview articles but without actual reviews, the plays are implicitly delineated as culturally interesting but not necessarily artistically compelling—although language (broadly considered) may be one of the salient issues at stake: when Okada's *Enjoy* (*Enjoi*) and his *Five Days in March* were produced in English by American directors and acting companies—the former at the 59E59 Theaters and the latter at La MaMa—both were prominently (and favorably) reviewed.[71]

New Japan-Related Work by American Artists is the name of a productive new series that got under way in 2001, supported by a grant of $1.25 million from the Doris Duke Charitable Foundation. Japan Society initiated the series to encourage established American artists to engage with Japanese culture. A portion of the income from the endowment is used, as Yoko Shioya has explained, "to commission non-Japanese artists to create new work which somehow relates to Japan, such as using traditional Japanese performing arts techniques or collaborations with Japanese artists."[72] For commissioned artists, the connection with Japan Society opens up access to a wide range of consultation services, ranging from opportunities to receive training in traditional performance techniques to getting help with Japanese copyright issues. Through the process of actively "'seeding' . . . Japan-related creativity in the U.S., the hope is that the artist's vision is allowed to grow beyond what was initially conceived."[73] The first commission went to composer Lee Hyla, whose *At Suma Beach* was performed at Japan Society in 2003 by the Chamber Music Society of Lincoln Center. "That cultural exchange fosters artistic inspiration has been an article of faith at least since the late 19th century, when international expositions awakened artists from Debussy to W.S. Gilbert to the wonders of the Far East," the *Times* review observed. "Today such exchange is often formalized through programs and institutions, like the 96-year-old Japan

Society." Hyla spent two months in Japan, where he became interested in noh. "'At Suma Beach' is less a setting of a Noh play than a delicate reduction of one, condensed like a clear stock into intense—but not dense—music."[74]

Commissions have also been awarded to puppeteer Basil Twist, Big Dance Theater, and choreographer Jeremy Wade. The idea for Twist's 2004 piece, *Dogugaeshi,* came from a type of Japanese folk puppet tradition that employs painted screens changed in rapid succession to the accompaniment of shamisen music. In *The Other Here,* which premiered in 2007, Big Dance Theater's artistic directors Paul Lazar and Annie-B Parsons referenced Okinawan pop music and traditional dance, as well as short stories by Masuji Ibuse. Wade's *there is no end to more* opened at Japan Society in December 2009. While in Japan to develop the project, the Berlin-based, American-born Wade "followed his interest in manga comic books and the country's aesthetic of extreme cuteness."[75]

"Mr. Zorn has connected downtown New York improvisation to other scenes worldwide, particularly in Japan."[76] The reference was to the first installment of the Tzadik Label Music Series, an alliance that began in 2006 between Japan Society and musician-producer John Zorn. Tzadik is the name of Zorn's nonprofit record label, which he launched in 1995. Series programs have included, in May 2006, "New Voices from Japan," featuring Keiji Haino, Koichi Makigami, and Eye Yamataka; in December 2006, "New Voices from Japan II: Power of the New Japanese Woman," focusing on the work of Afrirampo, ni-hao!, Yuka Honda, and Miho Hatori; in March 2008, "Ikue Mori: Celebrating 30 Years of Life, Love and Music in NYC," a concert by Mori and a retrospective of her improvisatory work on the drum machine and laptop computer; and, in December 2008, "A Tribute to Teiji Ito." (Ito, who died in 1982, was a Japanese American composer of experimental music.) The Tzadik series explicitly recognizes Zorn for his role as a conduit of experimental music from Japan to the United States through his record label (which includes the New Japan series), his downtown performance venue (The Stone), and his own artistic collaborations. It is also a way for the society to harness Zorn's reputation in order to associate itself authoritatively with the New York experimental music scene.

Scholars

Over the past two decades American scholars of Japanese theater, dance, and music have been important contributors to Japan Society's project of structuring and conveying knowledge of Japan through the performing arts. Their specialized books and articles inform and influence critics who review presentations, and their background and preview articles in newspapers and general-interest magazines become part of the archive of America's Japan.

Scholars also directly participate in the intercultural space to which Japan Society lays claim. They serve, for example, as members of the Performing Arts Advisory Committee, giving input and feedback on programming and helping the society strengthen the bond between it and the institutions that serve as destinations for US performance tours. The advisory committee in recent years has included John Gillespie (scholar, translator, businessman, and former director of the society's performing arts department) and professors David Goodman (University of Illinois), Laurence Kominz (Portland State University), Judy Mitoma (UCLA), and W. Anthony Sheppard (Williams College)—along with several other people associated with the arts, such as Philip Bither of the Walker Art Center, Margaret Lawrence of the Hopkins Center at Dartmouth College, and playwright John Weidman. Emeritus advisory committee members have included professors Donald Keene (Columbia University), James Brandon (University of Hawai'i), Karen Brazell (Cornell University), and J. Thomas Rimer (University of Pittsburgh); critic Akihiko Senda; and Ralph Samuelson, shakuhachi musician and former director of the Asian Cultural Council.

Scholars contribute to society programming as pre-performance lecturers, giving them visibility in a non-academic setting as designated and credentialed experts on Japan. The society in turn benefits from their presence in building its reputation as a source of significant and scholar-authenticated theater, dance, and music from Japan. Examples of pre-performance lectures include, in September 2005, Karen Brazell on *The Hawk Princess* (*Taka-hime*), a work of modern noh written by Mario Yokomichi and directed by Hiroshi Sugimoto and Tetsunojo Kanze; in November 2006, Patricia Welch (Hofstra University) on rakugo master Utamaru Katsura; in December 2007, W. Anthony Sheppard on the noh-inspired work *Delusion of the Fury* by composer Harry Partch; in March 2009, Jane Marie Law (Cornell University) on the Awaji Puppet Theatre; and in March 2010, Samuel L. Leiter (Brooklyn College) on kyogen presented by the Yamamoto Kyogen Company.

Forum-style conversations among scholars and directors, playwrights, and performers also supplement productions at Japan Society. Hosted by the Graduate Center, City University of New York (CUNY), they have included, in December 2003, "An Evening with Japanese Kyogen Actor and Director Mansai Nomura," with Nomura, Joanne Akalaitis (Bard College), and Samuel L. Leiter; and in March 2007, "An Evening with Takeshi Kawamura," with Kawamura, Carol Martin (New York University), and playwright Richard Foreman.

There have also been two symposiums for scholars held in association with Japanese Theater in the World, a cross-disciplinary program that included a major exhibition of masks, costumes, props, and other theater materials at the Japan Society gallery in the fall and winter of 1997–98—which then traveled in the spring of 1998 to the Museum Villa Stuck in Munich. It was, as Stanca Scholz-Cionca and Samuel Leiter have written, "the most comprehensive exhibition of Japanese theatre arts ever shown outside of Japan."[77] The two scholarly assemblies were Zeami and the Nō Theatre in the World (held at the Graduate Center, CUNY, in October 1997) and Japanese Theater in the World (held in Munich in the spring of 1998). There were subsequently two published volumes of papers—the one edited by Scholz-Cionca and Leiter and one edited by Benito Ortolani and Leiter.[78]

When dancer Akemi Takeya, who lives and works in Vienna, presented her *Body Poems—Reflections* at Japan Society in November 2005, Yoko Shioya described her, as noted in the introductory chapter of this study, in terms of her membership in "'the diaspora of Japanese artists,' creating hybrid work caught between Japan and the host country."[79] However, by presenting Takeya, Japan Society was automatically reconnecting her to Japan—given that it is a (if not *the*) preeminent presenter of Japan-related performing arts outside of the actual borders of the country. This default reconnection applies to all "nonresident" artists originally from Japan who stage their work at Japan Society—Eiko and Koma, Yoshiko Chuma, and Ikue Mori, among many others.

Increasingly, it seems, Japan Society must grapple with the ambivalent nature of "performing arts from Japan." In 2003, when Takeya first appeared at the society, she was one of the artists representing Japan in the Contemporary Dance Showcase. Although the program that year included a supplementary hour focusing on New York–based dancers "in the diaspora," no mention was made of the fact that Takeya was living and working outside of Japan. In 2008 Yun Myung Fee, a woman of Korean ethnicity who was born and raised in Tokyo, was one of the three Japan-based performers in the expanded Contemporary Dance Showcase + East Asia. The program booklet informed readers that Fee incorporates mate-

Fig. 11. Cover of the 1997–98 performing arts season brochure, in conjunction with the Japanese Theater in the World exhibition and ninetieth-anniversary celebration at Japan Society. (© 1997 by Japan Society, New York. Courtesy of Japan Society, New York.)

rial from Korean culture in her work. What was not alluded to, of course, is that (in all likelihood) she traveled to the United States on a Korean passport, given that ethnic Koreans are not automatically granted Japanese citizenship even if Japan is their birthplace and home. When Japan Society declared in publicity material for its fall 2009 Japan Transatlantic: Tokio-Berlin season that "Japanese culture is no longer confined to the geographical borders of Japan," the statement held more significance than was perhaps intended: it can be interpreted as saying that there should be recognition of the diversity of cultures within Japan, just as "Japanese culture" should be recognized as part of the diversity of cultures in the world at large.

The society's performing arts program has coupled issues of national and ethnic identity with those of gender. In conjunction with Making a Home: Japanese Contemporary Artists in New York, a Japan Society gallery exhibition that ran from October 2007 to January 2008, the spring 2008 performing arts season was called New York Woman: "The New York-based Japanese women artists featured this season shatter the stereotype of the 'Japanese woman' as subservient and quietly humble. With bold ferocity and poetic imagination, they have sculpted individual artistic visions that weave into the diverse cultural landscape of the extraordinary city we call New York."[80] The featured artists were composer, pianist, and singer Akiko Yano; electronic musician Ikue Mori (appearing in the Tzadik Label Music Series); playwright, director, and translator Aya Ogawa, who crafted *Frozen Beach,* the English translation of *Furōzun bīchi* by Keralino Sandorovich (the pen name of Kazumi Kobayashi) for the plays-in-translation reading series; and choreographer and dancer Yoshiko Chuma, who directed her School of Hard Knocks in a production of *POOM: A Page Out of Order M to M.* An unspoken point was that so many creative women had chosen to leave Japan.

Twenty-first-century performing arts programming at Japan Society also reveals the organization's sense of its own long history and how it defines its goals going forward. For the society's centennial celebration in fall 2007, the focus, in Shioya's words, was on "cutting-edge performing arts from Japan, as well as work from American artists inspired by Japanese culture." It was, moreover, a multi-institution New York event that took place throughout the city: "Discussion with many of our colleagues in the New York City performing arts industry began as early as 2005, when we first conceived of a campaign to celebrate Japanese performing arts for the occasion of Japan Society's centennial. We are thrilled that they were so enthusiastic about participating, and that seven presenters have come on board to present Japan-related programs."[81] Unlike the National Endowment for the Humanities' Japan Today festival almost thirty years earlier, this time the event was initiated by the society to build on its already well developed institutional relationships and to reaffirm its place as a leading presenter in New York and a national producer of contemporary Japan-related programming. The seven cooperating institutions were Dance Theater Workshop, where Big Dance Theater presented *The Other Here*; The Kitchen, which hosted a concert featuring electronic/underground musicians Kanta Horio, Atsuhiro Ito, Fuyuki Yamakawa, and a recital by choreographer-dancer Mika Kurosawa with experimental musician SKANK;[82] Danspace Project, the venue for the Yummy Dance troupe in *Bring Me a PPPeach* and Nami Yamamoto in *tony, and me*; Performance Space 122, where Sennichimae Blue Sky Dance Club appeared in *A Bowl of Summer*; HERE Arts Center, host of Theatre of a Two-Headed Calf's production of *Drum of the Waves of Horikawa*;[83] the Brooklyn Academy of Music, the venue for the Pappa Tarahumara dance-theater's *Ship in a View*,[84] also part of BAM's Next Wave Festival; and the CAVE New York Butoh Festival, which took place in various locations in the city. All of these are "downtown" venues—a noteworthy departure from the time when Japan Society partnered almost exclusively with institutions such as Lincoln Center and Carnegie Hall.

Japan Society stands in contrast to other performing arts organizations where theater, dance, and music from Japan are also presented. For Japan Society the performing arts are instrumental—as are its gallery exhibitions, films, lectures, language classes, and other programs. They are ways to mediate and circulate knowledge of Japan. Presentations at Japan Society risk being viewed solely as cultural demonstrations meant to represent Japan rather than as art subject to critical scrutiny. While Japan Society is a kind of anthropological space, inviting people to experience Japan in multiple ways, it is also a space for audiences to see and hear important works of theater, dance, and music that are open to critical evaluation and validation.

Many factors determine which productions are selected to appear at Japan Society—calculations involving what society administrators want to present, what New York audiences will come to see, which performers from Japan (and elsewhere) wish to perform on the society's stage, and the constraints of funding—both in terms of the amount of money that is available and the types of programs potential sponsors are willing to underwrite. Patrick Lonergan has identified three forms of cultural exchange: "international exchange (movement from one country to another), intra-societal exchange (movement from the margins of a society to its centre), and global exchange (the consumption of a global product by local audiences)."[85] Broadly speaking, Japan Society embraces all three. International exchange has been the main component of postwar performing arts programming at Japan Society. Intra-societal exchange takes the form of tours that circulate Japan-related programming—wherever it may originate—through a North American network that links arts centers and college and university campuses in the United States and Canada to New York. The global exchange component is evident in projects that draw attention to the multilayered-ness of performers' identities.

"The struggle," as Ivan Karp has observed, "is not only over what is to be represented, but over who will control the means of representing."[86] The Japan that John D. Rockefeller III conceptualized over a half century ago was defined strictly by its geographic borders. It would have been difficult at that time to imagine that Japan Society would one day need to come to terms with border-crossing artists who may have been born, raised, and educated in Japan but whose artistic practices challenge or deliberately reject conventional notions of border and identity. The society's performing arts program started in the 1950s as a way to give financial support to artists from Japan who were drawn to New York to further their education and training. The assumption was that they would get their Juilliard (or other) degrees and soon after return to Japan. However, many stayed in New York or later returned as residents. In the decades since then, numerous others have chosen to develop their careers in New York. Today a number of performers at Japan Society do not come by airplane. They come by subway, bus, car, and even on foot. And, those who do come by plane often begin their journeys from homes outside Japan. "The exhibitionary context cannot replicate what it represents. It necessarily recontextualizes what it shows, producing something new,"[87] as Fred Myers has written. Japan Society has a central role in the narrative of America's Japan. The ongoing construction of the image and idea of Japan through the performing arts at Japan Society is part of that "something new" that is produced.

3

De-familiarizing Japan at La MaMa E.T.C.

[I]n New York, where every square inch feels urban, downtown is a refuge from—a repudiation of—the conventionality of Midtown, and mid-everything. Downtown is a concept, and perhaps an archaic one.[1]

"The brilliant theatrical and dramatic upsurge in Japan in the late 1960s truly merits the appellation 'renaissance,'" Yasunari Takahashi has written. "It brought about a revolutionary change in the concept of theatrical representation, if not in the actual structure of society."[2] In 1970, just three years after founding the Tenjo Sajiki theater troupe in Tokyo, Shuji Terayama, one of the primary figures of that upsurge, made his American directorial debut in New York at La MaMa E.T.C. As Steven Clark has pointed out, Tenjo Sajiki was "one of the first Japanese theater companies to perform a significant number of plays abroad and it was the only one which was a full participant in the international experimental theater movement of the 1960s and 1970s."[3] Similarly, Takayuki Tatsumi has called Terayama the "*enfant terrible* of postwar Japanese decadent literature . . . a playwright whom we must recognize for having revolutionized the Japanese sensibility of the urban in the 1970s."[4]

Productions at La MaMa by Terayama and his former Tenjo Sajiki disciple and colleague Yutaka Higashi initiated important new cultural connections with Japan. The "uptown," timeless-culture image of Japan that took shape during the cold-war 1950s and 1960s was significantly challenged in the summer and fall of 1970 by two events at La MaMa. One was *The Golden Bat* (*Gōruden batto*), an exuberant Japanese-language rock musical performed by the Tokyo Kid Brothers under Higashi, the troupe's founder, director, and principal writer. The other, described by Carol Fisher Sorgenfrei as a "wildly comic" play "permeated with . . . ambiguities and inversions: crime and innocence, illusion and reality, truth and lies, female and male, sex and love, education and life experience,"[5] was *La Marie-Vison,* an English-language version of *Kegawa no Marī* written and directed by Terayama. *The Golden Bat* and *La Marie-Vison* gave New York audiences a breakthrough glimpse of Japan's experimental theater scene. In hosting the presentations, La MaMa brought Japanese theater downtown, thus helping usher Japan and its performing arts into new debates about cultural production and encounter, while at the same time solidifying the position of La MaMa as a leading voice in those debates.

This chapter examines how the exoticized image of Japan was de-familiarized through just over a decade of performing arts events that began with Higashi and Terayama at La MaMa in 1970 and culminated in the first appearance in the United States of butoh dance pioneer Kazuo Ono, which took place at La MaMa in 1981. The de-familiarization process was twofold, evident in the expanding number of performing arts organizations and other cultural institutions eager to present Japan to the American public and in the growing number and range of material and artists from Japan being introduced. By making new Japanese work an integral part of its program in experimental theater, La MaMa was the first institution to incorporate Japan fully within New York's competitive performing arts environment. La MaMa also became a model for other institutions in providing audience access to a de-familiarized Japan through the performing arts. In the 1970s and 1980s, work from Japan that had never been seen before in the United States—the rock musicals, innovative theater, and butoh and other heretofore little-known forms of dance featured at La MaMa—began attracting widespread interest and critical attention.

New Networks of Cultural Production in Japan

The late 1960s theatrical and dramatic upsurge to which Yasunari Takahashi referred had grown out of and in turn stimulated the development of powerful new networks of cultural production in Japan. "[L]ittle theater [early avant-garde theater] and modern dance were from their inception closely related,"[6] Akihiko Senda has observed, noting that Juro Kara, founder of the Situation Theatre (Jokyo Gekijo) in the early 1960s, studied under Tatsumi Hijikata, who developed butoh with Ono. In 1972 Akaji Maro, a prominent actor in Kara's Situation Theatre, established Dai Rakudakan, a troupe that made its US debut in 1982 as "the first company to introduce Japan's Butoh dance-theater on a large scale to the United States."[7] To cite an example unrelated to dance, Higashi had worked closely with Terayama in Tenjo Sajiki until leaving the troupe in the fall of 1967 and going on to launch the Tokyo Kid Brothers. Also, the experimental theater troupe Abe Studio, which made its first (and only) trip to the United States in 1979 as part of the Japan Today festival, was led by novelist, director, and playwright Kobo Abe. Abe was already approaching the end of his theatrical career, having been a central figure in Japanese avant-garde theater since the mid-1950s.

In the 1950s and 1960s, kabuki—along with gagaku, noh, kyogen, and bunraku—basically delineated the narrative of America's Japan through the performing arts. American critics and audiences at that time were almost without exception unacquainted with artists whose efforts were expressive of contemporary cultural issues and representative of contemporary movements in Japan. Although visits to the United States by figures such as Terayama, Abe, and Ono decontextualized them and their output from the networks with which they were associated in Japan, their ties to La MaMa in New York gave them a new, substitute context and "downtown" identity.

"La MaMa is an international theater"

This statement is by Ellen Stewart.[8] Stephen Bottoms has written of her as "the maverick impresario and self-appointed earth mother who founded Café La MaMa in 1962 . . . to provide young playwrights with a theater space in which they could develop work on their own terms, without fear of creative interference."[9] By 1967 La MaMa was "the most active producer in New York City, the most active theater center in America."[10] The opening of Stewart's new theater building in the spring of 1969 at 74 East 4th Street symbolized the "institutionalization of the alternative theatre . . . [and] La MaMa finally had the security and legitimacy it needed to survive."[11] Early on Stewart could take satisfaction that La MaMa was able to win major "uptown" recognition in the form of a crucial $65,000 grant awarded to her in 1968 by the Rockefeller Foundation.[12] The money was given to support her troupe and help defray the costs associated with the new building.

Driven by Stewart's vision and instincts, La MaMa embarked on a course that made it an important player in the field of cultural exchange. "She was one of the first to recognize the importance of international cultural exchange," Cindy Rosenthal has written. "Productions produced or directed by Stewart in the 1970s drew on many cultures . . . long before terms such as 'cultural collage' and 'multicultural,' 'intercultural' and 'transcultural' were the subjects of academic conferences and perfor-

Fig. 12. Program cover, La MaMa 47th Season. (Rendering of La MaMa E.T.C. by Adis Hughes. Courtesy of La MaMa Archives/Ellen Stewart Private Collection.)

mance studies courses."[13] *The Golden Bat* and *La Marie-Vison* were part of the early history of La MaMa; almost from the beginning Stewart invited artists from abroad. "More than any other New York cultural institution," *Times* theater critic Mel Gussow wrote in 1982, "La MaMa . . . is an international home for venturesome theater."[14] Stewart also began taking New York productions on tour outside the United States, eventually opening La MaMa branches in several countries. For Ellen Stewart "being international" was a basic tenet of La MaMa's artistic mission.

Rock Musicals

In midsummer New York, Golden Bat is a surprising tonic for which one can only say arigato.[15]

While the genre-defining rock musical *Hair* was still attracting large audiences on Broadway in the summer of 1970, in one stroke Stewart internationalized the category and de-familiarized Japan on the American stage with *The Golden Bat,* La MaMa's first from-Japan event.[16] For *Times* theater and dance critic Clive Barnes, who had covered the bunraku visit in 1966 and the reprise of kabuki in 1969, *The Golden Bat,* which he approvingly dubbed "a tribal musical in the tradition of 'Hair,'" was an eye-opening moment in his engagement with Japanese theater. "Of course, you expect the unexpected at the Café La MaMa," he wrote, "but I must confess I never expected anything quite so unexpected as the Japanese rock musical 'Golden Bat,' which I saw there last weekend." His words were expressive of US goodwill toward Japan in the cold-war era. "They are enchanting people," Barnes wrote about the Tokyo Kid Brothers, whose very name seemed intended to promote a family and friendship appeal. "They are clearly the post-Hiroshima generation of Japan. They offer love as if it were a flower and the whole world were their garden." The performers were not those who had waged war. They were a new generation, to be welcomed as well-meaning young people. He enthusiastically wrote that *The Golden Bat* was "a most marvelous and welcome ambassador for Japanese youth."

Not only did the Tokyo Kid Brothers stand for a friendly postwar Japan, but—in a conceptual leap of considerable proportions—Barnes also saw in them a more approachable downtown New York. They had "none of the abrasive condemnation of the Living Theater," he told readers, referring to the New York theater company founded by Judith Malina and Julian Beck. Barnes's review additionally signaled a newfound interest in Japan: "I have always wanted to visit Japan. 'Golden Bat' only reinforces that wish." Nevertheless, such was the pull of America's kabuki-Japan that he could not help writing that it "may be as up to date as tomorrow, but you are never allowed to forget that it comes from a country of long and noble theatrical traditions." It was an unconvincing assertion, insofar as it was backed up only by the vague observation that the rock music composed by Itsuro Shimoda "is given a particular Japanese accent, and the staging by the show's writer, Higashi Yutaka, is dazzlingly simple."[17]

The Golden Bat got a fortunate break and vastly increased visibility when

New York producers Kermit Bloomgarden and Arthur Cantor extended the show's run by moving it to the off-Broadway Sheridan Square Playhouse, where it continued for 139 performances. In "A Love Letter from Tokyo," an essay reflecting on the New York success of the musical, Broadway theater critic Walter Kerr wrote that the show was a "warm and moth-light and altogether winning Japanese rock entertainment." Like Barnes, Kerr saw in *The Golden Bat* a bridge linking *Hair* and Japanese culture: "It may simply be their Oriental theatrical heritage that makes their freedoms more disciplined and less urgently amateurish than ours ('Hair,' which I twice liked, is sloppy in spirit alongside 'Golden Bat'); but when, for instance, an occasional player moves directly into the auditorium perhaps to dance with a member of the audience, the confrontation works immensely better than I have ever seen it work here."[18]

Delighted with the successful reception of the Tokyo Kid Brothers in their summer 1970 debut, Stewart booked them for a return visit to La MaMa in October of the same year. Newly "designated as the La MaMa Tokyo troupe,"[19] reported *Time* magazine, Higashi and his company hired American actors and actresses to fill out the cast of a hastily assembled new show titled *Coney Island Play* (*Konī airando purē*). The Japanese performers seemed possessed of boundless energy—performing *Coney Island* at La MaMa at midnight on many of the same days they gave *The Golden Bat* at Sheridan Square. "I find these Japanese kids innocent, amusing and lovely," wrote Barnes, "and here they are joined by a talented bunch of American youngsters in the production of a kind of lighthearted and blithe rock revue that is unfinished but gentle fun." The critic mused about "East-West encounters" in an environment where people do not speak each other's language: "It is a mild entertainment, but it has a very special feel to it. . . . These Tokyo Kid Brothers and their new American friends are engaging people to spend an hour or so with."[20]

Having developed a solid relationship with Stewart at La MaMa, the Tokyo Kid Brothers continued in 1974 to serve as a conduit of youth culture from Japan to American audiences. Motorcycle gangs—icons of teenage rebellion and angst—had ridden into Japan's urban consciousness in the 1950s and 1960s. They found expression in *The City* (*Za shitī*), which Higashi's company presented at La MaMa in August 1974. "This time the Kid Brothers have revved up a motorcycle musical about a pack of young rebels united in their love of cycles and their opposition to the police and parents," wrote Gussow. "'The City' is their rock, and to return home would be a defeat." The postwar world in which the Japanese cast had grown up was one in which English had become a required subject in school. Whereas the language of *The Golden Bat* was Japanese, this time the Tokyo Kid Brothers decided to try using English onstage. However, Gussow pointedly noted, *The City* is "apparently in English, much of it unintelligible." Perhaps because he had found "charm" in *The Golden Bat,* the critic cut the Tokyo Kid Brothers some slack in his review. Noting the "curious time lag" in a show that seems "a child of the sixties," he wrote that even though the cast could not dance or sing very well—"which does not stop them from doing either"—the show "is high in energy and enthusiasm."[21]

The run of rock musicals from Japan ended with *Shiro* (*Shiro*), presented by the Tokyo Kid Brothers at La MaMa in November 1981. La MaMa made the show part of its twentieth-anniversary celebrations. A *Times* preview article characterized *Shiro* as "a gamble befitting the theater, a great throw of the dice. No one else in Japan but Mr. Higashi would risk the spectacle of fully armored samurai trundling about the stage in horned hats to music from a tiny rock combo, reinforced by the magical shakuhachi or bamboo flute." In sum, the production was "a magical mystery tour of ancient Japan."[22] For Gussow, *Shiro* evoked nostalgia for the "captivating" experience of *The Golden Bat* eleven years earlier. Labeling it a "'Japanesque' samurai musical," he wrote, "Four teen-agers of the 1980's . . . fall into a time warp and are carried back 350 years to the time of the samurai. The confrontation between contemporary street kids and medieval warriors is a promising idea, but the issue is confused in the telling. The dialogue is in long bursts of Japanese, followed by an often indecipherable bullet of English. Only a few of the actors are intelligible to American ears." He suggested that the troupe might well have altogether abandoned "the attempt at English." His reasoning was that when there was no English "we can sit back and enjoy the floating images and visual splendor."

It seems surprising that Higashi, creator of *The Golden Bat, Coney Island Play,* and *The City,* now appeared to play to a timeless, ahistorical image of Japan with his "Japanesque" musical. "[T]he La MaMa Annex stage has never looked more opulent, with a carpeted stage backed by frescolike curtains that change pictures from savage samurai to peaceful cherry blossoms," Gussow noted. The score, "though evidently influenced by 'Hair,' has an exotic Japanese flavor"—with instruments that included the shakuhachi and Japanese-style drums.[23] However, *Shiro* can be read as an attempt to satirize the Japan that America thought it knew and perhaps once again wanted—even within the walls of La MaMa. The United States in 1981 was in a period of recession. At the same time, Japan's seemingly unstoppable economic rise was making headlines, with growing public anger directed at Japan's challenge to American might. In *Shiro* Higashi served up to

American audiences a picture-book Japan, updated for the 1980s with a catchy rock tune.

Experimental Theater

Proclaiming Terayama "Japan's leading avant-garde playwright," the *Times* greeted his July 1970 American debut with a lengthy preview article published three days before the opening of *La Marie-Vison.* The title, "'There Will Be No Audience,'" highlighted Terayama's concept that those attending should consider themselves "guests of the house [the setting of the play]. They will find places to sit here and there in the various rooms." But there was unintended irony in that title, given that Terayama—despite being highly regarded in Japan and Europe—was as yet unknown in the United States. "Although the 34-year-old writer has a dozen plays, a number of film and radio scenarios, novels, essays, books of poetry and international prizes to his credit," arts journalist Elenore Lester pointed out, "he was not translated into English until the script of 'La Marie Vison' was prepared for presentation at La MaMa." Introducing Terayama to American audiences would not be easy. Trying, somewhat unsuccessfully, to summarize *La Marie-Vison,* Lester added, "Most of the action takes place on a level of poetic metaphor that makes it virtually untranslatable into narrative prose." Terayama himself did not make it any easier for Lester, telling her that physical deformity "stimulates the imagination. It is erotic." New York, he dryly commented, was a place where "there is much nudity but no eroticism. It is like a meat market. I am not interested in people who can take their clothes off without shyness."[24]

Claims made about Terayama's importance prior to his arrival in the United States had the almost predictable effect of inviting the skepticism of New York critics. "Shuji Terayama has been praised as Japan's leading avant-garde playwright, and his work, 'La Marie Vison' ('Mink Marie'), which he wrote and directed, has been praised as a masterpiece," Gussow's review began, only to conclude that "it appears to be an intriguing environment in need of a play." Although the play was presented in English translation with locally hired actors, the critic was not pleased. He found the use of "Japanese names in an otherwise American context" to be "jarring." "La Marie-Vison" was visually "stimulating," he wrote, but "lacking in insight and resonance."[25]

Terayama's arrival in the United States seemed to demand a fresh evaluation of culture from Japan. "Tokyo: Kabuki, Rock, and the Twain," for example, is a wry riff on contemporary Japan-US cultural exchange. The piece focused on the international release of a film version of Shusaku Endo's novel *Silence,* the star turn by kabuki actor Somegoro Ichikawa VI on Broadway in *Man of La Mancha,* and Terayama's production at La MaMa. *Silence,* Tokyo-based correspondent Takashi Oka wrote, "explores Mr. Endo's favorite theme—the great distance between East and West, the isolation and loneliness in which each dwells beneath a surface show of comprehension and good fellowship." Shifting his subject to kabuki, he complicated American understandings of the art form by writing that Somegoro "feels the scope for inventiveness [in kabuki] is limited." A segue to Terayama brought the observation that the "avant-garde playwright and director whose style and subject matter seem at first glance to be the complete antithesis of stately Kabuki . . . feels closer in spirit to Kabuki as originally performed in the 17th and 18th centuries than to the type of Moscow Art Theater realism of Japan's orthodox contemporary theater companies."

Terayama was perfectly aware of American audiences' predilection for traditional Japanese theater. "Kabuki as performed today is a museum piece," Oka quoted Terayama as saying, "but in its origins it was splendidly alive. The living theater we build up in each day's performance may be ephemeral, but it has the power to make history, not to repeat it."[26] Underscoring Oka's points, Steven Clark has written that Terayama's Tenjo Sajiki acting company "faced a strange paradox: at home the troupe typically fit into universal categories like the avant-garde or underground theater, but when they performed in Europe or America they often found themselves representing geopolitical particularities like 'Japan,' or even 'the East.' Terayama's plays, then, were not experienced as 'Japanese' until they left Japan." Terayama, Clark observed, did not define his plays "in relation to Japan as a national culture" but "engage[d] parallel processes of slippage between the categories of universal and particular." Terayama's project abroad was to explore "how that conceptual slippage can be manipulated and with what effects it has historically been exploited."[27]

Terayama's return to New York in 1980 was preceded a year earlier by the arrival at La MaMa of Kobo Abe's *The Little Elephant Is Dead: An Exhibition of Images* (*Kozō wa shinda*)—perhaps the single most important event in Japan Today, the three-month touring cultural festival discussed in chapter 2. As host of the production, La MaMa gave the Abe Studio a context that unambiguously emphasized the aim of Japan Today organizers to stimulate new understandings of Japanese culture. Gussow responded with enthusiasm, calling *The Little Elephant Is Dead* "experimental theater with a sense of humor" and citing Abe's "original and transforming" vision. "As action artist," Gussow wrote, "Mr. Abe is a grand performer and designer in the theater."[28]

Abe already had considerable literary renown in the United States. English translations of his novels, starting with *Woman in the Dunes* in 1964, were published by Knopf.[29] In 1969 Grove Press brought out a translation of his play *Friends.*[30] In 1971, with the launch of his Abe Studio, he expanded an already established reputation in Japan as one of the most important figures in postwar theater. As director and playwright of the studio, Abe gave free rein to his experimental imagination over a span of eight years. The 1979 US tour of *The Little Elephant Is Dead* was Abe's last playwriting and directorial project.

In retrospect the imminent closing of the Abe Studio gave added significance to the La MaMa run and the rest of the US tour of *The Little Elephant Is Dead.* Extensively interviewed by the American press in the five cities (New York, Washington, DC, Chicago, Denver, and Saint Louis) where productions took place, Abe told journalists, "I would like to share with you here a world, the kind of world that you surely could neither have experienced nor imagined without encountering this work."[31] It was a statement that resonated outside theater—a profound commentary on Japan Today as an opportunity to reframe and de-familiarize Japan. Nancy K. Shields, an American academic who became a close friend of Abe and other members of the Abe Studio, accompanied the twenty-eight-member troupe on its US tour. She has provided an eyewitness account of the de-familiarization taking place: "Talking with people in the lobby and eavesdropping on their conversations," she wrote, "I find that the American audiences expect to find the Abe productions to be distinctively Japanese, or at any rate filled with things that they have hitherto thought to be symbolic of Japan (kimonos, cherry blossoms, stylized traditional drama such as Noh or Kabuki). What they experience is something very different."[32]

Japan Today was long over, although its reverberations continued to be felt, when Terayama appeared again at La MaMa in June 1980 with his *Gulliver's Travels*–inspired *Directions to Servants* (*Nuhikun*). Members of the audience at La MaMa, Sorgenfrei has written, were witnesses to "the bizarre, sado-masochistic interactions between actors and machines, masters and servants, fiction and reality . . . [and] there was a strong sense of either being forced into the position of voyeur, or of being forbidden to see certain scenes that were nevertheless audible."[33] "Philistines of the world, take heed," critic John Corry wrote, "You have nothing to lose but your prejudices." In Corry's view, the work "is baffling and self-indulgent. It is also worthwhile and theatrical." Although the critic did not spell out who the "Philistines" were and the nature of their "prejudices," he was trying to make clear that *Directions to Servants* was not Japan as usual: "East or West, the egoism of directors can be boundless. We sense that Mr. Terayama, whatever his other motives, is in love with his own experimentation." For Corry it was that very experimentation that was the key to Terayama, and that made *Directions to Servants* "an important piece of work."[34]

Japan Society co-sponsored the eleven-day run of *Directions.* La MaMa needed the financing Japan Society could bring, which included a grant from the Japan-US Friendship Commission to underwrite the event. On its side, Japan Society benefited from a deepening association with New York's foremost experimental theater. The impact of Terayama's presence was maximized by weeklong workshops that he and his troupe held for actors. Publicity was also intensified with the concurrent showing at the Public Theater of Terayama's film *Pastoral Hide and Seek* (*Den'en ni shisu*).[35]

Butoh/Experimental Dance

Sensing its own expanding role as a world capital of dance, New York in the early 1980s was ready for the American debut of Kazuo Ono, "the 75-year-old father figure of Japanese avant-garde dance."[36] The performance took place at La MaMa in July 1981. Dance critic Jennifer Dunning wrote that Ono "never failed to fascinate." The dances that made up the composition *Admiring La Argentina* were "[w]onderful in their terrible abandon, touched by a glint of humor [that] proved Mr. Ohno to be a complete child of the theater." Dunning described his "clawed hands and body that curls in almost to the point of embrace,"[37] images that would become increasingly familiar as more butoh presentations from Japan quickly followed.

Ono's appearance at La MaMa marked the formal introduction of butoh to New York and symbolized the full unfolding of the de-familiarization narrative in theater and dance from Japan. Dunning had mentioned in passing that Ono began his career in Japan in the late 1940s but did not comment on the fact that it had taken an extraordinary amount of time for a US visit to take place. In a sense, La MaMa's invitation to Ono was recognition of the rapid increase in the number of dance artists from Japan who were arriving and in many cases, like Kei Takei, Yoshiko Chuma, Mariko Sanjo, and Eiko and Koma, settling in New York. "Not only are a great number of Japanese dancers in evidence these days, but they are among today's outstanding performers in the modern-dance world," Gwin Chin had observed in a 1979 *Times* essay."[38] Whatever the contributing factors—scholarships (such as Fulbright) for study in the United States and the sheer desire to leave Japan and "make it" in New York—Japan was helping shape the development of contemporary dance in the United States.

By the mid-1980s butoh was a major topic in American conversations about dance—ones in which La MaMa frequently continued to take part. Butoh artist Min Tanaka became a prominent figure on the La MaMa schedule, with his *Emotion* in 1983, *Mythos Oedipus* in 1984, and *Form in the Sky* in 1985. In "Dance That Startles and Challenges Is Coming from Abroad," dance critic Anna Kisselgoff wrote, "Ten years ago, the idea that [Germany, France, and Japan] would provide the leading new and unexpected dance currents that have begun spilling over to these shores would have seemed inconceivable. Modern dance appeared to be an American preserve." The work coming out of Japan to which she was referring centered on butoh, which she called "highly original."[39] American academics and theater professionals were also taking note of the dance form: the summer 1986 issue of *TDR: The Drama Review* alone published eight articles—covering sixty pages—on the subject. The special section opens with Bonnie Sue Stein's oft-cited "Butoh: 'Twenty Years Ago We Were Crazy, Dirty, and Mad,'" a history and overview of butoh in Japan and abroad.[40] Stein—a performing arts and Japan specialist who at the time was a program associate with Beate Gordon at Asia Society and now heads her own production company in New York—teamed with *TDR* editor Richard Schechner in bringing together a rich repository of interviews with and articles by Min Tanaka and Kazuo Ono.

An Expanding "Downtown" for Japan

La MaMa was at the center of a growing number of downtown spaces that included Japan-related theater, dance, and music in their programming. Such programming legitimized performing arts from Japan within the competitive New York marketplace—and, at the same time, helped establish the identity of the hosting institutions as centers for the presentation of international art.

One of the most important is the Brooklyn Academy of Music (BAM). Starting in the late 1960s under Harvey Lichtenstein, the century-old

Brooklyn Academy of Music (located across the East River from Manhattan but still considered "downtown") was being transformed into "America's premier showcase for cutting-edge performing arts from around the world."[41] Joseph Melillo, who succeeded Lichtenstein in 1999 as BAM's executive producer, had joined the institution in 1983 to run the Next Wave Festival—a major contemporary performing arts event and an important site for work from Japan. Japan-related programming was inaugurated at BAM in October 1973 when the organization followed La MaMa's lead in presenting a Japanese rock musical. Written, directed, and produced by Tsutomu Yamashita, founder of the Red Buddha Theatre company, *The Man from the East* was "a collage of Japanese life—ancient and modern, real and fantastic."[42] Other noteworthy productions have included, in 1988, *Comet Messenger-Siegfried* (*Suisei no shisha jīkufurīto*), a play written and directed by Hideki Noda and performed by his troupe Yume no Yuminsha; in 1989, *Japan's Traditional Dance—Now,* a selection of classics newly choreographed by Juraku Hanayagi; in 1990, a production of *Macbeth,* directed by Yukio Ninagawa and performed by the Ninagawa Company; in 1994, the dance piece *Noïject,* choreographed by Saburo Teshigawara and performed by Teshigawara and his company, Karas; in 1995, Yukio Mishima's play *Madame de Sade* (*Sado kōshaku fujin*), directed by Ingmar Bergman; in 1999, the dance piece *Kiyomeki,* choreographed by Ushio Amagatsu and performed with his company, Sankai Juku; and in 2006, the dance piece *Kagemi—Beyond the Metaphors of Mirrors,* also by Amagatsu and Sankai Juku.

The Joyce Theater, a center for contemporary dance that opened in 1982, is another particularly influential downtown venue. Its Japan-related programming has included, in 1985, *Closeup of Japan,* a weeklong butoh series featuring Kazuo Ono and Kuniko Kisanuki; in 1990, *Memory, Rust,* and *Passage,* choreographed and performed by Eiko and Koma; in 1992, a jazz-dance troupe from the Takarazuka Theatre; in 2000, *Secret Club,* choreographed and performed by H Art Chaos; and in 2008, *Hunger,* choreographed and performed by Eiko and Koma.

These and other "downtown" venues for Japan-related performances reflect the breadth of New York's experimental arts scene and the continuing influence of Japanese artists. From a biennial butoh festival organized by the Brooklyn-based CAVE Organization to the regular flow of theater, music, and dance offerings at the HERE Arts Center, The Stone, The Kitchen, the Village Vanguard, the Blue Note, Dance Theater Workshop, and Danspace Project, Japan is now as firmly rooted in the avant-garde side of New York culture as it is in the uptown institutions.

De-familiarization/Re-familiarization

In a 1984 essay on the sudden emergence of butoh performers as principal figures in cultural exchange from Japan, dance journalist Terry Trucco pointed to the enthusiasm of American (and European) audiences for Sankai Juku, a troupe that "uses the shocking and the grotesque to create powerful images." She noted, "In Japan, where Buto first evolved in the 1960's . . . [it] is still looked upon as a faintly distasteful underground art, well outside the mainstream. Performances are held in small theaters and jazz clubs, and nearly all of Japan's 40-odd performance troupes and individual dancers support themselves with outside jobs." Members of Sankai Juku, which made its American debut at City Center in 1984, "seemed pleasantly bemused at the warm reception they received."[43] Like Akaji Maro's Dai Rakudakan troupe, which traveled to the United States for the first time in 1982 in response to an invitation to appear at the American Dance Festival in Durham, North Carolina (where it received enthusiastic reviews), companies that may have been on the margins of the performing arts scene in Japan were being wooed by major arts presenters abroad. (The shock-style of certain butoh performers was made tragically evident in the United States when a member of Sankai Juku died after a rope holding him upside down off the side of a building broke during a 1985 open-air performance in Seattle.)

In counterpoint to the de-familiarization of Japanese culture through the performing arts that began at La MaMa with Higashi and Terayama in 1970 and culminated with Ono in 1981, there was an almost immediate reflexive attempt to re-familiarize it by rendering it timeless and ahistorical—the very discourse butoh vigorously rejected. To an extent America's kabuki-Japan neutralized Japan's butoh. Though accurately citing the influence of the form on US practitioners of experimental dance starting especially in the 1980s, Kisselgoff was nevertheless attracted to what she interpreted as a Japanese "essence" in the works she saw: "Butoh remains significantly Japanese—as in Haiku, it offers a remote rather than a literal image to convey the message at hand."[44] Kazuo Ono "uses abstraction: Minute gestures are abstracted, Kabuki style, to the point that they mean nothing literal but have a generalized meaning."[45] In reviewing *The Dead Sea* by Ono and his son, Yoshito, at the Joyce Theater, Kisselgoff wrote, "In some of the solos, Mr. Ohno is presenting the traditional Kabuki onnagata role (a woman played by man) in a grotesque modern version.

The references to an older Japanese tradition are visible, at the same time that the heritage of the West, especially in music and clothes, is drawn upon for shock effect."[46] Seeing a male Japanese performer in the role of a woman, the kabuki-knowledgeable critic made the dubious leap to *onnagata,* thereby firmly—and reassuringly for readers unsure how to interpret the dance form—placing butoh along a continuum with kabuki.

Even in a Broadway musical, kabuki was inescapable. For two months in the spring of 1970, twenty-seven-year-old Somegoro Ichikawa VI, one of kabuki's consummate cross-over actors, played the title role in *Man of La Mancha.* In addition to kabuki, his onstage résumé already included a long list of appearances in Japanese productions of Broadway musicals and contemporary plays. As *La Mancha* rolled out in theaters around the world with local casts, producer Albert Selden launched a Festival of International Don Quixotes. The idea was "to ask the Don Quixote of each major foreign production of 'La Mancha' to take the lead in the New York production for two to three months."[47] Preceded by actors from Mexico and England, Somegoro, who starred in a Tokyo production of *La Mancha* the previous year, gamely used English onstage for the first time when he came to New York. Billed as a "kabuki actor on Broadway," he cooperated with the American image-makers, telling the press, "I hope that, as my particular contribution to this festival, I can bring to my performance the good points of Kabuki without diminishing the special atmosphere and quality of this play."[48]

La MaMa occasionally deploys public reminders of its institutional history as a way to push back against attempts at re-familiarization. Over the course of three weeks in June 2002, Stewart and her staff paid tribute to Terayama and Higashi in a series of lectures, video screenings of productions directed by the two men, and an exhibition of related posters and other memorabilia. While the individual careers of both Terayama, who passed away in 1983, and Higashi, who died in 2000, received a substantial boost because of their association with La MaMa, their productions in turn did much to help establish the organization's own identity as a leading international, avant-garde institution. A great deal of scholarship has been published on Terayama. Although Higashi is less frequently mentioned, in February 2010 La MaMa presented a tribute to him alone in the form of *Hitohira 2010: The Last Golden Bat.* Like its namesake, the show was a musical—a pastiche nostalgically recalling the 1970 production—that was conceived and performed (with some additional actors) by Itsuro Shimoda and other original members of the Tokyo Kid Brothers. La MaMa's publicity materials made a point of telling theatergoers in 2010 that *The Golden Bat* had been "the first Japanese Avant-Garde theatre production to go Off Broadway."

Higashi and Terayama were important figures who helped begin the process of de-familiarizing Japan through the performing arts. La MaMa welcomed them "downtown"—into America's iconic space of resistance and experiment. By the time they made their first trip to New York, travel time from Tokyo had shrunk exponentially—and, with it, the psychological distance between the two cities. As Steven C. Ridgely has pointed out, "[T]he speed with which ideas, information, and even people could move between Paris and Tokyo, say, was functionally equivalent by the 1960s to their velocity between the East Village and Berkeley."[49] Productions at La MaMa (and soon other institutions) significantly broadened opportunities for performing arts from Japan to be viewed as "real" theater subject to critical scrutiny—rather than mainly as cultural demonstrations outside of the realm of criticism.

4

Claiming the New, Reclaiming the Old in "Music From Japan"

"In Japan we were for a long time influenced by the West," Mr. [Hiroyuki] Iwaki, the conductor [of the NHK Symphony] said. "But now America will be more influenced by Japan."[1]

"Today, the number of Oriental music students in this country has multiplied manyfold, and there has been a notable increase in soloists and orchestra players from Japan and South Korea (and, so far, a few from China). Orientals have placed high in or won all of the recent major music competitions. Their seemingly sudden appearance on our concert stages has been so remarkable that it has prompted tongue wagging in lay circles as to whether performers from the Far East can really understand or play Western music."[2] Although it seems as if these words had to have been written in a much more distant time, the year was 1980 and the publication was the *New York Times* Sunday magazine. The subject of this chapter is Music From Japan, an institution started in 1975 by Naoyuki Miura. Miura unequivocally challenged the kind of cultural ethnocentrism so manifest in the *Times* piece by creating a new kind of cultural exchange in the field of music—one that puts the focus on acquainting American audiences with the broad range of important new work being written by composers from Japan. Arriving in the United States in 1966 on a Fulbright grant, he studied at the Manhattan School of Music and Juilliard. He then went on to forge a successful career in the American music establishment as a double bass player with the American Symphony Orchestra and the New York City Opera orchestra. Miura left active performance in the late 1980s for a dual, binational career as president and director of Music From Japan in New York and as a professor at—and, for a time, president of—Fukushima College in Japan.

As an independent producer of concerts, Miura has used a variety of stages over the years—most frequently at Lincoln Center, Japan Society, Carnegie Hall, Asia Society, and Merkin Concert Hall. He also arranges performance tours to other US and, occasionally, international locations. In his annual programs of music by Japanese composers, which regularly attract the attention of critics, he has engaged many US- and Japan-based ensembles, orchestras, and soloists—such as Tashi, the Kronos Quartet, the Manhattan String Quartet, Pro Musica Nipponia, Reigakusha, the Junko Tahara Biwa Ensemble, the American Symphony Orchestra, the Brooklyn Philharmonic Orchestra, Aki Takahashi, Elizabeth Brown, Mari Kimura, and Mayumi Miyata. Whereas Ellen Stewart at La MaMa brought "Japan" downtown, Miura took new music from Japan into New York's uptown, establishment spaces—in which he already had attained a place as a performer. "There was a good deal of creativity [in Japan] that wasn't much recognized in Europe or America," Thomas R. H. Havens has pointed out in reference to Japanese musicians, dancers, and visual artists working in the 1950s.[3] When Music From Japan got under way, the works by the composers presented under its umbrella illustrated Havens's observation that in the postwar period there was a critical mass of musicians and other artists in Japan who

> sought to create a new culture that was neither imperially Japanese, as in the 1930s and early 1940s, nor postimperially American, as during 1945–1952. . . . A number of [artists] ended up producing non-Western or even post-Western contemporary art, although some of it was neutrally nonnational or even transnational in direction. Other avant-garde figures were more mimetic. Many of the most innovative works exceeded syntheses of domestic and Western idioms to develop radically new stances on the relationship between the spatial (Japan) and the temporal (the contemporary). In doing so, some of these works repositioned themselves as transcultural: now deterritorialized as place-specific to Japan and instead engaged in a dynamic, interactive process of cultural creolization that began early in the century and accelerated among artists around the world after World War Two.[4]

In documenting the history of Music From Japan, I identify several overlapping phases that have unfolded over the span of thirty-five years. During its first decade, it was in a way an iteration of what Yoshio Sugimoto has referred to as the "waves of 'learn-from-Japan' campaigns" that came to the fore at a time when US corporations were struggling to compete against the strong economic growth occurring in Japan.[5] Ezra Vogel's 1979 best seller, *Japan as Number One: Lessons from Japan,* became the primary textbook of such campaigns, arguing that Japan had a great deal to teach the United States in areas such as business and education. As a member of the New York musical establishment and with strong ties to the music world in Japan (where he had begun his professional career prior to attending Juilliard), Miura was in a unique position to help Americans learn about, and from, music from Japan. Music From Japan was in effect a way to speak back against the discourse of America's kabuki-Japan—"to show that current art was alive and well in Japan."[6] It was also a chance to present a more nuanced and cultured image of Japan—one that was unrelated to the unremitting stream of stories about business and the economy that was dominating the news.

In the second phase, starting in the mid-1980s, Miura began responding to and providing a platform for burgeoning interest around the globe in "new" sonic possibilities offered by traditional Japanese instruments, as well as in the application of computer technology to musical performance. Music From Japan became a more proactive arts organization by launching a robust commissioning program that gave composers in Japan the assurance that their work would be heard internationally. It also helped stimulate conversations between Japanese musicians and American critics, scholars, and the public by holding symposiums in conjunction with its concerts. In 1994 Music From Japan helped solidify its institutional presence in New York by opening a music library and information center in office space on East 20th Street. The collection, which is supplemented by a comprehensive online music database, includes hundreds of scores and thousands of recordings.

The third, and most recent, phase began with two events in the mid-1990s that definitively established Music From Japan as the principal cultural-exchange conduit in New York of new works originating in Japan that are written for "Western" instruments, as well as those written for "Japanese" instruments. One was the American premiere of *Kinkakuji* (*Temple of the Golden Pavilion*), an opera composed by Toshiro Mayuzumi based on the novel by Yukio Mishima. Presented at Lincoln Center's New York State Theater (now called the David H. Koch Theater), it was a co-production of Music From Japan and the New York City Opera. The other was a series of lectures and concert/demonstrations of "new gagaku" performed by Reigakusha, the ensemble that inaugurated Japan-related programming at the Lincoln Center Festival and would subsequently become a featured performer in Music From Japan programs. Music From Japan continues

Fig. 13. Brochure page, Music From Japan, Merkin Concert Hall, 2008. (Courtesy of the Merkin Concert Hall at Kaufman Center.)

to represent for New York—and, more broadly, American—audiences the wide scope of art music practices in Japan today.

Miura's task has not been easy, but he is a patient man. As the *Times* reported two and a half decades after he began his project, "What little New Yorkers do know about Japanese contemporary music is largely a result of efforts by Naoyuki Miura, the artistic director of Music From

Japan, which has presented the work of more than 100 composers and which next weekend celebrates its 25th anniversary with two concerts and a symposium at Merkin Concert Hall, near Lincoln Center."[7] The product of Miura's sustained vision and the strong music-world connections he cultivated in the United States and Japan, Music From Japan is a compelling example of cultural mobility and exchange.

Contextualizing Music From Japan

Prior to the mid-1970s, most Americans would have associated the phrase "music from Japan" with either Japanese performers of the classical "Western" repertory or Japanese koto, shakuhachi, and other instrumentalists (including the gagaku ensemble that visited in 1959) playing a traditional repertory. By way of contextualizing Music From Japan within the narrative of America's Japan, I begin by looking back to productions of *Madama Butterfly* in the 1950s as important examples of efforts to develop new connections with Japan through music. I also discuss several initiatives that in the 1960s and 1970s were intended to introduce musicians and music from Japan.

A More "Authentic" *Madama Butterfly*

At exactly the same time that Joshua Logan, Paul Green, and James Michener were advocating for kabuki, the first major Japan-related presentation to take place in New York in the postwar period was a 1952 production of the Puccini opera *Madama Butterfly*. If "Cold War imperatives," as M. J. Heale has written, "required that [Japan] be cherished by Americans,"[8] there was perhaps no better vehicle than *Madama Butterfly*, which had been attracting US audiences for nearly fifty years. Joseph Rosenstock's vision of cultural exchange with Japan took the shape of a cooperative venture between the New York City Opera and the Fujiwara Opera of Japan. Rosenstock, who was both conductor and general director of the New York City Opera, had worked in Japan before the war as head of the Japan Philharmonic Orchestra. Such was the esteem in which he was held by the music establishment in Japan that he was named honorary musical director and conductor of the Japan Broadcasting Corporation after the war ended.

Madama Butterfly calls up images of an aestheticized Japan long familiar to American audiences. In the joint productions that took place in 1952 and 1953 the Fujiwara performers took the Japanese roles and sang in Japanese. The New York–based company delivered the rest in Italian. Despite Rosenstock's good intentions, music and theater critic Howard Taubman seemed uncomfortable at the prospect of Japanese participation in Western high art. In a preview piece profiling Yoshie Fujiwara, director of the visiting company, Taubman expressed surprise that Fujiwara had developed a career as an "opera impresario," unilaterally asserting that "opera is almost as much of an exotic to the Japanese as their No-Drama would be to Americans." Despite Taubman's supposition that "the career of impresario is undoubtedly one of the rarest in Japan" (which could certainly be said about the United States as well), opera already had a long history in Japan. It appealed to an audience as sophisticated and self-selected as the one for noh drama.

Taubman's essay communicated the uncertainty of a critic called on at that moment in history—the Occupation of Japan had just ended—to evaluate performers from Japan who, some might say, were taking the places of Western performers on a professional Western stage. Noting that Fujiwara had trained and worked in Italy as an opera singer before returning to Japan and establishing the opera company that bore his name, Taubman hastened to tell readers, "Mr. Fujiwara does not pretend that [Fujiwara Opera] is in a class with a major American or European troupe. His company, for example, has no theatre of its own." He might have added that many highly regarded performing arts troupes in Japan use shared facilities. When Taubman reported on Fujiwara's enthusiasm for initiating his own future cultural exchange project, especially to introduce American audiences to the work of the Japanese operatic composer Ikuma Dan, Taubman neither concurred nor identified Dan beyond saying that Fujiwara "regards [him] as a gifted composer."

Fujiwara's seriousness of purpose, and that of his troupe, were lost in the fog of Taubman's depiction of the impresario as an exotic spectacle, whose very ethnicity was questioned: "Mr. Fujiwara has not only a strange occupation but also a strange background." The son of a Scotsman and a Japanese woman, Fujiwara had taken his mother's family name. His fluency in English was noted, although the pidgin-style quotations attributed to him were unmistakably condescending. Rosenstock invited the Fujiwara Opera company to the United States to introduce Japanese cultural authenticity into a familiar and popular work that could potentially serve as common ground in shared artistic pursuits. Like his contemporaries Joshua Logan and Lincoln Kirstein, Rosenstock believed that cultural exchange in the performing arts was an important way to build friendly relations between the United States and Japan. However, Fujiwara's mild criticisms of the

Orientalist elements that historically were accepted practice in productions of *Madama Butterfly* were turned into an Orientalist parody of his own speech: "'Every Cio-Cio-san I have ever seen in Europe and America walks like this,' Mr. Fujiwara said, and with his arms and shoulders he made the mincing, jerky moves that fit into the Western conception of the Oriental. 'But Japanese lady does not walk like this.'"[9]

Taubman conceded in his review several days later that there was "much more of Japan" in the opera, thanks to the visiting performers, their costumes, and their props. Although the sets brought from Japan could not be used—"they were not flameproof and were not properly processed for hanging in our theatre"—in the critic's eyes the stage "irradiated a flavor of Japan." Taubman praised "the movement of the Japanese singers [which] had the grace and design of a delicate ballet. The ladies did not walk with the mincing steps of manikins, so common in our conception of Oriental people, nor did they move like Western women. There was a gracious fluidity in their movements and gestures." The singing was, however, an altogether different matter. Taubman felt that the Japanese performers came up short: their voices were "not on a level with what we are accustomed to." One soprano's voice "has sweetness" but "it tends to tremble and go shrill." Another "lacks color." The men's voices "were even paler." Willing to give an A for effort, Taubman wrote, "[T]hese comments, probably too inhospitable in view of the charm of the visitors, should not keep prospective patrons from a rare experience in the theatre. This is a 'Butterfly' of remarkable delicacy on the Japanese side and of strong singing on the American side. . . . Puccini's music is still there, even if Joseph Rosenstock takes it a shade slowly now and then. The language shifts from Italian to Japanese and back again to Italian, but that does not matter, either. Somehow the Japanese filled the theatre with a special warmth."[10]

The Fujiwara Opera returned to the United States in 1953, repeating the joint, bilingual production of *Madama Butterfly* in a tour that culminated at City Center. Taubman's writing the previous year had given little credence to the idea of first-rate opera in Japan, but subsequent newspaper coverage of a Japanese diva named Michiko Sunahara clearly demonstrated that Japan was not such a neophyte in the art after all. The *Times* reported on the New York arrival of Sunahara: arrayed in a kimono, obi, and geta sandals—the clothing "customarily worn by fashionable Japanese ladies"—she had come directly from an engagement at the Opéra Comique in Paris and was heading to Los Angeles to join the Fujiwara Opera Company on its tour. On her way through New York she had time to tell the reporter, "We learn Italian opera in Japan just as you do in

America. . . . Japanese music is completely Westernized. We learn first the arias, in Italian, exactly as if we were studying in New York." Mixing Italian and Japanese in the same opera is "customary when Italian opera is played in Japan." Given the long history of translated work on the stage in Japan, she quite reasonably remarked that in Japan "the familiar arias are all sung in Italian, the recitatives in Japanese."[11] It was as if she were saying, don't you follow a similar pattern in the United States?

Sunahara's confidence did not win over the *Times* reviewer when she returned to New York in October. The unidentified writer seemed to be uncomfortable with round 2 of the "experiment" that the New York City Opera had "tried last fall." The Fujiwara troupe was rather dismissively referred to as "foreign visitors [who] brought their own costumes and properties and their own crisp, formal, fluttery manner of performing." The presence of the Japanese singers was judged to be no more than an attempt at "visual verisimilitude"—which the reviewer regarded as "not particularly important in this opera"—noting that *Madama Butterfly* "was composed by an Italian in Italian and the orientalisms in the scoring are only superficial. It remains an Italian opera that has to be sung in an Italian manner with a fullness of melodic outpouring by voices that can match the orchestral music in the sweetness and richness of their tones." While following Taubman's lead in concluding that the Japanese singers were simply not up to the job ("for the most part, [they] did not have weighty enough or fine enough voices"), the reviewer went a step further: "And they sang in Japanese, a language that does not blend well with Italian and which seems almost counter in character to Puccini's type of music."[12] Though vaguely disguised as an issue related to language as an artistic medium, the unmistakable message that ethnic/racial boundaries had somehow been violated was far from the outcome Rosenstock expected when he launched his cultural-exchange endeavor.

The Fujiwara Opera company intrepidly traveled to New York for a third and last time in 1956. Again they were performing *Madama Butterfly*, but on this trip it was mostly in Japanese—except for the roles of Pinkerton, Kate, and Sharpless, which were sung in English. The three-day run took place at the Brooklyn Academy of Music in a series that had the opera alternating with an American production of Gilbert and Sullivan's *Mikado*. In his review Harold C. Schonberg adopted a mellower view than his predecessors had on the issue of language: "'Butterfly' sung in Japanese is not as fearsome as one might have anticipated. In fact, the accents sounded down right mellifluous." While rating most of the singing as no more than "routine," he concluded, "As for authenticity, what could be more Japanese-looking than a group of Japanese girls dressed in native costume?"[13]

If responses to the Fujiwara troupe, especially in 1952 and 1953, exposed a degree of American anxiety over Japanese performers appearing in Western canonical forms, they also suggested that safe ground existed in arts fully identifiable with Japan. And, indeed, the Azuma Kabuki Dancers and Musicians arrived in 1954 to an unqualifiedly enthusiastic response. Nevertheless, the project of authenticating *Madama Butterfly* through cultural exchange persisted, taking a new turn in 1958 at the Metropolitan Opera House in a production that has been described as one of the Met's "glories."[14] John D. Rockefeller III was not the only wealthy individual willing to use his own funds to put Japan onstage. "'Met' Is Going Native in Restaging 'Butterfly'" was the title of an article announcing that for the first time in thirty-four years the Met would offer a brand new production of the opera—and that the theater had "engaged two Japanese theatre men to help in the new production." The invited guests were kabuki director Yoshio Aoyama and scene and costume designer Motohiro Nagasaka.[15] The project sponsor was businessman and philanthropist C. V. Starr, founder of the American International Group (AIG).

Like Rosenstock, Starr saw in *Madama Butterfly* an opportunity to have a positive impact on American attitudes toward Japan by enabling a production that would set new standards for cultural authenticity—for both Puccini and the Met. In "No Fireflies for 'Butterfly,'" opera critic John Briggs alerted *Times* readers to the changes they would see, and thereby implicitly critiqued the *Butterfly*-Orientalism that up until then had been accepted practice at the venerable opera house. "Butterfly's house will be authentically Japanese except that its proportions will be slightly larger than standard to go with the cavernous Metropolitan stage," Briggs wrote. Directing actors to walk with their hands hidden inside the sleeves of their kimonos and with "mincing steps," he continued, was typical of past productions, but it "actually is Chinese rather than Japanese" and would be revised. Audiences would also see the maid Suzuki kneel when Butterfly kneels before Pinkerton because Butterfly's maid should always remain lower than her mistress. Imitation fireflies, a "time-hallowed Metropolitan touch," were banished: "'In Japan,' Mr. Aoyama explains urbanely, 'we do not have fireflies during the cherry blossom season.'" However, nothing could be done to replace the music Puccini used when Butterfly commits suicide, which "in Japan is a well-known drinking song."[16]

Rosenstock's bilingual production had irritated Taubman. At the Met in 1958 there were no innovations in casting or language. It was the work done in other areas by the visiting director and designer that gave the opera "the unmistakable stamp, 'made in Japan.'" The production, Taubman wrote this time around, was "exquisite in taste and sensibility. The encrustations of tradition at its worst have been wiped away and have been replaced by a fresh view painted by the delicate brush of Japanese imagination." He felt that "this production liberates the stage so that it subtly enriches the mood and sentiment of Puccini's music. 'Madama Butterfly' has never seemed more wistful or more honest."[17] It can also be said that, in contrast to Rosenstock's humanistically ideal vision of a shared stage, the Met production articulated a disembodied Japan, one removed from the physicality of the "real" people who were the fictional characters in the opera.

Introducing Musicians and Music from Japan to American Audiences in the 1960s and 1970s

Starting in the early 1960s, Japan Society–sponsored recitals introduced musicians from Japan, such as Kenji Kobayashi, to New York audiences: "Kenji Kobayashi is a young Japanese violinist of taste and finesse. That helped to make Town Hall, where he made his local debut last night, a fine and musical place to be."[18] Former Juilliard students like Kobayashi, who had been studying music in New York since 1952, were already to an extent part of the American system. However, musicians arriving directly from Japan, especially institutional cohorts such as the Fujiwara Opera company, faced the hurdle of being scrutinized as outsiders. When the Japan Philharmonic was invited to New York's Philharmonic Hall in 1964, Schonberg observed, "It would be idle to pretend that the Japan Philharmonic is one of the world's leading ensembles, but it is an expert group and a cosmopolitan one." The concert "attested to the popularity of Western music in Japan that one has been reading about." While appearing to give a fair assessment of the artistic merits of the orchestra, the critic seemed slightly discomfited by the presence of an orchestra from Japan in New York's symphonic showcase: "The unfamiliar strains of the Japanese national anthem were heard last night in Philharmonic Hall, and on stage was the equally strange presence of 85 Japanese faces."[19]

If it was "strange" to see Japanese people playing Western music, it could be an agreeable sight if the music and instruments were Japanese. Among the "pleasures" of the event, wrote Ross Parmenter in his review of a Japan Society–sponsored koto recital by Kimio Eto at Philharmonic Hall, "were the many Japanese women in the audience who were wearing traditional kimonos. Mr. Eto was a picturesque figure, too, for he wore a white and gold hakama. . . . As he played he sat in the kneeling Japanese position behind his straw-colored instrument."[20] There were attempts to encourage American audiences to look—and listen—beyond the exoticism. Conductor, composer, and musical educator Leonard Bernstein, lauded by Japanese audiences on a 1962 New York Philharmonic tour, attempted to cultivate reciprocal respect for Japanese music in a television program nationally broadcast in the United States. "It was an altogether fascinating excursion," wrote Richard Shepard after the show aired, "although in this case it seems that even persuasive words can't inculcate affection for the strange sounds of the islands' music; it's more a question of habit than of talk."[21]

Kimio Eto, who gained widespread renown in the United States, hoped that the koto would one day attract the interest of musicians from around the world. He was a student of Michio Miyagi, leader of the New Japanese Music (Shin Nihon Ongaku) movement, which aimed "to bring Hōgaku [in this context, a reference to music written for Japanese instruments] closer to European music."[22] The ambitious and independent-minded Eto moved to New York in the 1950s "determined to carry on the work of his teacher and popularize the koto as a solo instrument in the Western world." His projects included American composer Henry Cowell's *Concerto for Koto and Orchestra,* which was "the first concerto ever composed by a Westerner for the 1,100-year-old Japanese instrument."[23]

Eto's efforts notwithstanding, the koto has remained a primary signifier of music from Japan—even occasionally referred to as "the national instrument of Japan."[24] It is the large taiko drum that, starting in the 1970s, has crossed over—popularized both within and outside of Japan by artists and troupes that, as is true of butoh dance, emerged as a postwar phenomenon in Japan. The first taiko ensemble to reach center stage in Manhattan was the Ondeko-za, which arrived in 1978 for a two-week engagement.[25] The visit was arranged by impresario Kazuko Hillyer, who booked the troupe into the Beacon Theater—the same venue that hosted Grand Kabuki in 1977 and again in 1979.

Ondeko-za, under founding director Den Tagayasu, immediately attracted attention as the young, Boston Marathon–running "demon drummers" whose sponsor was French fashion designer Pierre Cardin.[26] Taiko was viewed at first with a degree of uncertainty and even shock. John

Rockwell's review in the *Times* was an outcry against what he perceived to be a violation of Japan's classical arts.

> The show at the Beacon looks like a highly individual essay on certain aspects of Japanese culture, rather than any sort of actual re-creation of its traditions. . . . The thundering of the big drums . . . is initially engrossing. . . . For the rest, this observer found it all sadly vulgar. Traditional Japanese culture derives its power from the tight repression of violent passion into an art that is chaste and contemplative. . . . The result violates Oriental art into something that destroys the essence of the East yet is still too Eastern for most Westerners really to enjoy. Ondeko-Za may think of its work as a restoration of traditional Japanese values; to this eye it looks more like an agent and symbol of their adulteration.[27]

The taiko, however, quickly struck a popular chord, giving rise to many US-based troupes—such as New York's Soh Daiko. In time the sensual throbbing sound and visceral images of the drumming would even be used to convey auditory and visual excitement in American films and television commercials.

Music From Japan: Learning About—and from—Japan

Reflecting on the quarter-century history of the institution he founded in the mid-1970s, Naoyuki Miura wrote, "When I came to New York City in 1966 . . . I realized there was hardly any Japanese music played around the city. Back then, an average American's knowledge of things Japanese was quite limited. I had been exposed to contemporary music in Japan and knew the high quality of our composers' works first hand. I wanted to show that current art was alive and well in Japan." To accomplish his goal of having American audiences learn about and from Japan through the music originating there, Miura crucially chose to place the task of playing the work in the hands of resident New York performers: "We invited American musicians and groups to perform works whenever possible. This enhanced the Japanese works' international scope and quite often revealed unexpected elements in the music."[28] The non-ethnically Japanese performer was an important visual aspect of Music From Japan events at a time when, as the quote in the first paragraph of this chapter indicates, some questioned the musicianship of the "Oriental" artists appearing in increasing numbers on the American concert stage. At that time it was a reasonable calculation that US-based performers would possibly draw more serious critical and audience attention to the work of Japanese composers and thus bestow greater artistic validation on it than might be the case if cultural-exchange musicians from Japan were employed.

Miura originally called his project the Society for Contemporary Music From Japan, but soon shortened the name to Music From Japan—a more accurate appellation for an organization that also reclaimed the old by additionally embracing Japanese traditional music and instruments. Coincidentally, in March 1975, the same month that Music From Japan held its inaugural concert at Japan Society, Lukas Foss, conductor of the Brooklyn Philharmonia (now known as the Brooklyn Philharmonic), presented a program featuring Japanese composers in his Meet the Moderns series at the Brooklyn Academy of Music. Within the span of only a few days, New York audiences could experience the work of Joji Yuasa, Kenjiro Urata, Teruyuki Noda, Sesshu Kai, and Roh Ogura presented by Music From Japan, and music by Toru Takemitsu, Yuji Takahashi, Jo Kondo, and Toshi Ichiyanagi courtesy of the Brooklyn Philharmonia. "Japanese composers," as Rockwell wrote with a measure of deliberate understatement, "have made a significant mark on the international avant-garde scene in recent years."[29]

Unlike the concert by the Brooklyn Philharmonia and presentations by other New York ensembles, such as Continuum, which have occasionally showcased the work of contemporary Japanese composers, Music From Japan was from the beginning an institution with regularly scheduled, annual concerts that employ a widely diverse field of performers. However, critics viewed the strict geographic focus of Miura's project with a degree of skepticism from the start. What, after all, was "music from Japan" when applied to abstract work that did not have any obvious sonic associations with Japan? "Confronted with an event called 'A Concert of Contemporary Music From Japan,'" Donal Henahan wrote after attending the November 1975 program at Lincoln Center, "only the naïve listener would expect, nowadays, to hear anything identifiably Japanese. The so-called international style has such a firm stranglehold on composers that new music, whatever its national or regional source, tends to sound pretty much the same."[30] The four featured pieces were Ichiro Higo's *String Quartet* (1973), Hikaru Hayashi's *Shirabe* (1974) for three flutes, Ryohei Hirose's *Triste* (1971) cello concerto, and Michio Kitazume's *Relation* (1974) for percussion ensemble.

Within a year of launching Music From Japan it was clear that Miura was achieving a level of success in his bid to have New York audiences take notice of music by Japanese composers that was not, as Henahan had said, "identifiably Japanese." Although the *Times* did not run a review of the December 1976 concert, it published a lengthy preview essay by Rockwell that both gave recognition to and helped publicize Music From Japan as a significant new cultural forum. Rockwell called for better demonstration of "the tensions with which Eastern and Western notions coexist in Japanese music [and that] provide one of its principal sources of interest," adding, like Henahan, "The principal stylistic problem affecting all of this music is one common to most new music today—how to define a personal and cultural identity in the face of a gray internationalism of style." Although Miura would prove him wrong, Rockwell suggested that he "has something of a bias against music that uses traditional Japanese instruments, whether conservative or experimental."[31]

Starting in the late 1970s, the pace of Music From Japan events picked up. In June 1978 there was a live broadcast on classical music radio station WQXR that included Ichiro Higo's *String Quartet* (1973), followed in October by a concert at Carnegie Hall of work by Kenjiro Urata, Maki Ishii, and several others. A November program at St. Luke's Church in Greenwich Village took Music From Japan in a new direction: all of the pieces employed Japanese instruments, such as Tokuro Furuta's *Japanese Dances* (1975) for shakuhachi and harp and Teruyuki Noda's *Reflection* (1977) for shakuhachi, koto, and cello. In 1979 there were four concerts in all. Three were in New York—in January at the New York Public Library for the Performing Arts, in June a live broadcast on Columbia University's WKCR, and in November at Carnegie Hall. For the first time Music From Japan presented a concert outside of the city: the work of six composers (Teizo Matsumura, Jo Kondo, Teruyuki Noda, Kazuo Fukushima, Norio Fukushi, and Yasuo Sueyoshi) was presented at the Kennedy Center for the Performing Arts in Washington, DC.

Because of his own professional connections and the fact that he was able to secure funding from a variety of Japan- and US-related government, corporate, and private sources, Miura could establish an institution that employed first-rate musicians to perform in prominent venues. The 1979 concert at Carnegie Hall, with the American Symphony Orchestra under conductor Gerard Schwarz, offered three American premieres: Akira Miyoshi's *Festival Overture* (1970), Teizo Matsumura's *Piano Concerto no. 2* (1978), and Toshiro Mayuzumi's *Nirvana Symphony* (1958). The Mayuzumi piece—a highly experimental and expansive work that employs the full orchestra, a chorus, and several instrumental groupings in different locations around the hall—challenged music critic Raymond Ericson. "Like most non-Western music," he cryptically asserted, "the symphony is repetitive and hypnotically effective." For Ericson the measure of a work's value within the framework of Music From Japan was whether it was "spiritually Japanese" and evoked "a truly Japanese feeling,"[32] characteristics that he felt especially applied to the piece by Matsumura.

In February 1982 Harold Schonberg published an extended profile of Miura by way of previewing the upcoming Music From Japan concert at Carnegie Hall. Though praising Miura for his work, Schonberg displayed a remarkable lack of familiarity with the seven years of Music From Japan programs that had already entered the history books: "Japanese composers? Probably the only one whose name springs to mind is Toru Takemitsu. . . . Aside from Mr. Takemitsu, how many composers does one encounter?" Although he mentioned that "[n]ormally only American performers play Mr. Miura's programs,"[33] a complete shift had already taken place—in terms of both performers and composers. In a 1980 recital at Japan Society, pianist Aki Takahashi played the work of Japanese and American composers, including Ichiyanagi, Takemitsu, Ishii, John Cage, Charles Ives, and Morton Feldman. In 1981, again at Japan Society, marimba player Keiko Abe presented her own original work, as well as compositions by Yasuo Sueyoshi, Katsuhiro Tsubono, and David Crandall. Yet again at Japan Society that same year, tenor Katsuumi Niwa performed pieces by Japanese and American composers. Even the concert that was the subject of Schonberg's preview article included Akio Yashiro's *Concerto Pour Piano et Orchestre* (1967) performed by the American Symphony Orchestra with guest soloist Hiroko Nakamura, who displayed what Allen Hughes would call "pianistic brilliance."[34]

By the mid-1980s Music From Japan concerts were recognized as "annual features of our musical life,"[35] although the issue of cultural identity in music remained a primary topic of discussion. In response to a 1983 Music From Japan program at Carnegie Hall with works by, among others, Somei Satoh and Masanori Fujita, Hughes remarked, "The way things are going these days it appears that national differences in musical composition will soon be wiped out entirely, unless, of course, they have been already. This realization impressed itself anew last night during the 'Music From Japan' concert."[36] However, there was also evidence of the notion that the work of composers from Japan had to sound "different" lest it be considered unoriginal. The 1983 event at Carnegie Hall, wrote Henry Scott Stokes in a preview article filed from Japan, would have "little that the listener would immediately identify as purely Japanese." He added that "the music raises one of the hardest questions about Japanese cultural form: What is derivative and what is really Japanese?"[37] It was as if US critics and journalists were (without conscious intent, to be sure) trying to place Music From Japan within the framework of debates over the "Nihonjinron" theories of cultural essentialism then flourishing in Japan. For Miura, such debates were irrelevant: his purpose was to give voice to composers from Japan on the New York-equals-international stage.

New Sonic Possibilities

In continually seeking new ways of connecting with New York audiences, Music From Japan programming began to reflect the quickening pace of late-twentieth-century cross-cultural engagements with Japanese culture. The December 1983 concert at Asia Society featured John Cage's newly composed *Ryoanji* performed by the Kronos Quartet. "Inspired by the Zen Temple Garden of the same name in Kyoto," Rockwell wrote, "'Ryoanji' attains a meditative rapture that some of Mr. Cage's more abstract recent works have lacked."[38] At Carnegie Hall the following year, the presence onstage of taiko soloist Eitetsu Hayashi of the Ondeko-za troupe was both a response and a contribution to the growing interest in new sonic possibilities offered by traditional Japanese instruments. "It appears that in Japan, as everywhere else," Hughes wrote, "music is heading in many directions at once."[39] In response to a 1987 recital by Mayumi Miyata at Asia Society, Tim Page wrote that Miyata's reed instrument, the sho, which "is almost unknown in the United States," has "limited range but rare sonic beauty."[40] Almost all of the compositions presented at these events were contemporary works.

For Miura, as both musician and educator, Music From Japan was a meeting ground of ideas, and it became clear to him that there were potentially more ways to help generate and convey those ideas. He thus began scheduling public symposiums with a slate of guest panelists—composers, performers, critics, and academics—in conjunction with the concerts. Symposiums have been held on a range of topics—for example, the state of contemporary music in Japan, the impact of Japanese music on American culture, music education in Japan, the transmission of the traditional arts in Japan, and issues in cross-cultural music making. Preconcert lectures and post-concert "Q&A" sessions also became part of the programming. In addition, Music From Japan began fostering the creation of the very material it seeks to introduce to US audiences: it began commissioning new work from composers in Japan (a field that also embraces individuals with an interest in Japan), who have included Harvey Sollberger, Ushio Torikai, Takashi Yoshimatsu, Somei Satoh, Yuji Takahashi, Anthony Braxton, Richard Teitelbaum, Akira Miyoshi, Shoko Suzuki, and Toshi Ichiyanagi. Music From Japan, moreover, widened the geographic reach of its programs. In 1988, for example, it sponsored a tour by Pro Musica Nipponia that included stops in New York (at Asia Society and Lincoln Center), Michigan (at the University of Michigan and Detroit's Orchestra Hall), and Los Angeles (at the Japan America Theatre). The Tokyo-based ensemble, founded in 1964 by composer Minoru Miki, comprises musicians playing the koto, biwa, shakuhachi, and other Japanese instruments. In 1995, to give another example, a concert tour titled Masters of Tradition—with musicians Junko Handa (biwa), Reiko Kimura (koto), Meisho Tosha (noh flute), Seizan Sakata (shakuhachi), and Hidetaro Honjo (shamisen)—began in New York (at the United Nations' Dag Hammarskjold Library Auditorium) and went on to five locations in Brazil before making stops in California and Fukushima, Japan.

By the early 1990s Music From Japan was producing concerts exploring the intersection of traditional instrumental sound and computer technology. "Advanced Technology and Music Today: Koto and Voice-Aided Computers" was the title of a 1990 program at Asia Society focusing on work by Kazuo Uehara, Carl Stone, and David Berhman commissioned by Music From Japan. (Technical difficulties prevented the Stone piece from being presented as originally planned.) There was also an associated symposium titled Music/Technology/Audience. The compositions, Bernard Holland wrote, revealed "deeply embedded ritual [that] shook hands with modern technology. Everyone feels such culture clashes, but they are never more compelling than among the past-rooted and future-driven Japanese."[41] The following year brought a second installment of "Advanced Technology and Music Today," with work by Yuji Takahashi (whose *Tree* for digital piano, trombone, and computer system was commissioned by Music From Japan), Haruna Miyake, and George E. Lewis, as well as a symposium titled Artificial Intelligence in Live Performance. In 1994 Tradition and Innovation in Japanese Music was the theme of three concerts and a symposium held at Asia Society. "Shakuhachi, Koto, Shomyo, and Electronics," the specific title of one of the programs, presented two Music From Japan commissions: Mamoru Fujieda's *Night Chant no. 3* for shomyo and computer, and Hinoharu Matsumoto's *Dawn Bird* for shakuhachi, koto, and computer. Such programming exemplified, in Miura's own words, "new sound generated by the fusion of old and new [which] may be indicative of where modern Japanese music is generally heading."[42] It also helped spark new conversations about music as a medium of exchange. As Junichi Aoyagi observed, "How to transmit culture is a complicated question and one of interest to Japan. Some regard the Music [F]rom Japan format as a new, two-way approach to cultural exchange."[43]

Kinkakuji and Gagaku

Music From Japan took on its biggest project to date with the fall 1995 American premiere of the Mayuzumi opera *Kinkakuji*.[44] For Miura "the first production of a Japanese grand opera in this country" was "the crowning glory of all I have done with Music From Japan."[45] "'Kinkakuji' is not a profound success," wrote Holland in a *Times* review, "but it does what it does fairly well. Its only failure, if there is one, is as a truly Japanese opera. Mishima's violent chauvinism is founded on mistrust of Western sensibility. Mr. Mayuzumi dutifully incorporates Buddhist references in his music, but the washes of Impressionism and the imitative counterpoint betray a heart and intellect that have been left thousands of miles from home." Holland likened it to "a turn-of-the-century Parisian daydream of the exotic East—curio-shop japonaiserie fashioned by a native."[46] Despite whatever reservations critics may have had, the enormous visibility of the opera on the New York performing arts calendar helped further solidify the position of Miura's organization as the leading cultural-exchange producer in New York of new "classical" music from Japan.

"Attending some of the Japan-related programming around [New York City] recently," Miura commented in the inaugural issue of the *Music From Japan Newsletter*, "I was impressed with the sizable American audiences who could tolerate the most serene presentations that would test the limit of one's concentration and patience. At the same time I felt positive that Music From Japan, a tiny organization which somehow survived for 20 years, did make a contribution in nurturing this kind of special audience and appreciation for broader cultural activities in the United States."[47] Less than a year after *Kinkakuji*, Music From Japan took on another high-profile project as a producer, along with the Lincoln Center Festival, of the first New York appearances by the Reigakusha ensemble from Japan. Given the two-decade-long history of his organization, Miura could claim credit for helping foster a newly receptive American audience for gagaku thirty-seven years after the troupe from the Imperial Household arrived in

New York. The night before Reigakusha went onstage at the Lincoln Center Festival, Music From Japan hosted a lecture by gagaku scholar Steven G. Nelson and a concert/demonstration with members of the ensemble. The day after the festival presentation, Music From Japan's "Gagaku in the Flow of World Music" incorporated a talk on contemporary gagaku by ensemble artistic director Sukeyasu Shiba, a demonstration of the instruments narrated by Nelson, a performance by Shiba, and a panel discussion on gagaku moderated by composer William Duckworth.

"A Tribute to Toru Takemitsu," a two-day program of concerts, a lecture, and a symposium in February 1997 marked the beginning of Music From Japan's association with New York's Merkin Concert Hall as the mainstay venue for what are now its annual winter-weekend events. Subsequent programming has basically devoted one day to the work of a "Western-style" composer and one day to new works and standard pieces composed for traditional Japanese instruments. In 1998, for instance, a concert and lecture focused on the work of composer Shinichiro Ikebe and a recital by the Keiji Azechi Kokyu Ensemble. "What was particularly interesting about the contemporary works [written for the kokyu, a stringed instrument played with a bow]," Allan Kozinn wrote, "was their composers' eagerness to extend the techniques of the instruments without radically changing or distorting their sounds."[48] The next year Music From Japan looked at the music of Maki Ishii, while also offering the New York debut of shakuhachi musician Teruhisa Fukuda and a symposium titled Recent Changes in Japanese Music. In 2000, to give yet another example, one day was devoted to the work of Hikaru Hayashi and another to the New York debut of Tsugaru shamisen player Chikuzan Takahashi II, as well as to a symposium on the early history of musical practices in Japan. Music From Japan presentations continued to reach beyond New York—to Washington, DC, and other locations in the United States, as well as to Canada, Japan, and, for the first time, Kazakhstan and Uzbekistan.

Following a special twenty-fifth anniversary concert in 2000 of contemporary Japanese orchestral music performed by the Brooklyn Philharmonic at Carnegie Hall, twenty-first-century Music From Japan programs have carried on the two-pronged approach, with the focus split between the work of established and emerging composers from Japan and that of musicians specializing in Japanese instruments. Composers have included Akira Nishimura, Ichiro Nodaira, Joji Yuasa, Sunao Isaji, Keiko Harada, and Atsuhiko Gondai. Among the instrumentalists are shakuhachi players Akikazu Nakamura and Elizabeth Brown, Michio Yagi (koto), the

Junko Tahara Biwa Ensemble, Mayumi Miyata (sho), Mojibei Tokiwazu V (shamisen), and the Reigakusha gagaku ensemble.

Even within the set framework of the programming, Miura continues to explore and reconceptualize in a fresh way "music from Japan." In 2004, to give an illustration, a concert of work by Ichiro Nodaira was followed by "Music of the Ainu," which brought to New York musicians from the Ainu community in Hokkaido in a program of traditional and new pieces. An article previewing the Nodaira concert was notable for not trying to force an either-or, Asian-or-Western cultural identity on the composer. "Mr. Nodaira is clearly more interested in sound than in culture," as Matthias Kriesberg observed. "Asian composers have in recent years devised ingenious ways to pull elements of their native traditional music into their scores. But Ichiro Nodaira . . . couldn't care less. In fact, Mr. Nodaira makes a convincing case that even in music composition, it's perfectly possible to study Western practices, and then go out and beat us at our own game." Nodaira, whose studies in Paris included a period composing at IRCAM (Institut de Recherche et Coordination Acoustique/Musique [Institute for Research and Coordination Acoustic/Music], a world center for technological innovation in music), "has so thoroughly internalized Western music that he coolly resolves problems most composers either shrug off as too profound to deal with or don't even know they have." Although Nodaira returned to live in Japan, Kriesberg wrote that the composer's world "is hardly limited to establishing a Japanese perspective on European aesthetics." Nodaira may be a pianist who plays mostly classical music, but he "creat[es] works that initially preserve the melody lines of Bach, then proceed through broader transformations to undermine what is recognizable."[49]

If Nodaira's musical practice innovatively confronted cultural identity, so did that of Oki, the Ainu musician whose work was also part of Music From Japan that year. "We lost our land," Oki sang, "but soul and spirit never fade away." Lacking a privileged place in the matrix of sanctioned traditional Japanese cultural forms, Oki is among artists who speak up against a Japanese establishment that they feel has marginalized them. Noting Oki's use of the tonkori, a stringed instrument that originated in Sakhalin, Jon Pareles wrote, "The band sometimes joined Oki with electric bass vamps and percussion, and in one song the beat picked up behind Oki's fingerpicking to sound like West African pop built around a different harp, the kora. Fusions like that risk cultural loss by assimilation, but the dignified clarity of the tonkori came through even in modern trappings."[50] The point that Oki was trying to make was missed: what Pareles read as a fusion that risked cultural loss by assimilation was deliberate border crossing, a way to find a new voice for and thereby bring attention to what was left of Ainu culture within contemporary Japan.

Music From Japan's thirty-fifth anniversary concert in 2010 was a valedictory of sorts—a third appearance since 1996 of Reigakusha and a program of previous commissions along with two new ones, Hitomi Kaneko's *Almost Dusk* for string quartet and sho, and Yasuko Yamaguchi's *Wurzeln* for hichiriki, cello, percussion, and piano. Although Miura was not saying goodbye, there was a sense that no further proof was needed that this one-man institution had accomplished much of what it set out to do.[51] "For anyone interested in Japan's distinctive musical culture," Kozinn wrote in his review of the Reigakusha portion of the program, "Music From Japan has been a valuable resource since 1975, presenting concerts and festivals of traditional and contemporary works, and maintaining a valuable archive and database devoted mostly to modern Japanese composers."[52] It was a promise on which Miura had tirelessly delivered. A decade earlier, on the occasion of his project's twenty-fifth anniversary, Kriesberg wrote that Miura's "mission—to introduce a broad spectrum of Japanese composers and help secure a place for their work in the mainstream of American contemporary music—is paying off, he believes."[53]

Whereas Kozinn had noted in passing that "[a]rguments suggesting that music is a universal language are generally scoffed at now,"[54] a tenet of Music From Japan is that, as Miura has said, "Japanese music is very serious, and it can be difficult for Americans."[55] What could be taken as a "Nihonjin-ron-style" essentialism can more profitably be interpreted as Miura's attempt to speak back to those who would ignore or discount the contributions of Japanese composers and musicians. If appreciation follows exposure and understanding, Music From Japan—its concerts and accompanying lectures and symposiums—evolved as a principal agent to undertake those tasks. "[I]n the last 10 years, [Miura] has found, audiences have changed, more readily accepting non-Western artistic sensibilities. Of special fascination for Mr. Miura is the relationship that has developed between Japanese composers and the New York performers regularly engaged to interpret their work. 'American performers,' he said, 'are willing to ask questions in order to learn the special techniques required.'"[56]

In Rosenstock's and Starr's productions of *Madama Butterfly* and in the concerts and recitals of "music from Japan" presented under various auspices through the mid-1970s, the medium of cultural exchange was either the performer from Japan who knew his or her Puccini or Beethoven or the one who represented a heretofore unfamiliar style of music-making on instruments such as the koto, shakuhachi, and taiko. Miura conceptualized his project in a completely different way: to nurture recognition of and respect for Japan's contributions to the body of world music, he focused on composers whose works were introduced mainly by New York–based performers. But he was also cognizant of what American audiences immersed in the discourse of America's kabuki-Japan expected. "Currently in its 30th season," Jeremy Eichler wrote in 2004, "the group Music [F]rom Japan has long been a valuable contributor to New York concert life. It is best known for commissioning and presenting the works of contemporary Japanese composers, bringing new music that local listeners would otherwise have little opportunity to hear." He remarked, however, that the presentation of Reigakusha at Carnegie Hall that year was a response to "strong audience interest in more historic Japanese music" that had become evident in the previous decade.[57] Eichler's statement was incorrect: Music From Japan had long encountered resistance to work labeled "music from Japan" that did not sound "Japanese." Nevertheless, Miura had remained consistent in his vision. Although he had laid claim to the new, from the outset of his project he increasingly reclaimed the old, too, especially as growing numbers of composers, such as Sukeyasu Shiba, founder of the Reigakusha ensemble, broadened their explorations of new sonic possibilities for Japanese instruments. Whatever form the music has taken, Music From Japan has steadily shown, to again repeat Miura's words, "that current art was"—and is—"alive and well in Japan."[58]

5

Lincoln Center Festival's Japan

New York is an ongoing festival all the time. So you can ask, "Why do a festival at all?"[1]

"The processes of globalization," Patrick Lonergan has written, "have contributed to a subsequent festivalization of the performing arts industry, transforming festivals into the preferred sites for the promotion and consumption of high-end cultural products."[2] Since its first season in 1996, the Lincoln Center Festival, which runs for three weeks each July, has become one of the most prominent of the preferred sites to which Lonergan referred. "At Lincoln Center we have to create series of events that can stand out in the context of everything else in New York," festival director Nigel Redden told an interviewer. "That can mean big."[3] "Big" can mean sheer enormity of scale—manifested, for example, in the kabuki tent-theater brought in its entirety from Japan and erected on the grounds of the Lincoln Center campus for performances by the Heisei Nakamura-za troupe at the 2004 festival. It is also a more general, metaphorical reference to work that from the institution's perspective represents the highest level of artistic and technical sophistication in performing arts worldwide. In his "Note from the Director" on the festival's website, Redden states, "Lincoln Center Festival began with the idea of expanding the possibilities presented at Lincoln Center and bringing to audiences something that they could not see elsewhere. This is a challenging goal in a city as culturally rich as New York. . . . Central to the Festival has been an effort to look outside the Western European canon."[4] In this chapter I focus on how that effort has been realized to a considerable degree in the Japan-related productions that have been integral to the Lincoln Center Festival from its outset. Lincoln Center Festival's Japan has been constructed through "big" productions by artists such as Kanzaburo Nakamura XVIII, Amon Miyamoto, Simon McBurney, Yukio Ninagawa, and Saburo Teshigawara—

individuals whose work has conveyed new knowledge of Japan to New York audiences in the consciously global atmosphere of the event.

"Lincoln Center Plans an 'Intense' Festival"

Lincoln Center for the Performing Arts, located on New York's Upper West Side, is a sixteen-acre agglomeration of major arts organizations and their associated theaters and concert halls (including, among others, the Metropolitan Opera and the New York City Ballet).[5] It is, by its own description, "the largest performing arts presenter in the world,"[6] in terms of the total number of presentations offered, and the "world's leading center of superb artistic programming."[7] It opened in the mid-1960s. When planning for the project got under way a decade earlier, New York appeared eager to take the next step in the process of cementing its identity as a world capital of culture. In "New Cultural Vista for the City," Howard Taubman wrote, "New York stands on the threshold of a brave, new era in the performing arts. An integrated center to serve the theatre, opera and operetta, music and dance is well into the planning stage. If it is brought into being with boldness and vision, it could give a tremendous lift to the cultural tone of the city." There was an air of cold-war competitiveness in Taubman's words: "New York is not doing as well as it should as the capital of the performing arts. It is not using to the full its enormous resources of wealth, influence, potential audience and talent." The visits by troupes such as the Azuma Kabuki Dancers and Musicians at that time attested to New York's status as cultural-exchange power broker and destination for performing artists from around the world. Indeed, kabuki was one of the guests for which it was argued Lincoln Center should be built. Citing the need for better performing arts facilities in the city, Taubman concluded, "[V]isiting troupes from abroad, such as the Sadler's Wells Ballet and the Kabuki Theatre, should have a fitting place for their New York appearances."[8]

John D. Rockefeller III, who spearheaded the plan to build Lincoln Center, was the subject of a *Times* profile that reported on this "first Rockefeller to take an active role in the performing arts field" while foregrounding his strong interest in Japan. Rockefeller envisioned Lincoln Center in part as a showcase for the performing arts of Asia—much grander than the adequate but small stages in the buildings he would help underwrite for Japan Society and Asia Society: "Through his travels, through his growing awareness of the thought, the art, the culture of other peoples, Mr. Rockefeller came to believe 'in art, and the exchange of art, as vital in helping international understanding.' He would like to see the Kabuki Players of Japan perform in the Lincoln Center, or the Bolshoi Ballet, or the Balinese Dancers."[9] All of these visions would be realized.

The Lincoln Center Festival was a brand new entity that simultaneously transcended and stood apart from the normal temporal and spatial boundaries of Lincoln Center's other programming. The launch of the festival in the mid-1990s captured that decade's multicultural zeitgeist. When Lincoln Center announced in November 1995 that it was initiating a new annual summer festival, it was described as "an ambitious series that will draw on its resident companies and artists from around the world."[10] Board president Nathan Leventhal declared, "New York *deserves* a festival like this." The stock market was up, and there was a newly buoyant consciousness of the city's place as both a crossroads for and a home of the world's cultures. Troupes from abroad were to be regarded not merely as visitors but more expansively as "quintessentially New York"—given that it is "a city that is home to so many cultures."[11] The festival's first director was John Rockwell, a cultural correspondent and music critic at the *Times* since the early 1970s. He was succeeded in 1998 by Nigel Redden, who was already (and continues to serve as) head of Spoleto Festival USA. As Redden told an interviewer several years into his tenure, "We want to change the idea of Lincoln Center. . . . Throughout the year, the constituents of Lincoln Center (the New York Philharmonic, the Metropolitan Opera, the New York City Ballet, the Vivian Beaumont Theater and the Juilliard School among them) concentrate on works of the 19th century with a European background. The purpose of this festival is to move beyond that."[12] The dozen Japan-related productions that have taken place from the inception of the festival through 2011 have helped achieve Redden's goal.

Inaugurating the Festival: Reigakusha, 1996

The inclusion of the Reigakusha gagaku ensemble in the festival's first year was, in a way, a test of American understandings of Japan at a point in time long removed from the postwar 1950s—the decade during which the first visit by a gagaku troupe to New York had taken place. Among the other artists appearing in that inaugural year were the Lyons Opera Ballet, Merce Cunningham Dance Company, Thang Long Water Puppet Theatre, and Kirov Orchestra and Chorus. New York-based composer and director Tan Dun also had a slot on the program with his New Generation East ensemble, which offered works by contemporary composers from China, South

Korea, and Japan—the last represented by Toshio Hosokawa and Somei Satoh.[13] The gagaku concert in 1996 was not a return to the past. Unlike the Imperial Household troupe that arrived in 1959, Reigakusha had only a ten-year history behind it. The ensemble was brought together in 1985 by Sukeyasu Shiba, a gagaku musician, composer, and teacher who left a position with the Imperial Household troupe to devote himself to reinvigorating the gagaku repertory by opening it up to newly written pieces and by reviving forgotten works. His aim was also to cultivate new audiences for the art form by actively touring throughout Japan and the world.

The visual images transmitted by Reigakusha onstage through their richly woven attire and the "foreignness" of the instruments they played—not to mention the accompanying masked bugaku dances, such as one about a prince in the guise of a dragon—proclaimed to Lincoln Center Festival audiences "This is old Japan." The ensemble, as described by Jon Pareles, "made its entrance a ritual procession. The musicians, wearing robes and hats, arrived in single file and knelt silently until they were all in place; then they took up their instruments." The pieces that were played in the first half of the program—the traditional gagaku of bamboo flutes, the hichiriki double-reed pipe, and the strings of the koto and biwa—also evoked the past. Such music "[w]ith its deliberation and grace . . . stood apart from the commotion of everyday life. It seemed both transparent and monumental." However, the content of the second half of the concert—a rendition of Toru Takemitsu's 1979 *In an Autumn Garden*—drew audiences into a zone of experimentation that aficionados already knew to expect from the composer. The Takemitsu piece uses "gagaku elements—nearly motionless tempos, discrete musical gestures, notes that bend and slide—but applies them to Western scales and melodies, with vestiges of Debussy." Pareles described how the twenty-nine gagaku musicians were divided into four "antiphonal groups . . . placed around the stage, sharing or responding to one another's parts, playing mournful solos or building ensembles that soon dissolved." There was, to the critic's ears, "a modern sense of longing and loss" that he found "less balanced than the traditional gagaku."[14]

Reigakusha in 1996 captured a tension that has continued to play out in succeeding productions of Japan-related arts at the Lincoln Center Festival. Although the ensemble itself is a product of the late twentieth century, gagaku is a centuries-old art that has long been designated a national treasure in Japan—and is now on the UNESCO list of world treasures. "By admitting cultural forms associated with royal courts and state-sponsored temples, as long as they are not European, [UNESCO's] intangible heritage list preserves the division between the West and the rest," Barbara Kirshenblatt-Gimblett has observed.[15] Reigakusha, by both representing a national treasure and serving as a vehicle for new sound from Japan, enabled the Lincoln Center Festival to destabilize that long-established "West and the rest" division in a new and high-profile New York performing arts context.

The First Broadway Director from Japan: Amon Miyamoto and *Pacific Overtures*, 2002

"In reinterpreting an American musical about [Japan], Mr. Miyamoto and company have bestowed a great gift on New York."[16] In 1976 *Pacific Overtures*—with music and lyrics by Stephen Sondheim and libretto by John Weidman—channeled the early history of US-Japan relations through the medium of theater at Broadway's Winter Garden, where it ran for six months. The premise of the show is to imagine the "other" point of view—to present from Japan's perspective the mid-nineteenth-century arrival of Commodore Matthew Perry's "black ships," which led to the end of Japan's two centuries of almost total isolation. In 2002 the Lincoln Center Festival transported intact from Japan director Amon Miyamoto's version of the musical, which had taken shape two years earlier when it was the debut musical production at the New National Theatre in Tokyo. The government-financed theater opened in 1997 as a state-of-the-art center for opera, ballet, and modern and contemporary drama. The choice of Miyamoto to direct a musical there was an obvious one, given his longstanding reputation in Japan as the leading master of the form—a director who does "not merely recreate the original Broadway stagings" of musicals but "reimagine[s] their emotional topography."[17]

Miyamoto's *Pacific Overtures* at Lincoln Center used a quintessentially "American" form to speak back to US (mis)understandings of Japan. For director Harold Prince in 1976, *Pacific Overtures* was an opportunity to give American audiences a "kabuki-style" theatrical spectacle. Writing in the Lincoln Center Festival program booklet a quarter of a century later, Miyamoto diplomatically characterized his own interpretation of the work as "not in a decorative Kabuki style, but rather in Noh style." He deftly defined Noh style in the very general sense of a "simple setting [that] encourages the imaginative ability of the audience."[18] The Noh label, in short, was a way to reassure festivalgoers who were expecting to see elements of Japanese culture in the show that they would not be disappointed. However, words such as *kabuki* and *noh* had little relevance when, for example, a giant American flag was rolled out above the heads of the audience as Miyamoto's way of expressing the massive effect America's arrival had on Japan—or when the explosively choreographed final number, "Next," raced through several decades of US-Japan history "with a—Sondheim approved—strobe flash for Hiroshima-Nagasaki and a factoid about Sept. 11."[19] There was even a reference to longtime Seattle Mariners baseball star Ichiro Suzuki.

The original production of *Pacific Overtures* had been written off by some critics as "a failure: too unfamiliar for Broadway audiences, too formal, too complicated."[20] When Stephen Sondheim went to Japan in 2000 to receive a cultural achievement award from the Japanese government, the musical was coincidentally running at the New National Theatre. Sondheim and Weidman attended the show and thought the production was excellent. Sondheim's enthusiasm reached Nigel Redden, who invited Miyamoto to bring his *Pacific Overtures* to Lincoln Center's Avery Fisher Hall, which counts as part of the network of Broadway theaters. Immediately after the Lincoln Center Festival, the production traveled to Washington, DC, for inclusion in the Sondheim Celebration at the Kennedy Center.

"In the convoluted annals of cultural tourism," wrote Linda Winer, "there may be nothing quite like the Japanese 'Pacific Overtures.'"[21] For Miyamoto it had been Prince's 1976 production—which he had seen when it was broadcast on television in Japan—that was a strange experience: "When it was done originally, it had a sort of kabuki style. It was much more a spectacle. That way would have been too exotic for Japanese audiences."[22] Miyamoto's comments—and his own interpretation of the musical—took aim at the kabuki-Japan discourse in which Prince's version was rooted. Theater critic Ben Brantley of the *Times* understood Miyamoto's critique, writing that the new production was an "inspired reconsideration of the 1976 musical . . . directed with bountiful verve and imagination." It was a "highly original coup de théâtre."[23] Brantley's affirmation helped Kumiko Yoshii, a Japan-born, New York–based film and Broadway theater producer, hammer out an arrangement with New York's Roundabout Theatre Company. The resulting contract gave Miyamoto the unexpected chance to produce *Pacific Overtures* again in New York as part of Roundabout's 2004–5 subscription season—but this time using the original English-language script. Working with an Asian-American cast led by B. D. Wong, Miyamoto thus became the first Japanese artist specifically hired to direct a Broadway musical. The success of Miyamoto's "Japanese" production of *Pacific Overtures* within the context of the Lincoln Center Festival and its subsequent transition to a run during the regular New York

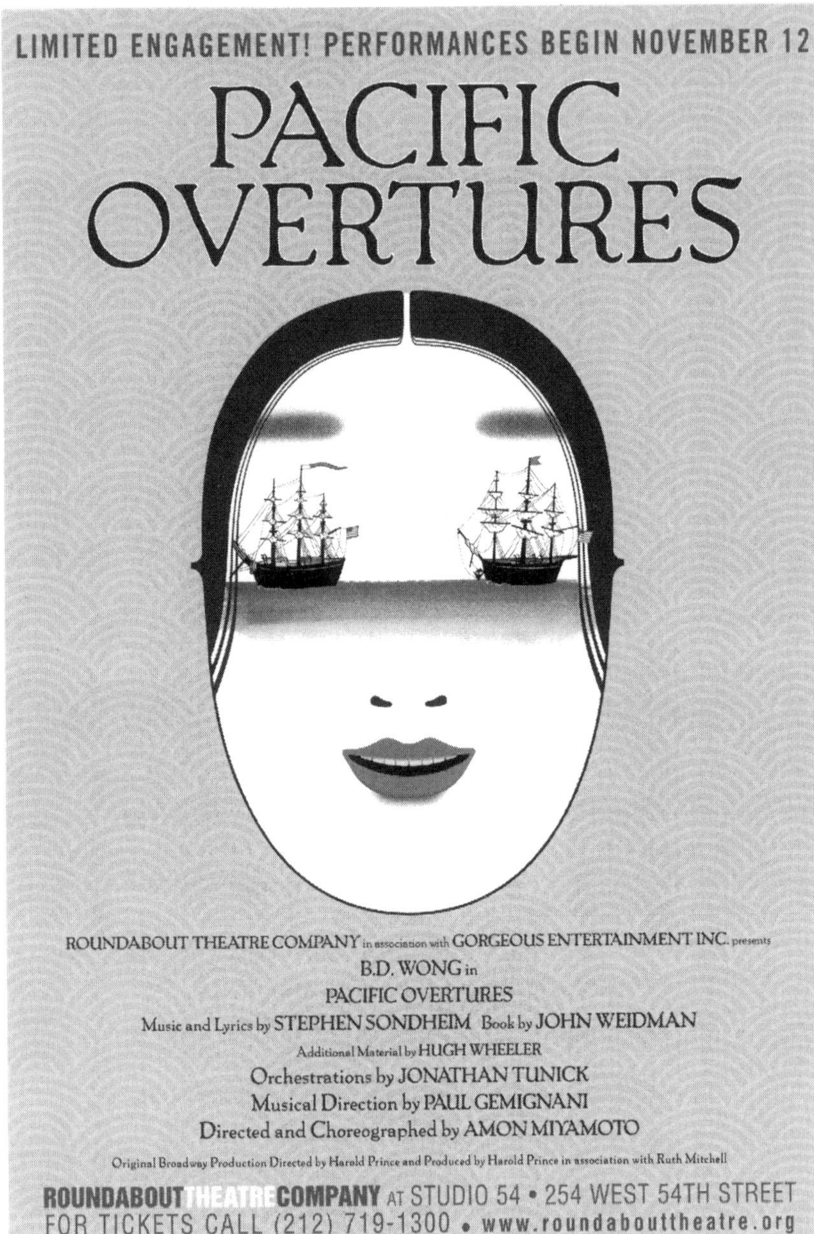

Fig. 14. Flyer advertising *Pacific Overtures,* directed by Amon Miyamoto, Roundabout Theatre Company, 2004–5. (Courtesy of the Roundabout Theatre Company.)

theater season established the director as a central figure in twenty-first-century cultural mobility and exchange from Japan.

K-Ballet: Celebrating Frederick Ashton, 2004

Tetsuya Kumakawa's Tokyo-based K-Ballet troupe was invited to the 2004 Lincoln Center Festival as one of a small group of "brilliantly assembled companies" participating in a retrospective of the work of British choreographer Sir Frederick Ashton, founder of London's Royal Ballet.[24] In 1999, deciding that they wanted to pursue their own projects, Kumakawa and a group of other Royal Ballet dancers (mostly British) broke away to form K-Ballet, which is now one of the world's leading companies.

The presence of K-Ballet in the Lincoln Center Festival Ashton program affirmed "Japan's" place among world-class performers in the field of ballet. Responding in 1970 to the "impressive" New York debut of ballet dancer Yoko Morishita, a member of the Asami Maki Ballet company in Tokyo, Anna Kisselgoff had described Morishita and her colleagues as "representative of their country's classic dancers"—calling them "the ballet counterpart of Japan's celebrated new breed of young virtuoso musicians [which] already exists."[25] The dance critic's reaction almost thirty-five years later to Kumakawa's K-Ballet stands in interesting contrast. In her review of the two-week Ashton tribute celebrating the centennial of his birth, an event that also included performances by the Royal Ballet of London, the Joffrey Ballet of Chicago, and England's Birmingham Royal Ballet, Kisselgoff focused solely on Kumakawa's place in the universe of ballet. When K-Ballet performed *Rhapsody,* Ashton's "virtuoso showpiece created in 1980 for Mikhail Baryshnikov" (who was in the audience), audiences witnessed "a signature piece for K-Ballet. . . . It is Mr. Kumakawa's bravura showcase. Although he adopts an understated tone and even blows an unexpected kiss to the audience, he executes unimaginable steps in the air."[26] The message of Kisselgoff's review was that Kumakawa in 2004 did not represent dancers of Japan. Rather, he represented "global" dance from his base in Japan.

Simon McBurney Interprets Haruki Murakami: *The Elephant Vanishes*, 2004

"There is a common belief among many Japanese that foreigners can never quite understand their country" was the lead-in to Todd Zaun's preview of

The Elephant Vanishes, a play written and directed by Simon McBurney.[27] Lincoln Center Festival productions originating in Japan encompass all of the categories of the taxonomy I propose in the introduction to this study: cultural heritage artists, internationalist and flexible-citizen artists, and artists inspired by Japan. Consistent with the global scale of the festival, the artists inspired by Japan are not limited to Americans. They include individuals such as the British-born director Simon McBurney.

Prior to its opening at the 2004 festival, McBurney's play—adapted from three stories ("The Elephant Vanishes," "The Second Bakery Attack," and "Sleep") by Haruki Murakami—had taken shape in Japan as a collaboration between McBurney's London-based Complicité theater company and the Setagaya Public Theatre in Tokyo. The show premiered at the Setagaya Public Theatre in mid-2003, then immediately went on to Osaka and London. Early the following year the production circled back to the Setagaya theater before going to the Lincoln Center Festival and on to a round of presentations in London, Paris, and Ann Arbor, Michigan.

McBurney has said that he does not consider himself a "British" director.[28] Complicité, which he founded in 1983, is based in London but defines itself through its wide-ranging projects and touring. Resisting geographic boundaries, it also resists stylistic ones. Productions have "ranged from entirely devised work to theatrical adaptations and revivals of classic texts. . . . Always changing and moving forward to incorporate new stimuli, the principles of the work have remained close to the original impulses: seeking what is most alive, integrating text, music, image and action to create surprising, disruptive theatre. There is no Complicité method. What is essential is collaboration. A collaboration between individuals to establish an ensemble with a common physical and imaginative language."[29] *The Elephant Vanishes* was the company's third project at the Lincoln Center Festival, following *The Three Lives of Lucie Cabrol* in 1996 and *The Street of Crocodiles* in 1998.

The Elephant Vanishes was a good fit for the Setagaya Public Theatre, which began operations in 1997 with a commitment to intercultural, collaborative productions. Its founding artistic director was Makoto Sato, who was succeeded in 2002 by Mansai Nomura, whose career extends far beyond his roots in kyogen. Over a five-year period, Complicité and the Setagaya Public Theatre worked on the project, which made extensive use of multimedia technology. McBurney told an interviewer, "Murakami puts his finger on something which we all feel. Sometimes people talk about an urban anomie or a dislocation, but I think it's much more specific than that. I think that in this ultra-consumerist society we live in, we are experiencing a disquiet particular to the way we are living."[30] *The Elephant Vanishes* coolly appraises present-day consumer culture in a deterritorialized, video-saturated space that suggests—but does not necessarily represent—Tokyo. The distinction is crucial. The play's characters, like many, if not most, of the actors who have brought them to life and the audiences who have seen the productions, are the inhabitants of world cities. Complicité and the Setagaya Public Theatre are two like-minded entities intent on transcending or even negating their specific physical located-ness. Their directors and the members of their acting companies are the restless "expressive specialists" who, as Ulf Hannerz has written, "know well enough that they are in the world cities to produce new culture."[31]

The *Times* published Zaun's preview essay on *The Elephant Vanishes* even though it hardly seemed necessary to smooth the way for a theater piece devised by McBurney, a well-known director with a long track record in New York, and based on material by Murakami, a best-selling writer with a wide readership in the United States. Indeed, Zaun wrapped up the article, which he filed from Tokyo, by quoting a Japanese woman who saw the play there. "It's basically a story about life in a big city," she said. "I think people in New York or London or any big city would understand it." Nevertheless, even recently written drama as cultural exchange often faces resistant audiences, which must somehow negotiate the "foreign" in terms of the languages being spoken and issues being explored. Zaun's approach was to focus on the reception to McBurney's work by Japanese audiences: "[B]y the end of the night, skeptical theatergoers seemed relieved of doubt that a foreign director could successfully guide a Japanese cast, using a Japanese script, in an authentic interpretation of work by Mr. Murakami, one of Japan's best-known contemporary writers." The responses of Japanese theater critics indicated that Tokyo viewers found merit in the work. Yoshio Ozasa was quoted as saying, "McBurney and the Japanese actors totally share Murakami's world even if they have different nationalities." Akihiko Senda found "some new possibilities in McBurney's stage direction. The visual effects express the characteristic of Tokyo really well."[32]

New York audiences unhesitatingly took up the challenge and responded in kind. Ben Brantley found *The Elephant Vanishes* a "fluent interpretation of Mr. Murakami's portraits of urban alienation." However, even in so unlikely a work, Brantley surprisingly felt the seemingly inexorable pull of the kabuki-Japan discourse: "The three overlapping tales told here deploy sophisticated lighting (by Paul Anderson) and sound (Christopher Shutt), as well as film and videotaped projections that in their blurring of live and recorded action bring to mind the internationally influential style of the

New York troupe Wooster Group. But there is also something purely and traditionally theatrical in the show that seems especially appropriate to the depiction of a Tokyo in which a centuries-old aesthetic infuses computer-dominated homes." The signifier of that aesthetic was McBurney's "subtle, simple use . . . of shadows on shoji screens."[33] The latticed, shoji-like form to which Brantley referred demarcated space within a structure that represented the interior of a home onstage and, simultaneously, served as a projection screen for videos that drew audience members' eyes—and minds—to worlds outside the one inhabited by the characters. That kabuki, which was also part of the 2004 Lincoln Center Festival, returned to New York after a long absence to play its sanctioned role as the representative classical art of Japan, is unremarkable. However, it is noteworthy that a "centuries-old aesthetic" was ascribed by Brantley, an authoritative analyst of new theater, to *The Elephant Vanishes,* a work that strongly projects a sense of postmodern temporal and spatial dislocation.

Kankuro's Kabuki in a Tent, 2004

There had never been a kabuki visit like it before. Kankuro Nakamura V brought to the 2004 Lincoln Center Festival his brilliantly subversive kabuki in a tent—erecting on the grounds of Damrosch Park (within the Lincoln Center complex) a portable kabuki theater that he had been using for several years in Japan but had never taken outside of the country. The US productions of Grand Kabuki were made-for-export assemblages of leading actors and musicians—of which Kankuro and his father Kanzaburo XVII had been part—performing a variety of best-of-kabuki scenes and dances chosen for their presumed appeal to American audiences. In 2004 the performers were Kankuro's own Heisei Nakamura-za, the troupe with which he regularly works in Japan, and the program was made up of a single, full-length play, *The Summer Festival: A Mirror of Osaka* (*Natsu matsuri naniwa kagami*).

As the symbol of Japanese traditional culture, kabuki hardly seems well suited to subversive expression. However, throughout the Tokugawa period (from the seventeenth to the nineteenth centuries) it was repeatedly the object of censorship decrees, proof that playwrights and actors often resisted political and cultural authority. Kankuro, who would return to the 2007 Lincoln Center Festival under his new name, Kanzaburo XVIII, is a leading figure within the kabuki world with a well-documented interest in reconfiguring the dynamics of kabuki presentation. In his hands—and since the mid-1990s in collaboration with the actor Hashinosuke Nakamura III and the director Kazuyoshi Kushida—the art form has been reimagined as a hybridized theatrical experiment, liberally referencing the "little theater" movement that arose in Tokyo in the 1960s. The collaboration was dubbed Cocoon Kabuki—named after Theatre Cocoon in Tokyo's Bunkamura art center, where it began and has continued to be staged. The purpose of Cocoon Kabuki, according to Kushida, was "not to preserve Kabuki as a classic, but to produce a living Kabuki for the present day."[34] Kankuro attributed the inspiration to take kabuki in a new direction to "a wildly energetic performance" of a work "written and directed by Kara Jūrō in 1977. It occurred to Kankurō that such vitality must have been a feature of Kabuki in its early days. Finding classical Kabuki to be somewhat staid, he wished to reintroduce this energy into new-style Kabuki performances."[35]

By conjuring up the past (the seventeenth century being his target time frame) in the shape of an enormous, 545-seat tent-theater that was fully equipped with a non-seventeenth-century air-conditioning system, Kankuro created at Lincoln Center a kind of theme-park/living-museum environment. Once past the ticket takers, but before entering the theater itself, audiences were invited to stroll along a row of booths in which artisans wearing cotton kimonos worked on various crafts, their wares neatly displayed around them in a replica of an "old Edo" street scene. (Until the latter part of the nineteenth century, Tokyo was known as Edo.) Inside the theater, most of the seating was on hard wooden benches. The brightly patterned, but wafer-thin, cushions that were provided proved no substitute for the usual well-padded theater seat. Life-size cartoon drawings of Edo-period theatergoers looked down from a two-dimensional balcony that ringed the interior of the building.[36] As curtain time approached, actors in period dress materialized and began milling through the aisles as if in search of their seats—giving delighted yells as they greeted similarly attired friends. Even a few well-timed scuffles broke out among the pretend kabuki-goers, as reportedly happened frequently at crowded Edo theaters.

There was a wonderful Disneyesque absurdity to Kankuro's "historically" re-created Lincoln Center Festival kabuki, giving "New Yorkers a jolting, healthy dose of cultural disorientation," as Brantley noted. The anachronistic absurdity of seventeenth-century kabuki brought to twenty-first-century New York reached its high point when the chase scene at the end of the play morphed into a portrayal of a romp through the streets of New York. The huge doors at the back of the stage were suddenly flung open, and actors who were waiting outside dressed as New York City police officers burst onto the stage. The line between Japan's kabuki fiction and New York's local reality hilariously collapsed, making it seem that maybe the cops had indeed arrived to save the day for the folks on stage. The up-to-the-minute urban streetscape "reveal" as the finale of the production was a device used by Kankuro in Tokyo, an idea borrowed from Kara and other 1960s experimentalists.

Brantley called the production "rock 'em, sock 'em theater that keeps the adrenaline pumping." But, despite Kankuro's best efforts, the kabuki-Japan discourse remained firmly entrenched. "Who would have thought," Brantley wrote, "that the most compelling alternative to this summer's action flicks would come from a Japanese theater troupe's resurrecting a ritualized centuries-old drama?"[37] The point was lost that Kankuro, who incarnated kabuki in its role as the paradigmatic representative of the "timeless culture" model, was trying to destroy that image by recovering the quality of newness that for most of its history had characterized the art form. He did so by breaking kabuki out of the cultural-cathedral-like environments of places like Japan's Kabuki-za theater—not to mention the Metropolitan Opera House, where kabuki had last been presented in New York in 1989—and relocating it to contingent, historically-pretend spaces in cities like Tokyo and New York. "This is real kabuki," proclaimed advertisements for Kankuro's kabuki in a tent at the 2004 Lincoln Center Festival. It was real, at the very least in the sense of creating a colorful critique of contemporary cultural myths.

Ninagawa Directs Mishima, 2005

For Yukio Ninagawa, a Japan-based director with an international reputation (especially in London) for "startling visual imagery and elaborate stagings"[38] in productions ranging from modern Japanese plays to classical Greek drama and works of Shakespeare, it was proving difficult to gain traction in the United States. The Brooklyn Academy of Music had presented his work on two occasions: *Macbeth* in 1990 and again in 2002. In 2005 the Lincoln Center Festival recognized Ninagawa's "global" artistry by offering his production of two modern noh plays written by Yukio Mishima.

Mishima's name, like Murakami's, was already well known to a sizable segment of New York theater audiences. As Brantley reminded *Times* readers in his review of the production, "Throughout his intense, brilliant career as a rule-breaking novelist and playwright, Mishima, who entered the annals of Japanese legend when he killed himself in a public ritual suicide in 1970, sought to infuse the increasingly Western modernity of his country with the form and ritual of earlier times."[39] Mishima borrowed the titles of his plays *Sotoba Komachi* and *Yoroboshi* from pieces in the noh repertory. There are links to the older works, but as presented onstage they appear fully contemporary.

Ninagawa started out as an actor in 1955 at the age of twenty, emerging as a director in Japan's avant-garde little theater movement just over a decade later. By the mid-1970s he was a leading director of commercial theater in Japan. In 1983 he began touring internationally, taking productions of *Medea* to Greece and Italy. His extensive work in England includes collaborations with the Royal Shakespeare Company and projects for the Royal National Theatre. "Ninagawa's desire in producing the works of Mishima is to open almost violently a metaphorically sealed room, a room built of words to which the only key is an actor."[40] In the "Director's Note" published in the program distributed to Lincoln Center Festival audiences, Ninagawa unapologetically described his approach as "[c]ontrary to Mishima's wish," writing that his "direction has added red camellias falling throughout the play in *Sotoba Komachi* and, in the last scene of *Yoroboshi,* live recordings of Mishima himself, in which he desperately shouts to members of the Self-Defense Forces prior to his death, after breaking into the headquarters. The screaming voice you hear from the stage is Mishima's voice before his suicide."[41]

Mishima used the term *modern noh* metaphorically, but it is the literal meaning of noh that resonates with American audiences that think of Japan mainly in terms of cultural continuity. Mishima's name and the term *modern noh* brought to Ninagawa American audiences looking for a familiar—and welcome—discourse. However, Ninagawa, like Kankuro the previous year, simultaneously took aim at the myth-making surrounding American conceptualizations of Japanese traditional culture. Brantley wrote, "At first, this production certainly does not feel like anything one might expect from the world of Noh." The critic appeared to understand that for both Mishima and Ninagawa "form and ritual," while important, were not foremost, concluding, "'Yoroboshi' operates both as a lyrical, abstract study of death-in-life and as a pointed social commentary."[42]

Teshigawara's *Bones in Pages,* 2006

When Saburo Teshigawara performed in 1992 at the Brooklyn Academy of Music's Next Wave Festival, he was categorized by Kisselgoff as "a post-Butoh choreographer." Making what the critic called his "belated New

York debut" that year,[43] Teshigawara seemed to baffle American presenters and critics alike. Like Ninagawa, he had cultivated enthusiastic audiences in Europe but in a way was shunted aside by American presenters wary of booking even the most serious and sophisticated artists from Japan whose work did not appear distinctly "Japanese." To label Teshigawara "post-Butoh" was a convoluted way of trying to identify him as a cultural heritage artist from Japan. As with Ninagawa, however, it was not until the Lincoln Center Festival was well under way that Teshigawara's "global" artistry was acknowledged by the institution.

The opening sentence of John Rockwell's review of *Bones in Pages* communicates frustration: "There is no doubt an answer to this question, but I don't know it: Why hasn't Saburo Teshigawara appeared more often in New York? Or in the United States for that matter?" It had been twelve years since the second of Teshigawara's two previous appearances in New York—like the first, also on the program of BAM's Next Wave Festival. "New York still likes to pride itself on being the, or at least a, dance capital," Rockwell added. "Yet here is a man widely regarded as Japan's most important choreographer, who has toured the world with his own company and staged ballets all over Europe. . . . The bitter good news, however, is that 'Bones in Pages' was magical, one of the most striking examples of imagistic dance-theater, or dance-art installation, that I have ever seen."[44] The comments were somewhat ironic, given that Rockwell, currently serving as the *Times*'s chief dance critic, had been the first director of the Lincoln Center Festival—a position that presumably would have given him the authority to bring about a much earlier visit by Teshigawara.

A Singaporean Artist Inspired by Japanese Culture: Ong Keng Sen's *Geisha*, 2006

At first it is difficult to understand how *Geisha* came to be included on the roster of Lincoln Center Festival productions. It seems retrograde, with publicity for the show inviting audiences to "[e]xplore the secret world of the enigmatic geisha . . . from the geisha's innocent childhood, to the stressful years of learning to excel at everything from flower arranging to proper kimono styling, to intricate wig and make-up techniques, to the subtle art of engaged conversation."[45] The production was conceived and directed by Ong Keng Sen, artistic director of the Singapore-based TheatreWorks company, which he founded in 1985.

Ong's project was not simply a riff on American fascination with geishas—which had recently been manifested in the *Memoirs of a Geisha* phenomenon ignited by Arthur Golden's 1997 novel and Rob Marshall's 2005 film. Rather, its intent was more far reaching, making it a lushly packaged critique of cultural assumptions and perceptions. The aim of the "half-playful, half-academic and disappointingly dull 90-minute collage of words, music and dance," Charles Isherwood wrote, was "to recast our perceptions of the geisha's role by both evoking and challenging familiar presentations of the tradition in Western art."[46] However, to understand the piece as being solely about geishas is to miss the point, as evidenced by the fact that there was no "real" geisha in the work. The title character was played—silently—by kabuki-dance master Masanosuke Gojo (who in 2008 succeeded to the name Tamami Gojo III). Theater experimentalist Karen Kandel delivered the voice of the character. The significance of *Geisha* lay in the gap that exists between the image of Japanese culture (embodied in the iconic geisha) and the reality (in this case, the male performer). It also lay in the fact that the audience's perception of that image was controlled and mediated by Kandel, an American whose role, appropriately enough, was labeled the "Dreamweaver."

Kanzaburo's Kabuki, 2007

Japan-related productions at the Lincoln Center Festival entered a new phase in 2007. Artists who had already appeared in previous iterations of the event were invited to return with new material, underscoring their prominence as global performing arts practitioners and allowing US audiences the opportunity to explore their work more deeply. Kankuro V, who had recently succeeded to the name Kanzaburo XVIII, came back in 2007 with his Heisei Nakamura-za troupe. Although there was no specially erected theater this time—only the stage of Avery Fisher Hall—there was again just one work performed, the eighteenth-century *Hokaibo* (*Hōkaibō*), a play, Isherwood wrote, that "incorporates all the essential elements of classic Kabuki: the all-male company of actors, exaggerated makeup, the stomping dances, the arresting, cross-eyed poses at moments of high drama that are recognized and applauded." The production, however, well supported Kanzaburo's project of making kabuki more accessible and meaningful to audiences today, starting with his own "audience-seducing brio that invites comparison to any great stage comic you could name." Isherwood perceptively noted that Kanzaburo's comic asides in English during the Lincoln Center Festival production "sometimes poke fun at some of the very traditions he is supposedly charged with maintaining."

An assumption of America's kabuki-Japan is that the traditional arts represent inviolable practices that have been—and continue to be—maintained intact. Referring to the murders and maimings stylistically depicted in *Hokaibo*—almost as if such violence is uncommon in American popular culture—Isherwood wrote that such scenes are a "reminder of the radical strangeness of Kabuki to Western audiences. Mr. Kanzaburo and his director, Kushida Kazuyoshi, have obviously taken steps to bridge the cultural gap between contemporary American sensibilities and the aesthetics of an art form steeped in firm adherence to performing tradition. Their stated goals, achieved with happy finesse in 'Hokaibo,' are to return Kabuki to its populist roots and to infuse it with new energy by opening it up to new influences."[47] The critic's final comment here suggests that in 2007 there was a much deeper understanding of Kanzaburo's seemingly contradictory assertion that in order for kabuki to have relevance for contemporary audiences within and outside of Japan it must also have a specific and recognized place in history.

Samurai Who Danced to the Tune of the Tango: Ninagawa's *Musashi*, 2010

"Behold the mighty samurai," Brantley wrote, "standing tall and vigilant, their hard faces fixed in forbidding scowls. Tremble as they draw their long swords and assume their martial positions. . . . Observe them as, still solemn-faced, they join a ritualistic chorus line, dancing delightfully across the stage to what sounds like accordion tango music." Director Yukio Ninagawa and the Lincoln Center Festival were taking a risk in 2010 with a three-hour, twentieth-century play from Japan dependent on English supertitles. The work was *Musashi,* written by the dramatist Hisashi Inoue. But there were the samurai, albeit ones who danced to tango music in what Brantley described as "an extended parable, which deals more in archetypes than specific psychological portraits . . . creat[ing] here a ravishing dialogue among forms of storytelling and theater, enacted with delicate precision and robust humor by the ensemble." The title character—based on a real swordsman/artist born in the sixteenth century—is an important figure in the Japanese cultural imagination, summarized by Brantley as "a superhero of folklore, literature, action movies and video games."[48]

Inoue, who died in 2010, "elucidate[d] the place Japan and the Japanese people should hold in the world."[49] Although Brantley seemed almost predictably compelled to find within the play evidence of Japanese cultural continuity, writing, "'Musashi' is, in some respects, a classic Noh drama, with that genre's ritualized rhythms and sounds,"[50] the critic's positive response to the nuances of the Lincoln Center Festival production suggested that contemporary drama from Japan had reached a new level of acceptance among US audiences.

Teshigawara's *Miroku*, 2010

Saburo Teshigawara was also on the 2010 Lincoln Center Festival program, with a dance piece titled *Miroku,* the Japanese name of the bodhisattva Maitreya, a symbol of benevolence. Despite the title's specific connotations of Japan and its cultural history, the work is a metaphysical exploration employing abstract movement, sound, and light. "In 'Miroku,'" as Gia Kourlas wrote, "three tall walls framed the performance area, allowing Mr. Teshigawara the opportunity to play with scale. His body was diminutive in comparison with the rest of the vast stage, which in turn became something of a canvas or a movie screen, amplifying the notion of the individual against the world." Evident in Kourlas's response to *Miroku* was the sense that a dialogue had opened up between Teshigawara and American audiences: "As Mr. Teshigawara has stated, 'What is important with dance is whether it is alive or not.' While the power of 'Miroku' ebbed and flowed, Mr. Teshigawara was not only alive, but also untouchable. You can't catch a spirit."[51]

Miyamoto Interprets Mishima: *Temple of the Golden Pavilion*, 2011

On the international stage especially, Yukio Mishima is usually thought of in connection with his modern noh plays rather than with a work that the Lincoln Center Festival described as "an intensely personal picture of Japan in the very troubled time surrounding World War II."[52] At the 2011 event, with the success of the two New York productions of *Pacific Overtures* behind him, Amon Miyamoto presented *Temple of the Golden Pavilion* (*Kinkakuji*), a musical drama adapted from the Mishima novel. In a ninety-second video message embedded in the *Temple of the Golden Pavilion* page on the Lincoln Center Festival website, festival director Nigel Redden summarized the show, referring to Japan's "uneasiness with the past that's reflected in [Mishima's] story" in a production that is an "attempt to make different parts of culture all come together." He told potential ticket buyers, "I think that if you want to understand Japan today, this is a terrific production to go to."[53]

It was not easy, though, to understand how American audiences were expected to interpret "Japan today" through Miyamoto's *Temple of the Golden Pavilion*. Indeed, the cursory *Times* review saw the play as little more than "a sprawling tale of madness" that "never really earns the crazy." New York audiences, it was suggested, "may leave this elaborate production feeling unfulfilled."[54] Although publicity material for the festival touted Go Morita, the actor playing the lead role of Mizoguchi (the troubled man who sets fire to the temple), as "a superstar of the Japanese boy band V6" and other "exciting young actors of this generation,"[55] that information would not have resonated with many festival ticket buyers.

On one level, "Japan today" was an allusion to Miyamoto as a highly acclaimed director of Broadway-style musicals in Japan, as well as to the popular singers and other performers in the cast, who also included dancers from the butoh company Dai Rakudakan. There was, in addition, another, more philosophical level to consider. Prior to bringing *Temple of the Golden Pavilion* to New York, Miyamoto had presented it several months earlier at the Kanagawa Arts Theatre in Yokohama, where he is artistic director. For Miyamoto, the character Mizoguchi represented a metaphysical quest to find meaning in twenty-first-century Japanese life: "The era when the Japanese people could live mindlessly under our capitalistic economy to achieve happiness has ended. So what is the value of life now? I'd like to ponder this with the audience through Mizoguchi's life."[56] Although the show was finished before the earthquake and tsunami occurred in March 2011, the disasters undoubtedly reinforced Miyamoto's interpretation of the work. The presence of the butoh dancers—whose artistry is often associated with the war's bleak aftermath in the 1940s and 1950s—could be seen as expressive of a Japan that feels confused, even lost. At the Lincoln Center Festival, *Temple of the Golden Pavilion* was a theater piece from Japan that challenged US audiences to delve beneath the familiar surface of "America's Japan today."

Following a trip to Japan in 2003, John Rockwell wrote that he attended a recital given by noh flute master Meisho Tosha at a temple in Kyoto that "summed up Japan, past and present. Here was an old, proudly non-Western instrument, played by a man in a costume and setting so formal and serene. The music was the aural image of the passions and intensity of Japanese drama, less alienating than hypnotically involving. The raked garden and the temple roof formed a visual image of the meditative serenity of Zen Buddhism. . . . And there was modern Japan, too: a train whistle and, later, the faraway roar of a jet." Those last sounds "represented the bustling, nonmeditative energy of contemporary Japan." For Rockwell, "Japan has always been the most distant, the most difficult of all world cultures to fathom, and in that sense the most fascinating." He noted, "[S]ome Japanese artists have proven themselves utterly and indistinguishably adept at Western idioms, like the pianist Mitsuko Uchida. Yet Mr. Tosha's flute playing suggested that maybe the best way to bridge gaps between cultures, and probably gaps between individuals, too, is to be true to yourself. His performance spoke deeply to Westerners because it conveyed something essentially Japanese. Embrace the world by embracing yourself."[57]

Saying that if Uchida, for example, wanted "to bridge gaps between cultures" she should be "true" to herself suggested, ultimately, that she would not be playing the piano. If American presenters like the Lincoln Center Festival were concerned with conveying "something essentially Japanese," an artist like Teshigawara would not have been invited to perform. And, yet, in the review Rockwell himself published in 2006 he wondered why Teshigawara did not appear more frequently in the United States. Teshigawara was required by the New York that was a world capital of dance, as Rockwell put it, but not necessarily by a New York that—given his 2003 essay—in some instances still narrowly defines what counts as "authentic" culture from Japan.

Under Redden the Lincoln Center Festival has given primacy to the singular "global" figure—individuals such as Kanzaburo, Miyamoto, Ninagawa, McBurney, and Teshigawara. If, through the performing arts, Japan Society helps New York (and, broadly speaking, the United States) develop a familiarity with Japan, La MaMa challenges conventional assumptions about Japan, and Music From Japan advocates for Japan, the Lincoln Center Festival states unequivocally that Japan is a major world presence. The repeated appearance at the festival of Japan-related productions helps forge and acknowledge Japan's prominent place in global cultural conversations that arise from and center on the performing arts.

6

Negotiating the Foreign

Language, American Audiences, and Theater from Japan

Among the things that are strange about Kabuki is the language.[1]

In his critically acclaimed US theatrical debut in 1979, Kobo Abe delivered a provocative collage of words, images, and sound. Onstage, amid the mutating figures of actors draped in large cloths, seemingly random English-language words and sentences were projected onto "costumes and whatever else was handy"—such as "Storm," "Leap," "Fake Fish," "Frozen Dreams" and "Look! The sea is falling into the sky!"[2] Perhaps for lack of a better term, one reviewer referred to the projections as "subtitles,"[3] but it would have been more accurate to say that they were stand-alone elements in a work in which dialogue was reduced to a minimum and "words were chosen as much for their sound as for their meaning."[4] Profiled in pre-tour press coverage as "the best-selling serious novelist in Japan and . . . the top-selling Japanese author in both the United States and the Soviet Union,"[5] Abe was well acquainted with the challenges of translation. *The Little Elephant Is Dead* is a humorously subversive piece of theater. It can be read as an intentional departure from and a pointed critique of the highly mediated commentary/explanation/partial-translation model of the theater-from-Japan experience that, as Abe well knew, US audiences had come to expect.[6]

Presentations in the United States of theater from Japan—an important segment of transnational cultural exchange—are sites of linguistic contestation and tension. Non-Japanese-speaking audiences rely on technologies of access to foreign words spoken (and cultures experienced) live onstage: supertitles, wireless earphone translation and commentary systems, and program notes. Such technologies of access become part of the audience's experience. The titles flashed on screens, the commentary transmitted through handheld, battery-powered devices, and the explanations printed in booklets constantly send audiences a message of remoteness, of difference, of a cultural "gulf."

My purpose here is to examine how language and the culture in which language is embedded have been negotiated over the past six decades in US presentations of theater from Japan. I look at critical responses to these events as a way to explore what Susan Bassnett-McGuire calls the "intercultural transfer" that has taken place.[7] The professional (and, invariably, non-Japanese-speaking) critic is a frontline negotiator with the foreign, a default interpreter who facilitates (or not) processes of intercultural transfer. Like American audiences in general, critics are not deeply versed in Japanese culture. Through their writings we can identify major modes of audience reaction to the unfamiliar. Critics' published reviews and related essays form the historical archive of intellectual engagement with and reception of theater (as well as dance and music) from Japan—in other words, the body of writing that constructs the narrative of America's Japan through the performing arts.

The analytical framework I propose, based on that archive, identifies three principal discursive strategies that mark critics' negotiations with the foreign. Advocating surrender allows pleasure and related rewards to be derived from a presentation even if the words or other aspects of a production are regarded as beyond the audience's ability to take in fully. Assuming universality is a corollary to surrender: what is labeled "universal" is seen as not necessarily requiring translation or explanation. Putting up resistance means that cross-cultural communication is judged to be extremely difficult or, in the end, not possible. There is a closing off, an attitude of incomprehension. Each of the strategies of negotiation is a response to words not understood from the stage. There is no neutral stance: language here inevitably calls attention to itself—and elicits a response.

I apply the terms *theater from Japan* and *translation* broadly—to spoken drama, as well as to dance and music events, which frequently are also sites of negotiation with the foreign. Even where there are no words per se, issues of "translation" easily arise in connection with genre, performance style, cultural references, or just the association with Japan-as-"other." The presenters hosting the events may thus offer audiences pre- or post-performance lectures by scholars, Q&As with directors and performers (channeled through bilingual personnel onstage), and program booklets replete with explanatory material. "For some time I have regarded the process of all theatrical translation as taking place on a continuum of accessibility," Jean Graham-Jones wrote in her introduction to an issue of *Theatre*

Journal devoted to this topic. "Do we translators make the play accessible to the audience, or do we make the audience accessible to the play? Do we attempt to do both?"[8] To build on Graham-Jones's point, in a metaphorical sense, translation is not just about the contents of a script. In the aggregate, translation may involve numerous people, tasks, and technologies that situate a production along a continuum of accessibility.

I begin by contextualizing my analysis in a discussion of the means by which audiences in Japan and the United States experience foreign theater. I discuss Japan's "theater of translation"—the ongoing project, more than a century old, of translating plays from abroad into Japanese and bringing productions of them with Japanese casts to the stage in Tokyo and other theater centers.[9] By contrast, the American practice in the case of theater from Japan has largely been to emphasize productions originating in Japan, while using increasingly sophisticated technological means to supplement the experience with interpretation and commentary in English. What might be called the linguistic domestication of foreign theater—in other words, the regular and ongoing process of translating and producing plays originating outside its borders—is the norm in Japan. I address this topic because language is a principal marker of foreignness in Japanese theater abroad—which mostly comprises works presented in Japanese by touring troupes from Japan.

There are few professional productions in the United States of translated work from Japan. Recognizing this fact, the New York–based Play Company ("dedicated to advancing an international view of contemporary playwriting") is trying to increase the number of such productions.[10] Under founding producer Kate Loewald, the organization presented Yoji Sakate's *The Attic* (*Yaneura*) at the 59E59 Theaters in February–March 2007. The director was Ari Edelson; the English translation was by Leon Ingulsrud and Keiko Tsuneda. (The play had its New York premiere two years earlier at Japan Society in a Japanese-language production, with English supertitles, by Sakate's Rinko-gun Theater Company.) In April–May 2010, The Play Company produced Toshiki Okada's *Enjoy* (*Enjoi*), again at the 59E59 Theaters, directed by Dan Rothenberg. The translation was by Aya Ogawa. At La MaMa, also in May 2010, Daniel Safer directed and choreographed an adaptation of Okada's *Five Days in March* (*Sangatsu no itsukakan*), based on a translation by Ogawa. (The US premiere of *Sangatsu no itsukakan*, with English supertitles, was presented by Okada's chelfitsch Theater Company at Japan Society in February 2009.) Other steps have been taken toward developing a more visible and sustained English-language theater of translation for modern and contemporary plays originally written in Japanese.[11] More works are being translated and published.[12] In Septem-

Fig. 15. Advertising card, *Enjoy,* a play by Toshiki Okada, produced by The Play Company at the 59E59 Theaters, 2010. (Artwork by Noah Scalin/Another Limited Rebellion. Courtesy of Noah Scalin/Another Limited Rebellion.)

ber 2007 the Japan Foundation and City University of New York collaboratively presented "Spotlight Japan," a program of staged readings of three translated works: Masataka Matsuda's *Auto-da-Fe* (*Autodafe*), Okada's *Enjoy,* and Mikuni Yanaihara's *The Blue Bird* (*Ao no tori*).[13] Since 2008 Japan Society has produced professionally staged readings of plays in translation. They have included Okada's *Enjoy, Frozen Beach* (*Furōzun bīchi*) by Keralino Sandorovich, *Women in a Holy Mess* (*Katazuketai onnatachi*) by Ai Nagai, and *Trance* (*Toransu*) by Shoji Kokami. Despite these recent efforts, translation into English is still very limited in comparison with Japan's one hundred years of absorption of foreign drama.

Language/Foreign Theater

Japan's "Theater of Translation"

In the essay noted above, Graham-Jones cited a *Village Voice* article by Tom Sellar as "a powerful invective against New York's limited reception of international theatre."[14] Sellar had made the point that "New York's larger, most prominent theaters rarely stage their own full productions of new writing in translation," adding, "[I]magine what additional voices we might discover if we had . . . [a] major institution exploring a *foreign* dramatist every year."[15] Starting with late-nineteenth- and early-twentieth-century productions of plays by Shakespeare, Ibsen, Chekhov, and others, audiences in Japan have been discovering on a regular basis the "additional voices" to which Sellar referred. *John Gabriel Borkman,* produced in 1909 at the Jiyu Gekijo (Free Theatre) in Tokyo under the direction of Kaoru Osanai, links Japan's theater of translation to the beginning of the theatrical movement called *shingeki* (literally, "new theater"), a label generally applied to translated Western and original Western-style drama in Japan. *Shingeki* places Japan's theater culture within a new/old dichotomy: "old theater" is kabuki, noh, and the other genres to which adjectives such as "traditional," "original," and "authentically Japanese" are typically applied. In contrast, the works of *shingeki* form the "history of Japan's attempts to modernize her drama."[16]

Issues of language and translation trigger heated discussion within the field of *shingeki* scholarship and criticism. M. Cody Poulton has argued that Osanai's legacy as a *shingeki* pioneer "was a dubious one if we are to consider not the introduction of Western drama, but the creation of an indigenous drama in Japan as the defining moment of modern Japanese theater. As we shall see, he prevented much Japanese drama from being staged. His first trip abroad (1912–1913) seems to mark a turn toward what he would later call a 'true age of translation' (*ma no hon'yaku jidai*) that frustrated many who had hoped the Free Theatre would remain a forum for the presentation of Japanese drama."[17] Poulton looks particularly at Osanai's Tsukiji Little Theatre (located in Tokyo), which was "often called Japan's first truly modern theatre."[18] The repertory there favored plays from abroad. In its five-year history, Tsukiji Little Theatre presented 114 plays—89 of which were translations of work by playwrights such as Chekhov, Tolstoy, and Gorky.[19]

Where translation led, imitation appeared to follow: "With the rise of *shingeki*'s emphasis on translation, the Japanese assimilation of Western culture also became less a matter of adaptation than adoption, an attempt to import whole new ideas and modes of expression."[20] Poulton cites J. Thomas Rimer's observation that "*shingeki*'s emphasis on translated drama would ensure for decades to come that modern Japanese theatre 'would remain an intellectual rather than an emotional experience.'"[21] Where translation led, cultural confusion also appeared to follow: "The general public was increasingly presented with improbable and alien ideals of thought and comportment and was less able to see itself presented onstage as it really was."[22] Overall, according to Yasunari Takahashi, *shingeki* "could never shake off a certain didactic posture, the air of being intellectually elitist and preaching from above."[23]

Poulton, Rimer, and Takahashi are certainly correct in problematizing translation and framing it within the history of ideological conflict that defines Japan's modernization. However, there is another way to look at the emergence and continuing vigor of Japan's theater of translation: the fact that for well over a hundred years Japanese audiences have had broad access through translation to the multiple forms and periods of world theater without needing to rely on titles, earphone systems, or program notes.[24] Such a reading foregrounds the transcultural mission of individuals such as Osanai early on and Tamiya Kuriyama (who recently served as artistic director of the New National Theatre, Tokyo) today.[25] To dismiss translation merely as an "entrenched dependence on Western theater,"[26] then, is to ignore that in a basic way it was an act of resistance against the government-imposed political, social, and cultural isolationism that is a central feature of Japan's historical memory.[27]

"Translation," as Maria Tymoczko and Edwin Gentzler have commented, "is itself very much involved in the creation of knowledge."[28] In Osanai's day, *shingeki* "was faced with a 'twofold learning process' whereby not only did its Japanese practitioners have to acquire new forms of expression, but on a more fundamental level, they had to try to embody the cognitive universe of westerners, acquire their sensibilities and behavior."[29] The old paradigm no longer applies. When discussing director Tadashi Suzuki's work (which includes Japanese-language productions of dramas by Euripides, Shakespeare, and Chekhov), Takahashi has pointed out that Suzuki is "neither an anachronistic chauvinist exploiting a 'samurai exoticism' nor a superficial cosmopolitan smoothing over undeniable differences."[30] Audiences that today buy tickets to "foreign" plays in Tokyo, like their counterparts in New York and London, for example, are informed by high levels of education, extensive travel, and exposure to the media in all of their variety, as well as possessed of considerable theatergoing experience acquired at home and abroad. Many are women, a number of whom are the internationalists who are the subjects of Karen Kelsky's research.[31] For these internationalists (some of whom are veterans of extended study- and work-abroad experiences), the West (especially) is seen as an escape from what they perceive to be a socially restrictive Japan. Expanding on Kelsky's thesis, I suggest that the theater of translation in Japan is an important space for linguistically barrier-free consumption of the West. In his comprehensive portrait of the performing and visual arts in Japan in the period between 1955 and 1980, Thomas R. H. Havens notes the growing popularity of translated Broadway musicals in the 1970s—which can be seen in Japan's flourishing Broadway-musical scene today.[32] Havens estimated that, during the two and a half decades that he looks at in his study, approximately half of the plays presented by modern and contemporary companies were translated works by non-Japanese playwrights.[33]

Referencing Homi Bhabha, Tymoczko and Gentzler have written that translation "has become *the* site for cultural production, the space where 'newness' enters the world."[34] Japan's theater of translation is where the ambitions of playwrights from abroad to have their work produced in Japan can be realized. Organizations and agencies interested in the promotion of national cultures, such as the French Society of Dramatic Authors and Composers (Société des Auteurs et Compositeurs Dramatiques), support their endeavors.[35] The society's November 2005–April 2006 newsletter, *Actes du Théâtre,* carried an article by scholar-translator Shintaro Fujii on the challenges facing French theater in Japan. Fujii highlighted the work of the Tokyo-based Théâtre Guy Foissy, which was established in 1977 to present dramas by French playwrights (with the focus on the work of its namesake, Guy Foissy) in Japanese translation. Theatre Ontario is another example. An article titled "Mining Canadian Theatre for a Japanese Audience," published in the organization's newsletter, opened with the question "Did you ever wonder how Canadian plays are produced in different parts of the world?" The piece profiled the successes of Toyoshi Yoshihara, "Japan's foremost translator of Canadian drama," in bringing the work of playwrights such as Anne Chislett, George Walker, and Michel Tremblay to the stage in Japan.[36]

Tamiya Kuriyama is an example of individuals who are ushering in a new kind of theater of translation in Japan, one aimed at helping Japanese artists assume a leadership role in the globalized theater world—and thereby rendering superfluous further acts of resistance to historical isolationism. During Kuriyama's 2000–2007 tenure as artistic director at Japan's New National Theatre, the emphasis was on "international communication among theatre professionals. . . . One of the mainstays of this effort is the commissioning and performance of new works by overseas playwrights."[37] An example is British playwright Shan Khan's *Cleanskins,* translated by Koshi Odashima, which had its world premiere (directed by Kuriyama) at the New National Theatre in April 2007. Also under Kuriyama, the New National Theatre launched a series titled Our Contemporary, with the goal of presenting the work of important contemporary playwrights from Japan and abroad in productions headed by noted "veteran" and "young" Japanese directors. Such work has included, in Japanese translation, *Die Frau von Fuhrer* by German playwright Roland Schimmelpfennig, *Shoot the Crow* by Irish playwright Owen McCafferty, and *Sixteen Wounded* by American playwright Eliam Kraiem.

Accessing Kabuki in America

Historically, issues of language in US presentations of theater from Japan are most sharply delineated in response to the highly publicized visits by kabuki troupes that have taken place since the 1950s. Writing about "the rapid expansion of heteroglossic theatre at the end of the twentieth century," Marvin Carlson has pointed out that the supertitle and "its close relative, the oral simultaneous translation" came to serve "as a presumably neutral extra channel that operated outside the actual aesthetics of the stage production itself."[38] When a Grand Kabuki troupe came to the United States for the first time in 1960, the introduction of a transistorized earphone system revolutionized the technology of access to foreign words spoken onstage. Until that time there had been no efficient, real-time method for delivering translations and commentaries to audiences. For relatively small-scale shows, one solution, used at a presentation of noh for non-Japanese-speakers residing in or visiting Japan, was to have "[f]ull program notes in English, coupled with numbered placards besides the stage synchronized with the development of the drama [that] enabled spectators to follow obscure passages in which a mere gesture or simple motion symbolized elaborate actions."[39] Precursors of the computer-based titling systems in use today, they are early (and literal) examples of language-and-culture-bridging "side texts," a term used by Carlson.[40] The enormous scale of a kabuki presentation makes placards at the side of the stage impractical.

Befitting a performing art with a cultural-diplomatic mission, the technological breakthrough for kabuki was inspired by the United Nations. Using "a simplified form [of the simultaneous interpretation system] employed in the conference rooms of the United Nations," the *New York Times* reported in advance of the 1960 visit, audiences attending the performances at New York's City Center theater would be able to follow the action onstage via "a running commentary in English" transmitted through earphone sets. One dollar covered rental of the handheld, wireless devices, broadcasting live the "partly descriptive and partly . . . lyrical translation of the dialogue." The system, developed by Matsushita Electric Company, was permanently installed in City Center to "be available for other future foreign-language attractions at the civic playhouse." In accepting the gift of the system, the chairman of City Center's board of directors said, "This marks the beginning of a new chapter in the City Center's history, and many attractions will be doubly welcomed from abroad."[41]

Audiences do not necessarily like such interventions despite their technological sophistication. "We rush for our headphones," Pulitzer Prize–winning critic Margo Jefferson has written about American presentations of non-English-language theater, "and tolerate the expressionless voice translating the dialogue several beats late, stumbling at points or sounding momentarily baffled. Some people relinquish headphones with a weary sigh and settle in for an evening of hard work, feeling thwarted by the language gap." Jefferson began her essay with the observation, "Unlike audiences in many places around the world, Americans rarely see plays performed in other languages."[42]

Reviewers' responses to kabuki reflected a sense of frustration. Writing about a scene from the play *Chushingura,* Brooks Atkinson, then "dean" of New York theater critics, pointed out, "Even with the aid of the transistor simultaneous translation and the ample program notes, a theatregoer ignorant of Japanese may find himself losing his place as the story slowly unfolds. The situation is further complicated by the fact that Onoe Shoroku II plays two of the leading parts."[43] Decades later, advances in the technologies of access notwithstanding, presentations of kabuki in the United States continue to face issues of language. Stung by criticism of the low quality of the English-language material transmitted over the earphone system during his troupe's appearance in 2004 at the Lincoln Center Festival, Kanzaburo Nakamura XVIII hired a professional actor to provide a better earphone experience for audiences when his troupe returned to the festival in 2007. (In 2004 Ben Brantley had written, "As rendered in simultaneous English translation via headphones, the dialogue can seem quaint to the point of parody."[44] The comment was a reference to infelicities Brantley detected in the translation itself.) Seeking ways to bypass technology in order to "engage in sympathetic communication with the audience,"[45] in 2007 Kanzaburo also directly inserted a number of joking English-language one-liners into his own dialogue in one of the plays—such as "Why is she always so damn slow?" (in reference to a female character who took her time moving and speaking) and "Next time, upgrade please!" (shouted good-naturedly at audience members seated in an upper balcony).[46] The effect, though, was not necessarily the "sympathetic communication" that Kanzaburo desired but audience amusement at the incongruity of such lines in a "traditional" kabuki play. Kanzaburo, whose career in Japan has emphasized attracting audiences by making productions more lively and spontaneous—in an attempt to re-create the raucous and unpredictable atmosphere of seventeenth-, eighteenth-, and nineteenth-century playhouses—was working well within the historic conventions of kabuki, which put a premium on humorous innovation. Even if American audiences interpret a few funny lines in English as a gesture of friendliness, the downside is that such lines may have the unintended consequence of highlighting even more the "foreignness" of the production's language and culture.

A Theater Translator Steps Forward

Lawrence Venuti has written, "The translator's invisibility is . . . a weird self-annihilation, a way of conceiving and practicing translation that undoubtedly reinforces its marginal status in Anglo-American culture."[47] However, during his long career as a New York–based translator/commentator and freelance writer who published widely on kabuki, Faubion Bowers was not content to remain in the background. For Bowers, a skilled linguist who became America's "voice of kabuki" (the earphone system's translator and commentator) starting with the Grand Kabuki visit in 1969, the art form could never be domesticated for American audiences: they would always need a helping hand, and he would provide it and thus make himself an integral and identifiable part of the audience's experience.

Bowers argued powerfully about the crucial role played by the person serving as translator/commentator in a 1970 *Times* article titled "Without Them, It's All Greek (or French, or Japanese)." Illustrated with a photograph of leading kabuki actor Baiko Onoe VII, the essay forthrightly addressed the issue of language: "Now that more foreign plays are being staged in their original form for American audiences, simultaneous translation has assumed considerable importance. It has, as well, stirred up some controversy. . . . How, in short, can an American audience understand plays from Japan, France, Poland, Russia, Thailand?" Bowers remarked that pre-performance explanations are not sufficient; neither are program notes, which require "undimmed houselights." He wrote, "After about 10 years of trial and error, on-again-off-again experimentation, the solution for all practical purposes and with all its drawbacks seems to be the voiceover translation more or less continuously spoken as the play progresses." The person providing the voice-over, he noted, "sits high up in the second balcony, watches the performance, and narrates it into a microphone while members of the audience wearing earphones [and holding receivers] hear his voice."

Bowers acknowledged that the voice-over system was hardly perfect. People found the system "maddening. The earphones hurt. Are they sanitary? . . . The voice is too loud, too soft. There's too much talk, no chance to hear the stage. There's not *enough* translation. The translator laughed and didn't say what was funny." Mechanical glitches could plague the system as well. For the kabuki presentations at City Center in 1969 fewer than three hundred of the eight hundred earphone sets were in working order, according to Bowers, who noted that "John D. Rockefeller 3rd fiddled with three before he found an adequate one on opening night."

Bowers expressed his understandable frustration with what he saw as the lack of respect shown those (such as Bowers himself) with the knowledge and skills to translate and interpret: "[C]ritics—I am speaking now of the theater—are cavalier, to say the least, about either acknowledging their debt to the translator or their need for one. During the Grand Kabuki, several reviewers reveling in the spectacle leaned exclusively on their 'intuitive perception' and let—how did the expression go?—the beauty flow over them like water."[48] Bowers did not mention that *Times* critic Clive Barnes had warmly praised him in a review published less than a year earlier, having written, "All the text is translated over transistors, which worked rather better, I thought, than is customary. Much praise is also due to the Western Kabuki expert, Faubion Bowers, who offers this excellent running commentary sensibly spiced with the occasional factual comment. This adds enormously to the pleasure of the evening."[49]

It was not just critics who annoyed Bowers; it was also the audience. "It is more to the audience in general that I direct my astonishment. Despite the boredom of watching a play without understanding a word of it, large numbers of people at all these performances of foreign plays refuse to avail themselves of the translation." Bowers wrote that he could understand "[o]n opening night, what with hairdos and so forth . . . the reluctance of women to wear a contraption which, at worst, does remind one of a hearing aid." But "their escorts and the others" had no such excuse. Audiences seemed shy, he observed, "about admitting [they] don't know a foreign language, but why should one be expected to know Japanese, for instance?"[50] Bowers might have used the opportunity to explain that much of the language used in kabuki requires negotiation for both American and Japanese audiences. In kabuki theaters in Japan, earphone systems are now available in both English and Japanese—the latter for the many Japanese speakers who also seek to comprehend as much as possible of the language and conventions used in the art form.[51]

In making the quite reasonable case that American audiences should do their best to understand kabuki using technologies that convey translation and explanation, Bowers at the same time presented himself as the particular individual with the insider's knowledge and skills to provide the needed help. Referring to the challenges facing "the transistor translator," he asked, "[W]here does he obey literally and where does he 'interpret'?" Citing a line from *Kumagai's Battle Camp* (*Kumagai jin'ya*), one of the plays presented on the 1969 Grand Kabuki tour, which can be rendered "It is battlefield training," he wrote that "its *meaning*, its emphasis, the arrow of feeling which reaches the knowledgeable Japanese spectator's heart, is 'Such are the horrors of war!' [Leading kabuki actor] Shoroku and I talked at length about how this pivotal line should be translated, and he asked me to make clear that 'horror of war' was inherent within the line."[52]

There is no denying Bowers's point that for American audiences kabuki can never be other than a mediated experience. There is also no denying that as mediator the earphone translator/commentator wields considerable power. The multiplicity of voices onstage is reduced to one. Proceeding from the assertion "The classical theater of Japan is easy to translate for, largely because it moves slowly," Bowers boiled down the difficulties of translating kabuki to "[t]he intricacies of the poetry, the double and triple meanings [that] can almost always be indicated by a single phrase of poetry to suggest to the listeners that there is more but here is just a taste." Even if readers had known that there are many more obstacles to kabuki translation—starting with the innumerable arcane historical and literary references—they were in no position to argue with Bowers on whose expertise they relied. Like a teacher trying to convince a recalcitrant student, Bowers ended the article by writing that, despite the annoyances of wearing an earphone and having "someone superimposing his idea of the play over your idea of the play" and the irritations of "'seeing' one language with eyes and hearing another with ears," earphones should be used "until theater lovers learn all languages."[53]

In the arena of cultural exchange, where kabuki is treated as a consummate representative of Japanese culture for American audiences, a description that has been applied to translators and literary theorists Germaine de Staël and Gayatri Spivak in an entirely different context could very well be extended to Bowers during his nearly two-decade tenure as kabuki translator/commentator. The two women, as Sherry Simon has shown, are "not self-effacing language mediators, but strong-willed, forceful culture brokers, well aware of the pedagogical role of translation, participating in and shaping relations between disparate cultures, and promoting their own agendas as they wield their influence."[54] In addition to Barnes's earlier praise, there were other occasions when Bowers got at least some of the public recognition that he sought. "[A]nyone listening to Faubion Bowers's excellent translation of the text and commentary via transistor headphones," wrote Anna Kisselgoff on the occasion of the kabuki visit that took place in 1977, "will easily find the human and emotional range for which Kabuki is also famous."[55] Richard Eder, reviewing kabuki in 1979, mentioned "Faubion Bowers—who provides, via earphones, a model of discreet and useful translation."[56] In 1985 Kisselgoff again credited Bowers's "excellent simultaneous translation" of kabuki.[57] All of these comments were testaments to the power wielded by Bowers.[58]

Negotiations

Surrender

In his study of language and theater, Marvin Carlson in effect defines surrender when he refers to "what international travelers have always known: that despite language barriers a surprising amount of communication can take place based upon context, nonverbal signs, and the goodwill and imagination of the would-be communicants."[59] Critics who adopt surrender as a strategy of negotiation see audiences as "giving themselves up" to the performance. As Bowers said (not approvingly), they let "the beauty flow over them like water."[60] John Martin's response to the Azuma Kabuki Dancers and Musicians in 1954 was an early example of surrender: "For the Western mind to grasp straightway the ancient traditions of Japanese theatre art and the intricacies of its organization would be asking a good deal, and there is certainly no way for us to approach the coming [run] except with complete relaxation and an open mind. It is quite useless to try to 'know' anything."[61]

Martin again employed this strategy in 1959 in his coverage of the first overseas performance tour of gagaku court music and dance by performers associated with the Japanese Imperial Household. "Remote? Alien? Impossible to understand? Absolutely. So what?" he wrote.[62] For Martin it was futile to try to appreciate the presentations fully: gagaku is a centuries-old art that "they" (people in Japan) can understand, but "we" (Americans) cannot. He wrote that gagaku "is totally remote from the occidental mind. . . . [It is] altogether alien from anything we have known before."[63] Because gagaku incorporates material going back to the seventh and eighth centuries from countries (an allusion to China and Korea) whose ancient cultures are not familiar to American audiences, its finer points "are not discernible to the Western eye and ear." Martin's advice was, "It is enough simply to lay oneself open to the spell of the dancers, and let the stately flow of movement and music exert its persuasions."[64] He dismissed the idea that people might prepare themselves ahead of time in order to enrich their experience at the theater, writing, "It is quite unnecessary (as well as virtually impossible) to 'bone up' on Gagaku in the effort to enjoy it. . . . The mind should be kept a blank, or it will get seriously in the way of the exquisitely sensuous communications of grace and spirit."[65]

Surrender to difference was also the theme of gagaku coverage in *Time* magazine: "To a Western audience the dance fragments with their muted accompaniment of drums, flute or plucked strings may at first seem too contained to be powerfully stirring. But once the spectator grows accustomed to *Gagaku's* own laws of time and space, the dance becomes an unforgettable illustration of the unsuspected beauties of repose, the high drama that can be compressed in small-scale patterns."[66] It was, however, a limited surrender, with an aestheticized Japanese culture reduced in these comments to Orientalist clichés such as "muted," "contained," and "small-scale."

Recognizing the profound "foreignness" of the art form, Lincoln Kirstein, as host of the visit, made special efforts to provide audiences with background and context. Those attending performances could purchase a thirty-three-page illustrated booklet titled *Gagaku: The Music and Dances of the Japanese Imperial Household,* written by ethnomusicologist Robert Garfias, who also served as interpreter on the tour. Rarely have program notes been provided with such detailed coverage of topics such as the history, dance styles, music, and costumes of an art form. However, reviewers did not read—or simply ignored—the section of the booklet on gagaku in present-day Japan. Garfias made it clear that the art form was not well known in Japan: "[W]ith its almost strictly ceremonial usage for five hundred years, there has been little opportunity for the public to appreciate it"—adding that it was not until 1956 (only three years before the New York visit) that public performances in Japan were inaugurated. "Its audience," Garfias wrote, "is composed primarily of scholars who are interested in its history, composers who are interested in the possibilities offered by its unusual tonal textures[,] and the generally curious."[67] A relatively large-scale presentation for a broad-based, ballet-opera-theater-going audience, as was the case in New York, would have been unimaginable in Japan—and just as "foreign."

Surrender often gives way to bewilderment rather than opening up new ways of understanding. Succeeding encounters may only reinforce earlier responses—thus suggesting that knowledge cannot be gained through accumulated experience. In 1969, when the second visit of Grand Kabuki took place, Barnes wrote, "We are glimpsing an alien culture and, to appreciate what Kabuki has to offer, most of us have to give ourselves up to it completely." He even rejected the idea that the nonverbal parts of the kabuki repertory might prove more accessible to American audiences: "Certainly Kabuki dance dramas are no more easily appreciated than Kabuki plays—if anything they may be even more difficult for Western audiences to apprehend."[68] Jennifer Dunning's response to noh in 1982 was similar: "[It] is probably one of the hardest of Asian performing arts for the uninitiated to grasp. . . . One can open oneself to its stylized abstraction as if to a state of mind, suspending impatient Western expectation."[69] The title of a 1993 review by Jack Anderson, "Sitting Back and Enjoying What Can't Be Understood," also exemplifies a strategy of surrender. Here it is applied to a work by contemporary dancer-choreographer Yoshiko Chuma. Anderson's comment that "[t]he events in this work . . . made no sense" should be read within the historical context of encounters with Japan-related performances. They were not necessarily expected to "make sense."[70]

Surrender often carries with it justifications for ignoring the spoken word. Mel Gussow's response to an experimental work performed in 1975 at the New York Public Theater by the acting company headed by Katsuhiro Oida (who performs under the name Yoshi) was "The language is Japanese, but, as intended, an understanding of the specific words is not necessary to comprehend the mood and flexing tempos of the piece."[71] The insertion of "as intended" offered permission to American audiences to bypass language. Similarly, in a review of Shuji Terayama's *Directions to Servants* at La MaMa in 1980, John Corry wrote, "Mr. Terayama's work . . . is in Japanese. Therefore, you can't understand it, and an English translation makes it clear this doesn't matter. (Dahlia: 'You! You eavesdropped on the chinless man's joke box. You drowned the ungrammatical cat.') Mr. Terayama is not concerned with words, but with images, and with images he succeeds wonderfully well."[72] Reviewing the kabuki run at the Metropolitan Opera House in 1982, Dunning wrote, "Headsets were available for simultaneous English translation, but they were really necessary only for an occasional bawdy pun. All is there on the stage, expressed in the vivid sights and sounds of the Grand Kabuki."[73] D. J. R. Bruckner, attending Hideki Noda's *Comet Messenger—Siegfried* at the Brooklyn Academy of Music in 1988, noted that the presentation was "in rapid-fire Japanese." He told readers, "It is best to just sit back in wonder for two and a half hours without puzzling over the meaning . . . [for] what you see is so entertaining that what you miss in the dialogue hardly matters."[74]

Audiences of foreign theater, Margo Jefferson suggested, should look beyond words for their reward—to, for example, the "visual and emotional" aspects of a director's style.[75] However, this can be limiting and misleading. Surrender cannot substitute for the rewards of actively embracing all parts of a performance. It is dismaying to read critics' suggestions that audiences (including themselves) should feel free to suspend their normal mode of engagement simply because the performances (or the performers) are Japanese. Such attitudes might have been understandable forty or fifty years ago, but after many hundreds of Japan-related presentations, bypassing essential elements of works has worn thin.

Assuming Universality

In his foreword to the program booklet written by Robert Garfias for the gagaku visit in 1959, Lincoln Kirstein argued for the universality of gagaku.

> American dancers and lovers of dancing will welcome Gagaku, not alone as a magnificent gift from a splendid culture, but as an examplar [*sic*] of the sources of our theater, our one world-theater, which was first of all, ordered movement to honor the changing seasons, the survival of life, love and creation. Gagaku is a wonderful show, but something more. It is an embodiment of truth framed in every splendor human hands and minds have contrived to praise the principle that may, if we can manage to realize it, help us in our own struggle towards perfection.[76]

As a strategy for negotiating the foreign, assuming universality is the view that difference is irrelevant or can be transcended. "A privileged object of discourse called Japan," Naoki Sakai has observed, is "constituted in order to show *us* the supposedly concrete instance of particularism, in contrast to which *our* universalism is ascertained."[77] As the following examples illustrate, critics often find it difficult to escape "the centrality of the West as the universal point of reference."[78]

When the Edo Festival Music and Pantomime troupe performed in New York in 1971, Kisselgoff wrote, "There is, of course, no language barrier for a foreign audience. A 'Lion Dance,' performed by a dancer who gave his character some rather coy and human attributes, spoke a universal tongue. This was true as well of the remarkable musical ensembles whose drums and flute produced unexpected nuances."[79] In a similar vein, Anderson enthusiastically responded to the presentation of "torchlight" kyogen in the plaza of Lincoln Center in July 1984, writing, "Although the dialogue was in Japanese, the stage action was in a body language that required no translation."[80] Assuming universality often articulates an attitude of acceptance and goodwill toward visiting performers, as seen in other comments Martin made about the Azuma Kabuki Musicians and Dancers in 1954. Though labeling it "an art so utterly different," he assured readers that "[t]he fine performer makes himself felt no matter what language he speaks or what traditions of art he practices, and the level of performance here is very high indeed."[81]

Assumptions of universality typify responses to Japanese productions of canonical Western works. After seeing director Yukio Ninagawa's *Medea* at the Delacorte Theater in 1986, Gussow wrote, "The play is performed in Japanese, without translation; though one misses the Euripidean poetry (in one of the various English translations), there is no difficulty in following the emotions of the eternal story."[82] The thrust of Gussow's review of Ninagawa's *Macbeth* at the Brooklyn Academy of Music in 1990 is captured in the title of the article: "Universality of 'Macbeth' in Japanese."[83] The very existence of a Japanese production of *Macbeth* attested to the "universality" of the play.

Universality is sometimes—though not always, as the next section will show—assumed in responses to presentations of music from Japan. Writing about the "New Voices from Japan" program of experimental music curated by John Zorn at Japan Society in 2006, Jon Pareles commented, "Among these musicians there was little East-West contrast. They're all part of an international downtown where every noise holds possibilities."[84] Reviewing an *onkyo* (literally, "sound," a term that here refers to computer-generated music) concert at the same location the previous year, Anthony Tommasini went further: "Onkyo challenges almost every assumption about the way new music is composed and performed. Even the traditional understanding of musicianship becomes irrelevant."[85] For Tommasini, work from Japan introduces the possibility of a reconfigured universality: hearing *onkyo*, the receptive listener potentially develops a new approach to all music.

Assuming universality is a corollary to surrender. In fact, it can be seen as a less-aware form of surrender. Like surrender, it downplays or even ignores altogether the tension inherent in cultural difference. The assumption of universality falsely assures audiences that they already possess the intellectual background to experience in full a performance from

Japan. Assuming universality runs the risk of closing off the possibility that theater from Japan adds something fresh and unexpected to conversations about culture.

Resistance

Taking the position that efforts to fathom the foreign are likely to fail is in itself a strategy of negotiation. Music, contrary to the commonplace claim that it is a "universal language," provides some of the most striking examples. As B. H. Haggin unequivocally said in a review of the Azuma Kabuki Dancers and Musicians, "Most of us get nothing out of Japanese music."[86] Indeed, even scholars have addressed the difficulties of accessing some genres of Japanese music. An article by University of Michigan musicologist William Malm, a specialist on Japan, published prior to a concert of *nagauta* (a style of kabuki recitative and instrumental accompaniment) at Japan Society, noted, "[M]usic is not necessarily an international language. To appreciate nagauta as music rather than simply as exotic sounds, a special approach to listening is necessary." In contrast to what American audiences may expect in a musical piece, in *nagauta* "themes are not repeated, nor does the ending of a piece resemble the beginning."[87]

Resistance was forcefully expressed by John Rockwell, who wrote in 2004 that Japan "is part of the Western world economically and politically but not in its traditional music."[88] Some years earlier, in a review of a concert featuring a shamisen and hayashi ensemble at Asia Society, Rockwell said:

> Japanese art forms have always seemed about as distant as one could imagine. "Different" does not mean unapproachable, however; if one has faith in the universality of human expression, great art from any culture should be able to appeal outside itself. But classical Japanese art can still seem to come from very far away, both in place and time. And when it is the greatest, most highly differentiated art, and it is being executed with unusual skill, that sense of distance is all the more accentuated.

He concluded, "[T]he total effect, like so much of Japanese culture, was a strange and tension-filled dialectic between savagery and ethereal calm."[89] For Rockwell incomprehension is an inevitable response to what he saw as the "distance" of Japanese culture.

Resistance is often called forth by what are perceived to be transgressive border crossings. Bernard Holland's response to a Music From Japan concert in 1995 was that "[t]he six pieces demonstrated the felicities and disappointments of trying to express one's own sensibilities through the cultural means of others. The composers were Japanese, but with the exception of the sho (a distant relative of our harmonica) used in Toshi Ichiyanagi's 'Music for Violin, Sho and Piano,' here was Japanese culture forcibly filtered through instruments embodying European ideas of tuning, interval and sonority."[90]

Transgressive border crossings extend to language. In reference to the reception of work produced by Ninagawa in England, Tetsuo Kishi and Graham Bradshaw have observed an interesting pattern.

> When the production was in Japanese[,] which the critics could not understand, they loved it. When the production was in English[,] which they understood perfectly well, they hated it. They did not seem to realize, however, that Ninagawa is an extremely consistent artist. . . . So why did they respond positively to the Japanese-language productions? The obvious answer would be: they loved them because they were able to concentrate on non-verbal aspects of the productions without being bothered with what the actors were saying.[91]

I interpret the phenomenon somewhat differently. When Ninagawa's productions are in Japanese, they are remote and exotic—and "safe" to like. When they are in English, they become transgressive—and subject to critical disapprobation.

Failure to communicate may be an unintended consequence of the very technologies of access that are meant to facilitate the process. The information relayed through the transistorized translation system at the presentations of bunraku in 1966 led Barnes to conclude, "The ideas here are alien to us not only in the matter of time—so, for example, are those of John Webster—but also in the matter of our own Western humanist tradition."[92] It may also be a case of "mechanical" failure: a 1973 presentation by the Red Buddha Theatre at the Brooklyn Academy of Music was "unintelligible from the stage," wrote Barnes, "and barely visible through the misty spectacles of lengthy program notes."[93] Alternatively, the possibility exists that, technology notwithstanding, failure is inevitable: despite explanations provided by an onstage narrator for a 1967 dance concert by Rankei Fujima, Don McDonagh wrote, "Total understanding of Miss Fujima's tales eludes the first-time viewer [of her work]."[94]

Resistance is at times coupled with unambiguously Orientalist-inflected condescension or even derision. In 1969 Harold Clurman commented,

"The sounds emitted by Kabuki actors, musicians, [and] narrators, are frequently weird, startling or laughable to the Occidental ear. The movements, deliberate, pigeon-toed—the men playing women's parts walk with a slight break at the knees—are also peculiar."[95] Similarly, for Rockwell the theatrical enactment in 1973 of a Buddhist ceremony at the Brooklyn Academy of Music left the impression of "shouting and gabbling better than any contemporary avant-garde chorus."[96]

The view that communication cannot take place is sometimes framed by analysis reminiscent of—or even directly borrowed from—Ruth Benedict's *The Chrysanthemum and the Sword: Patterns of Japanese Culture* (1946). (Benedict, as mentioned in chapter 1, wrote her national character study on Japan for the US Office of War Information.) For example, "Samurai Saga," published in *Time* magazine in 1969, told readers that the "Grand Kabuki illuminates the paradox in the Japanese character, an outward decorum of almost inhuman restraint masking an inner fury of almost demonic feelings."[97] Reviewing the four butoh ensembles from Japan that appeared at the American Dance Festival in the summer of 1982, Kisselgoff described Japanese society as one that "accepts both flower arranging and hara-kiri."[98] She made the same observation almost two decades later in her assessment of the Japanese dance troupe H Art Chaos, writing, "To wonder how the same culture could [at] once produce kamikaze pilots and flower arrangements is to delve into the kind of protest that 'Secret Club' [the title of the troupe's presentation] embodies on an oblique but multilayered level."[99] In an essay on Japanese dance written in 2006, Rockwell invoked Benedict and her idea of "an inherent tension between aesthetics and bellicosity in the Japanese character."[100] References to "bellicosity," "demonic feelings," "kamikaze pilots," and "hara-kiri" call up images of Japan as wartime enemy, suggesting that "restraint" and "flower arrangements" are merely an aestheticized mask.

Resistance is negotiation by non-negotiation, a reluctance to concede that true understanding is possible. Critics employing this strategy are thus on guard so to speak against the notion that attempts to receive foreign performance on its own terms can ever succeed. Thus, they can find themselves reduced to superficialities and clichés, ostensibly out of respect for differences that are too great to bridge. When they adopt a posture of incomprehension they are negating the very idea of cultural exchange.

"[T]he Japanese language spoken in the theatre," J. Thomas Rimer has written, "gains much of its power from its very ambiguity, and any translator must perforce trim back those suggested overtones, leaving a sometimes luxurious tree with only a few bare branches."[101] For audiences solely dependent on technologies of access, the branches may be even fewer and considerably more bare. Nonetheless, critics have to find a way to respond intelligently and analytically to Japan-related theater in all of its variety. In their negotiations with the foreign they may advocate surrendering to the pleasures and rewards of performances without being concerned with literal intelligibility. Another strategy is to assume that theater from Japan contains enough universally accessible content to transcend issues of language and culture. A third strategy involves putting up resistance to the very possibility of cross-cultural communication.

There is a complex relationship between critics' reception of theater from Japan and the technologies of access used in presentations. When *The Doll Sisters* (*Ningyō shimai*), a play written by Taeko Tomioka and directed and designed by Setsu Asakura, was presented at La MaMa in 2008, supertitle technology was rejected by Asakura. She believed that it would be more distracting than helpful. Non-Japanese-speaking audience members had no choice but to consult the abbreviated summary printed in the program brochure that was distributed as they took their seats. In fact, they were exhorted by the house manager several times to read the material before the lights went down. *The Doll Sisters* is an important play about contemporary women and psychological struggle. Following its successful debut in Japan in 1976, the production traveled two years later to La MaMa. In 1978 computerized supertitle systems did not exist, and audiences necessarily had to rely on less sophisticated "technologies"—such as program notes. In 2008 the director's choice not to use supertitles marked a kind of paradoxical return to an exoticized, linguistically incomprehensible Japan. *Times* critic Anita Gates wrote:

> Let's call them Eager Sister and Skeptical Sister. One wants to run away with her new romance. The other thinks she's insane, because men are no good and will only hurt her. At least I believe that's what's going on with the battling lead characters in "The Doll Sisters," the genteel and seductive play-with-marionettes now at the Annex Theater at La MaMa E.T.C. I can't vouch for the subtlety of the dialogue, because it is all in the original Japanese, and there are no sub- or surtitles, only a brief plot synopsis in the program. But I can vouch for the fervent emotional truth in the performances of Kazuko Yoshiyuki and Mieko Yuki as the sisters.[102]

Had the director chosen to provide real-time access to words spoken onstage (even in the form of incomplete and potentially distracting supertitles), the array of strategies in the critic's reaction may well have been different.

American critical responses to theater from Japan have been constrained by unresolved linguistic contestation and tension. Even continuing technological advances do not carry the promise of substantially mitigating the effects of these constraints. However, should an American theater of translation of works from Japan become more firmly established beyond the occasional production that takes place today, far more nuanced responses to theater from Japan overall would likely be the outcome.

7

Closure and Counterpoint

The JapanNYC Festival, the Earthquake and Tsunami Benefit Concerts, and Circuits of Mobility and Exchange, 2010–2011

For the last few decades, the pendulum of Japan's images overseas has swung back and forth between positive and negative poles, and between universalist and particularist approaches.[1]

In his introduction to *Cultural Mobility: A Manifesto* Stephen Greenblatt cites the "urgent need to rethink fundamental assumptions about the fate of culture in an age of global mobility." Some cultures, he notes, "are routinely celebrated for their depth, authenticity, and wholeness." Others "are criticized for shallowness, disorientation, and incoherence."[2] Within the narrative framework of America's Japan, *both* celebration and criticism regularly—and sometimes simultaneously—characterize the reception of the performing arts. When I started this project, I could not have predicted the two sets of Japan-focused performing arts events that provide a ready-made endpoint for my look at how "Japan" and "Japanese culture" have been discursively constructed, reconstructed, and transformed in response to productions of theater, music, and dance that have taken place in New York since the postwar 1950s. There was the JapanNYC festival—which ran from September 2010 to April 2011—initiated, coordinated, and in part hosted by Carnegie Hall. And there were the post-earthquake and tsunami marathon concerts, which were swiftly and skillfully pulled together by composer-musician John Zorn in March and April 2011 to raise money for Japan Society's relief fund.[3] Both sets of events unfolded against the backdrop of the ongoing flow of Japan-related programming that also happened to be scheduled around the city during the same period.

JapanNYC was huge, with its multitude of presentations and venues easily constituting the single most extensive (mostly)-live-arts-Japan initiative ever to take place in New York. There were the concerts at Carnegie Hall—the Saito Kinen Orchestra conducted by Seiji Ozawa with soloists who included Mitsuko Uchida (piano), Yukio Tanaka (biwa), and Kifu Mitsuhashi (shakuhachi); the NHK Symphony Orchestra under André Previn; and the Bach Collegium Japan led by Masaaki Suzuki. Shamisen artists Yutaka Oyama and Masahiro Nitta also appeared at Carnegie Hall, as did violinist Midori; pianist Aimi Kobayashi; and jazz pianist, conductor, and composer Toshiko Akiyoshi. "A Tribute to Toru Takemitsu" was the title of another Carnegie Hall festival program with guitarists Kazumi Watanabe and Daisuke Suzuki, accordionist Coba, and percussionist Tomohiro Yahiro. Asia Society offered a concert by the rock band Shonen Knife in conjunction with its art museum exhibition Yoshitomo Nara: Nobody's Fool. Le Poisson Rouge hosted experimentalist rock musicians Deerhoof. Lincoln Center was the setting for the Kodo Drummers and the Martha Graham Dance Company (in pieces featuring sets designed by Isamu Noguchi). Lincoln Center also presented the Juilliard Percussion Ensemble under Daniel Druckman and the New Juilliard Ensemble under Joel Sachs playing works by contemporary composers from Japan. Soh Daiko gave performances at the Brooklyn Center for the Performing Arts and at Lehman College. Two separate programs at Columbia University's Miller Theatre—"Glories of the Japanese Traditional Music Heritage: Winds and Strings of Change" and "Glories of the Japanese Traditional Music Heritage: Japanese Sacred Court Music and Ancient Soundscapes Reborn"—included musicians Yukio Tanaka (biwa), Kifu Mitsuhashi and James Schlefer (shakuhachi), Yoko Nishi (koto), Hitomi Nakamura (hichiriki), Takeshi Sasamoto (ryuteki), and Mayumi Miyata (sho). Eiko and Koma appeared at the Baryshnikov Arts Center. The Kashu-juku noh theater was at Japan Society, which also was the locale for Bye Bye Kitty!!! Between Heaven and Hell in Contemporary Japanese Art—a gallery show based on the work of fifteen artists "who reject the outworn narratives of cuteness and infantilism fashionable in Western presentations of Japanese contemporary art."[4] Also under the JapanNYC umbrella were the Film Forum's two-week series of films scored by Toru Takemitsu and the Brooklyn Botanic Garden's exhibition of bonsai from the C. V. Starr Bonsai Museum—the same C. V. Starr who in 1958 underwrote the new Metropolitan Opera production of *Madama Butterfly* crafted by kabuki director Yoshio Aoyama and scene and costume designer Motohiro Nagasaka.

In some ways it was puzzling why Carnegie Hall would hold a festival celebrating Japan in the first decade of the twenty-first century. Publicity material invited audiences to "[d]elve into the dynamic artistic world of a country with a beguiling, ever-changing cultural tradition. Hear the best Japanese musicians—including two orchestras that festival Artistic Director Seiji Ozawa founded—and explore Noh theater, manga, film, butoh dance, and pop art at partner institutions throughout New York City."[5] Such wording seems reminiscent of an earlier era (the 1980s, for example), when "Japan was both the apex and the enigma of global modernity, especially among North Americans transfixed by the contrast between the nation's emerging economic power and its idiosyncratic local practices."[6]

Even given that "Japan" is never seen as entirely familiar—and is thus subject to being "introduced" over and over again to US audiences—there were other dynamics at work. One was that JapanNYC was the kind of exercise powerful institutions like Carnegie Hall conduct to confirm, assert, and broaden their authority to mediate culture on a large scale. "Clive Gillinson, in his six years as executive and artistic director of Carnegie Hall, has developed an ever more expansive view of its mission and constituency," James Oestreich has written. With programs such as JapanNYC, "Carnegie has increasingly ventured beyond its walls."[7] Another is that the festival was a tribute to Seiji Ozawa. The trajectory of Ozawa's career encapsulates Japan's postwar recovery and successful ascent to a position of economic and cultural strength and influence. As a Japanese conductor of orchestras worldwide he incarnates Carnegie Hall's position at the epicenter of globalized "Western" classical music.[8]

Addressing prospective ticket buyers in the JapanNYC publicity brochure, Ozawa said, "We have so many things to be proud of in Japan today. I want you to see our culture—not from 50 or 30 years ago, but today. And I hope American audiences find something truly unique in these performances and events. That is my dream and my hope."[9] For anyone taking the words literally, however, it was not entirely clear what "our culture" and "today" meant in relation to the content of the Carnegie Hall programming. Although work by Takemitsu, Atsuhiko Gondai, Jo Kondo, Hiroya Miura, Somei Satoh, Ushio Torikai, and several other composers from Japan was featured, so was music by Strauss, Prokofiev, Beethoven, Brahms, Schubert, Chopin, Ravel, Schumann, Bach, and Haydn. "As the world's most prominent Japanese violinist and a frequent visitor to Carnegie Hall," Allan Kozinn wrote in one of the festival reviews, "Midori undoubtedly had a guaranteed berth in Carnegie's JapanNYC festival." For her festival concert Midori "could have assembled a program of Japanese music" or "could also have played a standard recital and not seemed out of step." Her choice was "an installment in her continuing series of new-music programs, with one work by a Japanese composer [Toshio Hosokawa]."[10] The rest of the pieces were by composers from England, Australia, Scotland, and the United States.

Neither was it entirely evident what "our culture" and "today" meant with respect to the lineup of festival performers. A number of the participating artists—like Midori, Akiyoshi, and Eiko and Koma—are long-time residents of the United States, where they developed and base their careers. Ozawa's own résumé shows nearly three decades as conductor of the Boston Symphony Orchestra. The artists arriving directly from Japan for JapanNYC included musicians who presented classical Japanese works on traditional instruments. The troupe of noh and kyogen actors that traveled to New York were "providing," as the festival brochure explained, "this rare opportunity for American audiences to experience the 600-year-old tradition of noh and kyogen performed back-to-back."[11]

Ozawa's statement was clearly not to be interpreted strictly in terms of temporal or geographic boundaries. Rather, it expressed the wish that Americans conceptualize Japan and Japanese culture in terms of a wide-ranging, border-challenging present-ness, rather than in terms of a geographically restrictive, narrowly conceived past-ness. It was an understated rejection of the ahistorical tenets of America's kabuki-Japan—represented by the youthful Tsugaru shamisen musicians Oyama and Nitta, who "bring a modern sensibility to an ancient, highly percussive folk music."[12]

What makes JapanNYC particularly significant from the perspective of this study is that it brought together a roster of individuals with long and successful careers in the United States already behind them. In doing so the festival paid tribute not just to Ozawa but also to others—such as Eiko and Koma and Akiyoshi—as key figures in America's postwar cultural relations with Japan, while at the same time symbolically capping off that long chapter in history. Within the context of JapanNYC, the careers of these artists embodied the successful realization of John D. Rockefeller III's vision of friendly relations between the United States and Japan.

Ozawa's ill health imparted to the event a special urgency and poignancy. Months before his first scheduled appearance, there was palpable worry that the conductor's condition might prevent him from traveling to the United States. Oestreich reported from Japan that an obviously frail Ozawa was able only partially to carry out his work as conductor of the Saito Kinen Orchestra, which was scheduled for a December appearance at JapanNYC, "Carnegie's major festival of the season."[13] He wrote that no one better symbolizes Japan's "intense fascination with Western classical music" than Ozawa, "who has maintained a booming career in the West over half a century."[14] Shortly before the scheduled December appearance in New York, Oestrich again pressed home the point—in an article titled "Ozawa's Illness Shadows Festival He Inspired"—that the "assimilation of Western classical music" in Japan is "well exemplified" by Ozawa.[15] The concerts went on as planned, although Ozawa gave over some of his conducting duties to colleagues. "[O]nce the music started," noted Anthony Tommasini, Ozawa "conducted with balletic gestures and complete absorption and, as is his way, from memory."[16] In the end, the conductor's role in JapanNYC was in fact curtailed: his scheduled return to New York during the latter part of the festival with the Seiji Ozawa Ongaku-juku (the youth-focused Seiji Ozawa Music Academy Orchestra) was canceled because of an operation he needed to undergo.

There was also poignancy in the appearances of Eiko and Koma and Akiyoshi—all of whom had already been signaling to New York audiences the inevitability of their departure from the stage. For JapanNYC Eiko and Koma offered multimedia exhibits, performances, workshops, and discussions "[c]elebrating 30 years of innovative beauty."[17] The performances, collectively titled *Naked: A Living Installation,* were "part of a three-year, nationwide retrospective project of the couple's work," as Roslyn Sulcas wrote. "The performers are on a tiny island of earth, black feathers, vegetation and sticks, surrounded by darkness, water dripping slowly somewhere behind them. . . . The intimate scale of 'Naked,' our proximity to Eiko and Koma, is important here. We can see their stomachs and chests moving as they breathe, almost feel the tiny shifts of a finger or a foot. Their lives, their deaths, playing out before us, are absorbed into our bodies, become our own."[18] On her side Akiyoshi was presented as the "legendary pianist-composer [who] leads a tour through the history of jazz piano."[19] For the better part of a decade, she had also been taking stock of her past. In 2007 she was accorded "lifetime honors" by the National Endowment for the Arts, which designated her an NEA Jazz Master—"the nation's highest honor in jazz."[20] "She is 73," Ben Ratliff had written in a Carnegie Hall concert review four years earlier, "and her intent is to focus more on her piano playing. So while she conceived the performance . . . as a three-decade retrospective of big-band compositions, she also said it would be her last ever with [her big band], and appeared to mean it."[21] At JapanNYC Akiyoshi took the stage with only her husband, the tenor saxophone and flute player Lew Tabackin, and two backup musicians.

Other artists, too, captured the end-of-an-era sensibility. There were the various events in honor of Takemitsu (who passed away in 1996), with whom Ozawa had a long and close relationship. In 1967 Takemitsu's *Novem-*

ber Steps, a work for orchestra, shakuhachi, and biwa commissioned by the New York Philharmonic for its gala 125th anniversary concert, brought renown in the United States to both the composer and Ozawa as the Philharmonic's young guest conductor on that auspicious occasion. (Ozawa was already at that time musical director of the Toronto Symphony Orchestra.) The end-of-an-era sensibility was projected even by Midori, who had made her sensational US debut with the New York Philharmonic in 1982 at the age of eleven. It was just two years before that, as noted in chapter 4, that the *Times* had published an article that alluded to doubts "in lay circles as to whether performers from the Far East can really understand or play Western music."[22] In the ensuing decades Midori has repeatedly shattered any doubts that may have existed. From her perspective, as shown in the pieces she selected for JapanNYC, which were written by composers from around the globe, her birth in Japan and her ethnicity were mere biographical facts at the service of festival organizers. The presence of Soh Daiko, the New York taiko drum ensemble founded in 1979, was a further example of the festival's end-of-an-era sensibility. The joint appearance at Japan Society in 1987 by Soh Daiko and the Japan-based Kodo taiko troupe had helped definitively sanction the authenticity of the New York performers. By booking both troupes, albeit in separate appearances, JapanNYC recalled that moment and paid tribute to Soh Daiko as the leading example in New York of taiko drumming as "one of the most globally successful performance genres to emerge in postwar Japan."[23]

The marathon concerts benefiting Japan Society's Japan Earthquake Relief Fund were a counterpoint to JapanNYC, marking a transition from Seiji Ozawa to John Zorn as the symbolic interface between Japan's performing arts and New York audiences. The concerts took place at Columbia University's Miller Theatre on 21 March, at the Abrons Arts Center on 8 April, and at Japan Society on 9 April. Although not all of the performers had an obvious connection to Japan, Zorn's focus on "downtown" experimentalists imbued the concerts with the flavor of a scaled-up version of his ongoing Tzadik Label Music Series at Japan Society. The Miller Theatre event included Yoko Ono and her Plastic Ono Band, Cibo Matto, Sonic Youth, Mike Patton, and Mephista with Ikue Mori on laptop. The Abrons Arts Center double-bill lined up Norah Jones, Ned Rothenberg, Thurston Moore, Jesse Harris, and Ikue Mori, among others. The Japan Society concert, where the participation of Philip Glass, Laurie Anderson, and Lou Reed made it seem "it was like the 1980s again,"[24] also brought together the Japan- and New York-based rock groups Suzan, Hard Nips, Me & Mars, and Echostream. Other performers, representing the broader range of

Japan Society performers, included singer-pianists Akiko Yano and Ryuichi Sakamoto, James Nyoraku Schlefer (shakuhachi), Yumi Kurosawa (koto), and Mari Kimura (violin).

A generation after Ellen Stewart brought theater and dance from Japan downtown to La MaMa, John Zorn played an analogous role in music through Lower East Side locations such as Tonic, where he was a regular curator and performer, and The Stone, which he opened in 2005 and where he holds the position of artistic director. Zorn is a contradictory figure in the narrative of America's Japan. Despite the prominent place he gives to female performers in his Tzadik series at Japan Society, Zorn's own compositions appear to reference a retrograde America's Japan (and America's Asia) in works like *Forbidden Fruit* and *Osaka Bondage*. This has attracted the scholarly attention of Ellie M. Hisama, who has studied pieces by Zorn "that represent Asians or Asian women in their music, texts, and accompanying visual images."[25] She argues that work such as *Forbidden Fruit,* which employs a female voice speaking in Japanese about sexual activity, "steadfastly positions the Asian female under a male Orientalist gaze"—adding that other works by Zorn "hold her there with an even tighter grip."[26] Nevertheless, it cannot be denied that Zorn is among a handful of individuals who have a significant record of opening up space within the United States for performers from Japan—through his own venue, the ones over which he is occasionally invited to preside, and his record label. The spring 2011 benefits arranged by Zorn were a warm expression of US friendship toward Japan at a time of crisis. They were also an affirmation of the position of Japan Society—the site of one of Zorn's concerts and administrator of the relief fund that received the proceeds from all of them—as the main stage, not just in New York but everywhere outside Japan, for structuring and conveying knowledge about Japan through the performing arts. In his role as one of the society's established guest curators, Zorn himself directly contributes to the way the organization shapes such knowledge.

JapanNYC and the benefit concerts took place against the backdrop of "regular" Japan-related programming that also happened to be scheduled in New York in the August 2010 to July 2011 period. It included butoh troupe Sankai Juku at the Joyce Theater in October; concerts at Le Poisson Rouge by "noise" experimentalist Merzbow in September and jazz musicians Satoko Fujii, Natsuki Tamura, and their ma-do ensemble in June; and electronic experimentalists Carl Stone (whose performance and teaching career is closely tied to Japan) and Ikue Mori in separate appearances during the year at The Stone. The rock band X Japan, "[t]he biggest Japanese rock band the average American has never heard of,"[27] made its New York debut in October at the Roseland Ballroom. On the 2010–11 Japan Society calendar were actor Yoshi Oida, the Contemporary Dance Showcase, and musicians Akiko Yano, Hikashu, and Tomoe Shinohara. The annual February concert of Music From Japan took place at the Baruch Performing Arts Center. There were also performances by dancer-choreographer Yuko Takahashi in the Battery Dance Company's Downtown Dance Festival at Battery Park in August; jazz composer and pianist Hiromi at the Blue Note, also in August; koto player Yumi Kurosawa at the Rubin Museum of Art in December; and violinist-composer Mari Kimura at the Tenri Cultural Institute in June. *Temple of the Golden Pavilion* was directed by Amon Miyamoto at the Lincoln Center Festival in July. Roughly speaking, avant-garde visual/sound artist and composer Ryoji Ikeda bookended the year with his concert presentation *datamatics [ver. 2.0]* (along with a related gallery installation, *the transcendental*) in September 2010 at the French Institute Alliance Française (FIAF)'s Crossing the Line Festival and with his sound and light installation, *the transfinite,* in May and June 2011 at the Park Avenue Armory.

Whereas JapanNYC and the benefit concerts unequivocally emphasized connections between the United States and Japan, the ongoing flow of Japan-related programming that took place within established circuits of cultural mobility and exchange varied in the degree to which it foregrounded a Japan identity. Even though director and choreographer Ushio Amagatsu and the members of the Sankai Juku butoh troupe work and tour in Japan, they have been based in Paris since the early 1980s—a fact that some critics seem almost inclined to suppress. In a review titled "From Japan, a Reminder That We Are Dust, and to Dust We Return," Sulcas began by reminding readers that butoh is "the dance form that developed in Japan in the late 1950s."[28] Though mentioning Sankai Juku's success in France, she did not clarify that the artists are based there.

Music journalists celebrated both JapanNYC and the Music From Japan series as offering "myriad opportunities" during the 2010–11 season to "those interested in learning about Japanese culture."[29] "Flutes from the East and the West," a segment of Music From Japan's winter 2011 program, featured American composer and musician Elizabeth Brown and Japan-based instrumentalist Kohei Nishikawa. Pieces included a duet composed by Brown, in which she played the shakuhachi and Nishikawa played the noh flute. There was an interesting contrast in how the two artists presented themselves onstage: Brown, the American artist influenced by Japanese culture, wore a dress and performed throughout in a standing position. Nishikawa, the cultural heritage artist who was attired in a formal kimono and hakama "trousers," kneeled on a bright red mat when playing classical works on the shakuhachi.

Mari Kimura is an artist who directly and publicly addresses her Japanese identity. Like Ryuichi Sakamoto and Ikue Mori, she appeared in both the regularly scheduled 2010–11 programming and in one of Zorn's earthquake benefit concerts. Kimura, whose awards include a 2010 Guggenheim Fellowship, has been described as "a virtuoso playing at the edge."[30] She is renowned worldwide for her musicianship across the spectrum of the classical and experimental repertory—and for having introduced subharmonics as a musical technique that involves producing "pitches that sound up to an octave below the violin's lowest string without retuning."[31] A review of her breakthrough New York debut in 1994 incorporated a statement she made in the program notes: "I wanted to free myself from the boundaries of Western musical idioms, associated with traditional violin literature, to reflect my own Japanese heritage in my compositions."[32] Again speaking directly to audiences through the program notes for "Tradition/E–novation," which she curated for Music From Japan in 2009, Kimura said:

> When I go back to Japan, I see Japanese culture from the outside, but from the point of view of someone who used to be inside. My perception of contemporary Japanese music and artists may be quite different from what an American person, for example, would perceive as "Japanese music." I tend to look for contemporary Japanese composers who neither make too big a feature of their "Japanese-ness," nor have their European training so much at the forefront that there is little originality to tell them apart. I am most interested in the individuality of artists, Japanese or otherwise, who share a common background: Japanese land, air, food, and language that may have shaped their soul.[33]

By saying "Japanese or otherwise" in her statement Kimura was intriguingly inclusive, expressing an openness to artists who share a connection to Japan though they may not in fact be "Japanese" in terms of their ethnicity or nationality.

Reception/Japan

"Reception is consistently undertheorized as a space filled with both risk and potential—the risk of misunderstanding, and the potential for activist response (i.e., intervention)," Deborah Wong has written. "Given the susceptibility of American audiences to orientalist pleasure—their willingness to give themselves over to it—I must ask what happens when performers think they are saying one thing and audiences hear something else entirely, and whose responsibility it is to redirect the reading."[34] It has been the aim of this study to theorize the reception expressed in the writings that form the archive of America's Japan through the performing arts. The writings are not just about art: they are the product of and at the same time mold understandings of nation, race, and gender.

Talking about visual artists, Midori Yoshimoto has observed:

> In the 1950s and 1960s, most New York avant-garde artists and their supporting critics were still predominantly white men—with few exceptions. Ironically, by moving to their dream city, Japanese women artists were doubly removed from the center of the American art world by their ethnicity and gender. Memories of World War II, especially the Japanese attack on Pearl Harbor, had not faded in the minds of older generations of Americans. For more than three decades, racial and gender barriers were among the factors that obstructed these artists' recognition and led to their marginalization in American art history.[35]

In the case of the performing arts, however, there is evidence to suggest that their appearance as exotically attractive, kimono-costumed figures was crucial in bringing some Japanese women a level of recognition and respect for their art. The kimono-attired Tokuho Azuma, "a lovely creature to look at,"[36] pleased audiences and critics with a kabuki performance that radiated the image of "traditional" Japanese femininity. In 1956, the same year that the Azuma troupe was also in New York, twenty-six-year-old jazz pianist Toshiko Akiyoshi, who had arrived in the United States only months earlier to study at the Berklee College of Music, was already being lauded at the Newport Jazz Festival for her extraordinary musical talent. As the *Times* reported in one of a number of articles that took notice of her early on, "Toshiko Akiyoshi, a Japanese pianist who plays in the cool jazz idiom, looked very much in character in a flimsy blue and red kimono that was flicked by the damp wind."[37] There is no doubt that she was advised by her mentors to wear the kimono. The striking image of a young jazz-playing Japanese woman in a kimono (and a "flimsy" one at that) enabled Akiyoshi to slide past the fact that had she been a Japanese man at that moment in history it is far less likely that she would have been invited onto that stage.

Akiyoshi quickly won national acclaim for her musicianship—but the kimono remained useful. "When she opened in Manhattan last week," *Time* magazine noted in 1957, "a pressagent [*sic*] told Toshiko that she should wear a kimono all the time because she was, after all, the only female jazz pianist from Japan. As a concession, she wears a kimono on Saturday nights (the obi is apt to be too tight for really freewheeling playing, she complains), but the rest of the time she performs in Western cocktail dresses." Even though the anonymous writer observed that her playing—"clearly some of the best jazz piano around"—"demonstrates that she need not rely on costume for her success," it was instrumental in allowing her to establish her identity as a musician in the United States.[38]

A quarter century later, in a 1981 review of a koto recital by Reiko Kamata at Carnegie Hall, Allen Hughes's praise for the music was coupled with "Beautifully attired in traditional Japanese dress, she knelt on a bright red rug while she played."[39] Actually, as Hughes commented, she was so low on the stage that she was invisible to a large portion of the audience, but the implication was that she perfectly projected the stereotyped image of Japanese feminine beauty. The very next year, in what was otherwise an important profile of Naoyuki Miura and his Music From Japan project, Harold Schonberg described Miura as a "short, quiet, intense 40-year-old."[40] The first adjective, "short," stands out, not just as a neutral description of height but also as a reminder of Japanese male stereotyping that reverberates back to the war years. It was Schonberg who in 1964 had referred to the Japan Philharmonic Orchestra in terms of the "strange presence of 85 Japanese faces."[41]

"Imagine trying to sort out what parts of counterculture were Japanese and which were Western," Steven C. Ridgely has written in his study of Shuji Terayama.

> The globalization paradigm would inevitably gravitate toward claims about the enduring nature of Japanese cultural patterns, that against all odds we could still find group orientation, vertical society, minimalist aesthetics, and some hint of the samurai code in as unlikely a place as the "Japanese version" of a hippie. Alternatively, assuming the 1960s youth to still be shell-shocked from the war (over before most of them were born) and somehow resentful of America is a thinly glossed update to the old Orientalism. . . . Such an approach would serve only to rein in and tame Japanese counterculture, to sever the ties it made, and to undo what it achieved.[42]

Well into the twenty-first century, Anna Kisselgoff, as head dance critic for the *Times,* was writing, "An accent on the wacky and original makes the Japanese Contemporary Dance Showcase a hot ticket every year, as proved again on Friday night at the Japan Society." The five troupes in the eighth annual showcase "demonstrated that experimental dance in Japan is as lively as ever." But what did "experimental dance" mean? Kisselgoff found in soloist Kaiji Moriyama a "stunning Noh-like purity and fierceness." The Sennichimae Blue Sky Dance Club was populated with "gleeful schoolgirls in a pop brand of Butoh."[43] Japan, as David Novak has noted, emerged in the twentieth century as "the site of an idealized foreign tradition, but also a bizarre world of arbitrary postmodern hybridity. Japan became the 'mirror of modernity,' whose avant-garde refractions of the West filtered out through the incommensurable prism of the 'Japanese version.'"[44]

In the postwar 1950s America's kabuki-Japan formed in response to a cold-war American imperative to secure Japan as a friend in Asia through cultural diplomacy—manifested in the ultimately successful project to bring a Grand Kabuki troupe to the United States. By the 1970s and into the 1980s, having emerged as the second-largest economy in the world, Japan put considerable emphasis on cultural exchange as a way to foster better relations with an American public barraged and angered by reports of US-Japan trade friction. The Japan Foundation was established in 1972 as the principal source of administrative support and funding for cultural exchange in the performing arts (and other areas). Despite the onset of recession in the early 1990s, Japan found an eager global market for its cultural products—especially animation and computer games—but the frisson of "cool Japan" could potentially attach itself to any medium, even the "high art" theater, music, and dance produced by Japan Society, Music From Japan, the Lincoln Center Festival, and La MaMa (where Japan had long been cool, following the visits by Terayama and Higashi in 1970).

Looking back over the sixty-year period of this study, no one needs reminding that the mediascape and culturescape have vastly changed. The critics, correspondents, and scholar/experts—the privileged few who once regularly spoke authoritatively for and to audiences in wide-circulation newspapers and magazines—have all but given way to a much more fragmented input. This input comprises the voices of the audience members themselves, people who readily find digital outlets for opinions and information they want to share. Faubion Bowers's long run as the go-to expert on Japanese culture (especially the performing arts) for institutions such as the *New York Times* would be unimaginable now. He taught people a great deal through his articles and books, and he likely inspired a number to go out and learn more on their own, but his enormous enthusiasm for his subject matter morphed into mythic representations that were all too often accepted as fact.

The narrative of America's Japan through the performing arts is open-ended. Kabuki-as-metaphor is just one bit of evidence. "Discussions of authenticity and inauthenticity are legion within the ever-expanding field of cultural studies," Phillip Vannini and J. Patrick Williams have written.[45] Kabuki, along with the other traditional forms, once epitomized an aestheticized authenticity put forward by American opinion leaders to replace images of wartime Japan. Nowadays, traditional theater/music/dance from Japan fulfills a more generalized desire for a kind of anti-globalization authenticity, the components of which are defined by the adjectives *unique* and *local.* At the same time, Japan is widely regarded as an attractive source of new and interesting cultural products for the world at large. The fact that the French Institute Alliance Française (FIAF), whose job is to promote French culture, spotlighted Ryoji Ikeda in 2010 at its cutting-edge Crossing the Line Festival in New York easily makes the point.

Even so, America's Japan does exhibit a degree of historical inertia. In his foreword to *A Guide to the Japanese Stage: From Traditional to Cutting Edge,* Mansai Nomura felt the need to remind readers that "[t]he world of Japanese theater today presents a very complex picture."[46] The necessity of such an assertion reflects the continuing weight of America's kabuki-Japan even while so much of the complexity to which Nomura referred had already been amply shown to US audiences through cultural exchange. Ellen Stewart's death in January 2011 was an occasion to recall her launch of La MaMa in the early 1960s as a pioneering venue for experimental American and international theater. Tributes to Stewart specifically mentioned her role in introducing new Japanese performance to New York. In 2007 she was awarded the Japan Art Association's prestigious Praemium Imperiale. The prize, awarded annually to leading artists from around the world, was established in 1989 to honor the memory of Prince Takamatsu, former governor of the association and a sponsor of the visits to New York by the Azuma Kabuki Dancers and Musicians. Her selection for the prize can be read as a sign of Japanese weariness with America's kabuki-Japan. It helps send the message, as Stewart began doing forty years ago, that Japanese theater is *not* all about kabuki.[47] As the large number and manifold character of the Japan-related performing arts events that took place over the course of 2010 to 2011 suggest, America's kabuki-Japan has perhaps finally given way to a more nuanced and dynamic conversation about artistic production and encounter.

Notes

Introduction

1. Clive Barnes, "Twain Meet in City Ballet's 'Bugaku,'" *New York Times,* 21 June 1977.

2. "Presenter Interview: New Developments in the Japan Society, a Promoter of Exchange between Japan and the U.S. for 100 Years," Japan Foundation, Performing Arts Network Japan, 13 October 2007, http://performingarts.jp/E/pre_interview/0709/1.html (accessed 29 February 2012).

3. John Rockwell, "The Enigmas, the Oddities: What to Make of Dance from Japan," *New York Times,* 20 January 2006.

4. Clyde Haberman, "Skirmishes on the Economic Frontier: Trade Tensions with Japan May Get Even Worse," *New York Times,* 5 January 1986. As M. J. Heale has noted, "In 1981 the US trade deficit with Japan was about $10 billion; by 1985 it was a staggering $50 billion—the largest trade imbalance ever recorded between two economies." M. J. Heale, "Anatomy of a Scare: Yellow Peril Politics in America, 1980–1993," *Journal of American Studies* 43, no. 1 (2009): 24.

5. David Brooks, "Weekness [*sic*] and Endurance," *New York Times,* 18 November 2010. "In the 50 years since the American entry into World War II," Susan D. Moeller has written, "the American press has been the pre-eminent institution directing what the American public sees of Japan and the Japanese." Susan D. Moeller, "Pictures of the Enemy: Fifty Years of Images of Japan in the American Press, 1941–1992," *Journal of American Culture* 19, no. 1 (1996): 29. Daniel Marcus has referred to outlets such as the *New York Times* and *Time* magazine as "organizations [that] have set the agenda and determined the tone for most of the other reporting in the United States . . . [and have served as] central mediators of political discourse." Daniel Marcus, *Happy Days and Wonder Years: The Fifties and the Sixties in Contemporary Cultural Politics* (New Brunswick, NJ: Rutgers University Press, 2004), 6.

6. Sally Banes, "Introduction," in *Reinventing Dance in the 1960s: Everything Was Possible,* ed. Sally Banes (Madison: University of Wisconsin Press, 2003), xiv.

7. H. D. Harootunian, "America's Japan/Japan's Japan," in *Japan in the World,* ed. Masao Miyoshi and H. D. Harootunian (Durham: Duke University Press, 1993), 200.

8. Harootunian, "America's Japan/Japan's Japan," 216, 220.

9. Harootunian, "America's Japan/Japan's Japan," 215–16.

10. Clive Gillinson, "A Unique Journey of Discovery," in Carnegie Hall Festivals, *JapanNYC: Music and Arts from Today's Japan—Over 65 Events Citywide on Sale Now* (New York: Carnegie Hall, 2010), 2.

11. While Zorn's fund-raising concerts headlined the outpouring of goodwill and generosity from the New York performing arts community toward the people of Japan, there were numerous other charitable theater, dance, and music initiatives in the weeks and months after the catastrophes.

12. Jon Pareles, "Allies in Improvisation and in a Cause," *New York Times,* 28 March 2011.

13. Christina Klein, *Cold War Orientalism: Asia in the Middlebrow Imagination, 1945–1961* (Berkeley: University of California Press, 2003), 13.

14. Klein, *Cold War Orientalism,* 103.

15. Klein, *Cold War Orientalism,* 132.

16. Christopher Benfey, *The Great Wave: Gilded Age Misfits, Japanese Eccentrics, and the Opening of Old Japan* (New York: Random House, 2003), xv.

17. Sally Banes, *Greenwich Village, 1963: Avant-Garde Performance and the Effervescent Body* (Durham: Duke University Press, 1993), 10. For a history of New York's downtown theater—including the development of La MaMa—see Stephen J. Bottoms, *Playing Underground: A Critical History of the 1960s Off-Off-Broadway Movement* (Ann Arbor: University of Michigan Press, 2004).

18. Klein, *Cold War Orientalism,* 9.

19. Stephen Greenblatt, "Cultural Mobility: An Introduction," in Stephen Greenblatt, with Ines G. Županov, Reinhard Meyer-Kalkus, Heike Paul, Pál Nyíri, and Friederike Pannewick, *Cultural Mobility: A Manifesto* (New York: Cambridge University Press, 2010), 5.

20. Banes, *Greenwich Village, 1963,* 3.

21. Paul J. Yoon, "Asian Masculinities and Parodic Possibility in Odaiko Solos and Filmic Representations," *Asian Music* 40, no. 1 (2009): 101.

22. Deborah Wong, *Speak it Louder: Asian Americans Making Music* (New York: Routledge, 2004), 219.

23. Takeshi Matsuda, *Soft Power and Its Perils: U.S. Cultural Policy in Early Postwar Japan and Permanent Dependency* (Washington, DC: Woodrow Wilson Center Press; Stanford: Stanford University Press, 2007), 257.

24. Saskia Sassen uses the term *spaces of authority* in connection with the tall buildings that signify corporate culture in an urban context. The phrase, I think, well applies to the high-profile arts institutions I cite here. Saskia Sassen, "Analytic Borderlands: Race, Gender, and Representation in the New City," in *Representing the City: Ethnicity, Capital, and Culture in the 21st-Century Metropolis,* ed. Anthony D. King (New York: New York University Press, 1996), 191.

25. Douglas McGray, "Japan's Gross National Cool," *Foreign Policy* 130 (May–June 2002): 44–54.

26. Tadashi Uchino, *Crucible Bodies: Postwar Japanese Performance from Brecht to the New Millennium* (New York: Seagull Books, 2009), 4.

27. Uchino, *Crucible Bodies,* 23.

28. David Leheny, "A Narrow Place to Cross Swords: Soft Power and the Politics of Japanese Popular Culture in East Asia," in *Beyond Japan: The Dynamics of East Asian Regionalism,* ed. Peter J. Katzenstein and Takashi Shiraishi (Ithaca: Cornell University Press, 2006), 232.

29. Heritage studies, as William S. Logan and Laurajane Smith have written, "sees 'heritage' as a social and political construct encompassing all those places, artifacts and cultural expressions inherited from the past which, because they are seen to reflect and validate our identity as nations, communities, families and even individuals, are worthy of some form of respect and protection." William S. Logan and Laurajane Smith, "Series General Co-editors' Foreword," in *Intangible Heritage,* ed. Laurajane Smith and Natsuko Akagawa (New York: Routledge, 2009), xii.

30. See Barbara E. Thornbury, *The Folk Performing Arts: Traditional Culture in Contemporary Japan* (Albany: State University of New York Press), 1997.

31. For example, an article announcing the visit to New York of a kyogen troupe headed by Manzo Nomura noted that the sixty-six-year-old actor "has been declared an 'intangible cultural property,' the highest honor conferred by the Japanese Government on an artist." Louis Calta, "Japanese Actors Perform Kyogen: Manzo Nomura and 2 Sons Show Ancient Art Here," *New York Times,* 6 February 1964.

32. I have addressed the general topic of the performing arts and cultural diplomacy in Barbara E. Thornbury, "The View from Japan: The Traditional Performing Arts as Cultural Ambassadors Abroad," in *Japanese Theatre and the International Stage,* ed. Stanca Scholz-Cionca and Samuel L. Leiter (Boston: Brill, 2001), 213–27.

33. Examples of the articles in *Gekkan bunkazai* [Cultural treasures monthly] 275 (1986) include, followed by page numbers, Chikashi Mogi, "Kabuki," 4–10; Ichiro Ichikawa, "Kabuki no kaigai kōen are kore" [Some thoughts on kabuki productions abroad], 12; Shizuo Goto, "Bunraku," 14–20; Minosuke Yoshida, "Bunraku kaigai kōen no zuisō" [Reflections on bunraku productions abroad], 21; Makoto Kodama, "Nō," 24–28; Mansaku Nomura, "Kyōgen no kaigai kōryū" [Overseas exchange of kyogen], 30; Yoshihisa Oshida, "Gagaku," 32–39; Junichi Yoshinaga, "Minzoku geinō" [Folk performing arts], 40–43; and Kazuaki Kubo, "Kokusai Kōryū Kikin ga okonatta dentō geinō no kaigai kōryū" [Overseas exchange of the traditional performing arts carried out by the Japan Foundation], 44–46. Toshio Kawatake's name should also be mentioned among those scholars who have chronicled the cultural-exchange role played by kabuki, with essays such as "Kabuki no kaigai kōryū" [Overseas exchange of kabuki], *Gekkan bunkazai* 201 (1980): 4–11, and "Kaigai kōen sanjū-nen" [Thirty years of presentations abroad], *Engekikai* [Drama world] 42, no. 9 (1984): 74–77.

34. Kazuyoshi Nishi and Matsuda Tamotsu, eds., *Nōgaku kaigai kōen shiyō* [A history of noh productions abroad] (Tokyo: Kinseisha, 1988).

35. Chikashi Mogi, ed., *Kabuki kaigai kōen no kiroku* [A history of kabuki pro-

ductions abroad] (Tokyo: Shochiku, 1992). An English-language edition was also published: Shochiku Company, ed., *Grand Kabuki: Overseas Tours, 1928–1993* (Tokyo: Shochiku, 1994).

36. See Mansaku Nomura, *Tarōkaja o ikiru* [To live as Tarokaja] (Tokyo: Hakusuisha, 1984); and Mansai Nomura, *Mansai de gozaru* [I am Mansai] (Tokyo: Asahi Shinbunsha, 1999).

37. Hiroko Miura, *Nōgaku nyūmon (1): Hajimete no nō/kyōgen* [Introduction to noh (1): Seeing noh and kyogen for the first time] (Tokyo: Shogakkan, 1999).

38. John Rockwell, "Sounds of Exotic Cultures Enter the Musical Mainstream," *New York Times*, 3 November 1985.

39. Chiori Miyagawa, "Artistic Statement: Chiori Miyagawa," in *Global Foreigners: An Anthology of Plays*, ed. Carol Martin and Saviana Stanescu (New York: Seagull Books, 2006), 263.

40. "Song-Dance-Skill," *Newsweek*, 1 March 1954.

41. See, for example, Holly A. Blumner, Julie A. Iezzi, Alice E. Luhrmann, and Kathy Welch, eds., *101 Years of Kabuki in Hawai'i* (Honolulu: Department of Theatre and Dance, University of Hawai'i at Manoa, 1995).

42. Mark Walsh, "Everything's a Dollar!" *New York*, 19 December 2005.

43. Klein, *Cold War Orientalism*, 22.

44. Rockwell, "The Enigmas, the Oddities."

45. John Rockwell, "A Bento Box Brimming with New Moves from Japan," *New York Times*, 23 January 2006.

46. Eric Homberger, *New York City: A Cultural and Literary Companion* (Oxford: Signal Books, 2002), 124.

47. Seymour Peck, "New York: Stage for All the World," *New York Times*, 30 October 1955.

48. Leslie Bennetts, "City in Performing Arts: No. 1, with a Difference," *New York Times*, 5 March 1983.

49. Yuiko Fujita, *Cultural Migrants from Japan: Youth, Media, and Migration in New York and London* (New York: Lexington Books, 2009), 30.

50. Gwin Chin, "Japanese Dancers in America: What Draws Them?" *New York Times*, 2 December 1979.

51. Related studies on the topic include Midori Yoshimoto, *Into Performance: Japanese Women Artists in New York* (New Brunswick, NJ: Rutgers University Press, 2005).

52. Weld Royal, "On Avenue A, Living on Tokyo Time," *New York Times*, 24 August 1997.

53. Yoshimoto, *Into Performance*, 3, 36. Experimental musician Ikue Mori, who moved to New York in 1977, told an interviewer that she "always wanted to be out of Japan. . . . It seemed like the most interesting things were happening in New York around that time." Quoted in Tara Rodgers, *Pink Noises: Women on Electronic Music and Sound* (Durham: Duke University Press, 2010), 73.

54. Vincent Canby, "Mishima's View of Marquis de Sade," *New York Times*,

9 June 1995. In the same year, a survey of Japanese theater scholars and critics reported "that Mishima was Japan's greatest postwar playwright, and that his play, *Madame de Sade,* is Japan's finest twentieth-century play." Laurence Kominz, "Introduction," in *Mishima on Stage:* The Black Lizard *and Other Plays,* ed. Laurence Kominz (Ann Arbor: Center for Japanese Studies, University of Michigan, 2007), 1.

55. I apply the term differently from H. D. Harootunian. For Harootunian, Japan's Japan—like America's Japan—"simply managed to supplement (not in a Derridian way) the image already authorized by the representation constructed by both the Occupation and its later theoretical projection and empirical verification." Harootunian, "America's Japan/Japan's Japan," 200.

56. Patrick Lonergan, *Theatre and Globalization: Irish Drama in the Celtic Tiger Era* (New York: Palgrave Macmillan, 2009), 72.

57. See "TPAM," http://www.tpam.or.jp/ (accessed 28 February 2012).

58. "FESTIVAL/TOKYO," http://festival-tokyo.jp/en/about/effect.html (accessed 14 February 2010). See also http://festival-tokyo.jp/en/ (accessed 28 February 2012).

59. See "Mapping/Zapping 'J' Theatre at the Moment," chapter 7 of Uchino, *Crucible Bodies.*

60. Uchino, *Crucible Bodies,* 158.

61. Uchino, *Crucible Bodies,* 25.

62. Takao Norikoshi, *Hyper: Kontenporarī dansu tettei gaido* [Hyper: Contemporary dance perfect guidebook] (Tokyo: Sakuhinsha, 2003).

63. Aihwa Ong, *Flexible Citizenship: The Cultural Logics of Transnationality* (Durham: Duke University Press, 1999), 15.

64. Wendy Perron, "Dance: The Power of Stripping Down to Nothingness," *New York Times,* 7 November 1999.

65. See, for example, Jack Anderson, "Kumiko Kimoto's Map of the Clouds," *New York Times,* 13 November 1988.

66. "koosil-ja/danceKUMIKO: about," http://www.dancekk.com/ (accessed 2 April 2012).

67. Marilyn Ivy, *Discourses of the Vanishing: Modernity, Phantasm, Japan* (Chicago: University of Chicago Press, 1995), 1.

68. Steven C. Ridgely, *Japanese Counterculture: The Antiestablishment Art of Terayama Shūji* (Minneapolis: University of Minnesota Press, 2010), ix.

69. Howard Taubman, "U.S. Performances Set for Asia's Ancient Arts," *New York Times,* 5 October 1971.

70. Laurajane Smith, *Uses of Heritage* (New York: Routledge, 2006), 3.

71. Amanda Kearney, "Intangible Cultural Heritage: Global Awareness and Local Interest," in *Intangible Heritage,* ed. Laurajane Smith and Natsuko Akagawa (New York: Routledge, 2009), 211.

72. See Intangible Heritage Lists, http://www.unesco.org/culture/ich/index.php?lg=en&pg=00011#results (accessed 28 February 2012).

73. Taubman, "U.S. Performances."

74. Rockwell, "Sounds of Exotic Cultures."

75. Pierre Bourdieu, *Distinction: A Social Critique of the Judgement of Taste,* trans. Richard Nice (Cambridge: Harvard University Press, 1984), 2.

76. Ruby Shang, "A Taste of Japanese Dance," *New York Times,* 4 July 1982.

77. A program sponsored by the Japan Foundation, "Hogaku: New Sounds of Japan," has taken place on several occasions at Asia Society, scheduled to coincide with the annual conference of the Association of Performing Arts Presenters. According to Sugiura So, "In its broader definition, *hogaku* includes the ancient *gagaku* and *shomyo* music forms and the *Noh-Kyogen* or *Heike biwa* music of the middle ages, but in general use the term *hogaku* refers to traditional Japanese music born during or after Japan's Edo Period (17th to mid-19th centuries), including music for shamisen, koto, shakuhachi flute, biwa, etc." Sugiura So, "An Overview: Basic Knowledge about Pure Hogaku, Traditional Japanese Music," Japan Foundation, Performing Arts Network Japan, 19 January 2005, http://www.performingarts.jp/E/overview_art/0501/3.html (accessed 28 February 2012). In her discussion of Japanese music terminology, Carolyn Stevens notes that *hogaku* "is still widely used in the commercial sense" to mean "Japanese" music—though it does not subsume styles that are separately given labels such as "J-pop" or "J-rock." Carolyn S. Stevens, *Japanese Popular Music: Culture, Authenticity, and Power* (New York: Routledge, 2008), 16.

78. See, for example, "Instrumentalists: Eto and the Koto," *Time,* 8 January 1965.

79. In 1981, after Ondeko-za founder Den Tagayasu left the group and founded a new Ondeko-za, the remaining members of the original group adopted Kodo as their name. See Shawn Bender, *Taiko Boom: Japanese Drumming in Place and Motion* (Berkeley: University of California Press, 2012), 96–97.

80. Several small American productions of Mishima's modern noh plays followed a few years after the publication of Yukio Mishima, *Five Modern Nō Plays,* trans. Donald Keene (New York: Alfred A. Knopf, 1957). See Louis Calta, "Two Noh Plays by Mishima: Both on the Theme of Shattered Romance," *New York Times,* 16 November 1960; and Howard Taubman, "3 From Japan: Program of Modern Pieces at Players," *New York Times,* 4 February 1961. The 1961 production included a traditional work of noh, also translated by Keene. More recent productions include *Sotoba Komachi* and *Yoroboshi,* directed by Yukio Ninagawa at the Lincoln Center Festival in 2005. See Ben Brantley, "A Cycle of Destruction from Love to Despair," *New York Times,* 30 July 2005.

81. Mari Yoshihara, *Musicians from a Different Shore: Asians and Asian Americans in Classical Music* (Philadelphia: Temple University Press, 2007), 188.

82. Ong, *Flexible Citizenship.*

83. Ong, *Flexible Citizenship,* 6.

84. E. Taylor Atkins, *Blue Nippon: Authenticating Jazz in Japan* (Durham: Duke University Press, 2001), 11.

85. Miyamoto had made his American directorial debut in September 2001

with *I Got Merman,* an original musical he co-wrote with Dan W. Davis, which had its Tokyo premiere in 1987. Although the show had a limited run at the Rich Forum, part of the Stamford Center for the Arts in Stamford, Connecticut, it was, as Miyamoto has written, the first stage in the fulfillment of his dream to direct a musical on Broadway. See Amon Miyamoto, *Araibu: Boku ga ikiru imi o mitsukeru made* [Alive: Until I find the meaning of life] (Tokyo: Nihon Hoso Shuppan Kyokai, 2001).

86. Carol Lawson, "Yoko Morishita: Japan's 'Pioneer' Prima Ballerina," *New York Times,* 11 July 1976.

87. See, for example, Allan Kozinn, "Calligraphy Made of Sound," *New York Times,* 24 March 2011.

88. Philip Shenon, "East Meets West in Dancing of Junko Kikuchi," *New York Times,* 28 September 1984.

89. John Rockwell, "5 Poems in Movement by an Artist in Between Countries," *New York Times,* 7 November 2005.

90. In addition to the awards already mentioned, in 2012 Eiko and Koma were in the first group to receive a Doris Duke Performing Artist Award: "Twenty-one of America's most vital and productive performing artists in contemporary dance, jazz, theatre and multidisciplinary work were announced today as the first class of Doris Duke Artists, sharing a total of $5.775 million awarded in an unprecedented new initiative of the Doris Duke Charitable Foundation (DDCF)." "Doris Duke Charitable Foundation, Press Release, April 19, 2012," http://www.ddcf.org/Arts/ (accessed 23 May 2012).

91. Anna Kisselgoff, "Two Dancers from Japan in 'Fur Seal,'" *New York Times,* 25 February 1978.

92. "Eiko & Koma: Information," http://www.eikoandkoma.org/information (accessed 29 February 2012).

93. Roslyn Sulcas, "Poetry of Stillness, in a Moment Stretched to Infinity," *New York Times,* 30 March 2011.

94. Deborah Jowitt, "David Parker and Yoshiko Chuma Ride Different Ranges," *Village Voice,* 10 June 2009.

95. Interview, WNYC (New York Public Radio), 31 October 2008

96. Claudia La Rocco, "That Solo, That Look, and That Handstand," *New York Times,* 6 October 2007.

97. "In 2003 the New York choreographer Yasuko Yokoshi met a woman who changed her life. A relationship had brought her to Tokyo for a year, and she was at loose ends. 'I wanted to chill out,' she said. 'I thought it would be interesting to learn traditional Japanese dance—to just kind of kill time.'" Gia Kourlas, "Close Collaborators with Little in Common," *New York Times,* 11 March 2010.

98. "Yasuko Yokoshi, Julie Alexander, and Kayvon Pourazar in Conversation with Beth Gill and Danielle Goldman," 24 February 2010, http://movementresearch.org/publishing/?q=node/664 (accessed 1 June 2010).

99. Quoted in Steven McElroy, "Answering a Movie and a Nuclear Horror," *New York Times,* 10 May 2009.

100. Kerri Allen, "Newark's Brazen Voice," *New York Times,* 5 February 2006.

101. Phoebe Hoban, "A Complex Tale of Two Tales, Complete with a Puppet," *New York Times,* 1 March 2006.

102. "Thousand Years Waiting," http://www.crossingjamaicaavenue.org/tyw.htm (accessed 29 February 2012).

103. "Sonoko Kawahara," http://www.womenarts.org/network/profile_7.html (accessed 29 February 2012).

104. "Thousand Years Waiting." Otome Bunraku was introduced to New York audiences in September 2000 at Japan Society.

105. Quoted in McElroy, "Answering a Movie."

106. Chiori Miyagawa and Caridad Svich, "Communing with Culture: Chiori Miyagawa in Conversation with Caridad Svich," in *Trans-global Readings: Crossing Theatrical Boundaries,* ed. Caridad Svich (New York: Manchester University Press, 2003), 107.

107. Yoko Shioya, *New York City Is Turning Japanese: A City-Wide Celebration Commemorating Japan Society's Centennial* (New York: Japan Society, 2007), 1.

108. Deborah Jowitt, "Seeing Truth in the Dark," *Village Voice,* 11 September 2001.

109. See Gia Kourlas, "Recombinant Japan: Carp and the Modern Why," *New York Times,* 9 February 2007.

110. Yayoi Uno Everett, "Intercultural Synthesis in Postwar Western Art Music: Historical Contexts, Perspectives, and Taxonomy," in *Locating East Asia in Western Art Music,* ed. Yayoi Uno Everett and Frederick Lau (Middletown, CT: Wesleyan University Press, 2004), 9.

111. Rockwell, "Sounds of Exotic Cultures."

112. Robert Sherman, "From Tchaikovsky to Shostakovich," *New York Times,* 27 March 1994.

113. Edward Rothstein, "Soprano: Nan Nall," *New York Times,* 4 March 1982.

114. Alex Ross, "Review/Music: Shakuhachi, from School in New York," *New York Times,* 12 January 1994.

115. "Pop and Jazz Guide," *New York Times,* 22 June 2001.

116. Founder of KiSuiAn, "the largest and most active" shakuhachi school outside of Japan, Seldin also teaches at New York University and the City University of New York. "Nyogetsu—Biography," http://www.nyogetsu.com/biography.html (accessed 29 February 2012). Schlefer, a composer, performer, and grand master of the shakuhachi, is artistic director of Kyo-Shin-An Arts, which is "dedicated to the integration of Japanese classical instruments—specifically shakuhachi, koto and shamisen—in Western classical music." "Kyo-Shin-An Arts: Our Mission," http://www.nyoraku.bizland.com/kyoshinan/index.php?section=about&subsection=our_mission (accessed 29 February 2012). He teaches at the City University of New York. Marco Lienhard, a former member of Ondeko-za in Japan, is a master of the shakuhachi, fue, and taiko. He is now based in New York, where he performs, teaches, and is founding director of the Taikoza ensemble.

Samuelson performs and teaches at a variety of venues. He retired in 2009 as the director of the Asian Cultural Council, a major funding agency for US-Asia cultural exchange.

117. Yoon, "Asian Masculinities."

118. Paul J. Yoon, "'She's Really Become Japanese Now!' Taiko Drumming and Asian American Identifications," *American Music* 19, no. 4 (2001): 422.

119. See, for example, Tim Page, "Japanese Percussion," *New York Times,* 10 November 1985; and Robert Palmer, "Japanese Music," *New York Times,* 1 March 1987.

120. Yoon, "'She's Really Become Japanese Now!'" 433–34.

121. "Dance: Decay of the Angel," *New Yorker,* 12 April 2004.

122. In a sense, Garnica and Moriya picked up where choreographer and producer Brechin Flournoy left off. In 1995 Flournoy launched the San Francisco Butoh Festival, which ran for eight seasons.

123. Allen Hughes, "East-West Ballet: 'Bugaku,' New Work by George Balanchine, Is the Result of Many Heritages," *New York Times,* 22 March 1963.

124. Barnes, "Twain Meet in City Ballet's 'Bugaku.'"

125. The name Grand Kabuki signifies the authenticity of the troupe—especially in contrast to the female-led Azuma Kabuki Musicians and Dancers who performed in the United States in the mid-1950s.

126. John Rockwell, "A Workshop at 40, and Full Speed Ahead," *New York Times,* 9 November 2005.

127. Mary Louise Pratt, *Imperial Eyes: Travel Writing and Transculturation* (New York: Routledge, 1992), 7.

128. Kandice Chuh and Karen Shimakawa, "Introduction: Mapping Studies in the Asian Diaspora," in *Orientations: Mapping Studies in the Asian Diaspora,* ed. Kandice Chuh and Karen Shimakawa (Durham: Duke University Press, 2001), 7.

129. Anthony Lane, "A Critic at Large: Waiting—Samuel Beckett's Life in Letters," *New Yorker,* 30 March 2009.

130. Elizabeth Heilman Brooke, "Taking Taiko, Japan's Big Drum, into the Hip-Hop Age," *New York Times,* 24 September 2002.

131. Susan Bassnett-McGuire, *Translation Studies* (New York: Routledge, 1991), xvi.

132. Greenblatt, "Cultural Mobility," 4.

Chapter 1

1. Mansai Nomura, "Foreword," in Ronald Cavaye, Paul Griffith, and Akihiko Senda, *A Guide to the Japanese Stage: From Traditional to Cutting Edge* (New York: Kodansha International, 2004), 18.

2. John Rockwell, "Music: Shamisen Solo and Hayashi Ensemble," *New York Times,* 20 September 1981.

3. Masao Miyoshi and H.D. Harootunian, "Japan in the World," in *Japan in*

the World, ed. Masao Miyoshi and H. D. Harootunian (Durham: Duke University Press, 1993), 7.

4. Brooks Atkinson, "Theatre: Superb Clown: Kabuki's Kanzaburo Stars as a Drunk," *New York Times*, 17 June 1960.

5. Christina Klein, *Cold War Orientalism: Asia in the Middlebrow Imagination, 1945–1961* (Berkeley: University of California Press, 2003), 13.

6. Marlene J. Mayo, "To Be or Not to Be: Kabuki and Cultural Politics in Occupied Japan," in *War, Occupation, and Creativity: Japan and East Asia, 1920–1960*, ed. Marlene J. Mayo and J. Thomas Rimer (Honolulu: University of Hawai'i Press, 2001), 269.

7. A goal of those promoting a kabuki visit was to develop on Japan's behalf what would now be called *soft power*, a term coined by Joseph S. Nye in *Bound to Lead: The Changing Nature of American Power* (New York: Basic Books, 1990). Writing about Japan's soft power in the context of its relationship with its regional neighbors, David Leheny has observed (as I partially quoted in the introductory chapter), "In one variant, it represents a peaceful Japan. . . . In another, it offers the opportunity to convince other people that Japan's development as a normal country, with a normal military, is not to be feared, because this is a nation that has only the best of intentions. If people just get to know the Japanese—through their songs, their television hits, their anime—they will realize that they are kind and decent, creative and curious, and not to be feared." David Leheny, "A Narrow Place to Cross Swords: Soft Power and the Politics of Japanese Popular Culture in East Asia," in *Beyond Japan: The Dynamics of East Asian Regionalism*, ed. Peter J. Katzenstein and Takashi Shiraishi (Ithaca: Cornell University Press, 2006), 232.

8. Prior to the war, a Grand Kabuki troupe made one trip abroad—to the Soviet Union in 1928.

9. The foundation of America's kabuki-Japan was laid during the Occupation, as is made clear by studies that examine kabuki censorship during that period. They include James R. Brandon's "Myth and Reality: A Story of *Kabuki* during American Censorship, 1945–1949," *Asian Theatre Journal* 23, no. 1 (2006): 1–110; Samuel L. Leiter's "The Good Censors: Evading the Threat to Postwar *Kabuki*," in *Rising from the Flames: The Rebirth of Theater in Occupied Japan, 1945–1952*, ed. Samuel L. Leiter (New York: Lexington Books, 2009), 89–107; and Mayo's "To Be or Not to Be." All address at length Faubion Bowers's role as a censor.

10. Paul Green, "Tribute to the Kabuki Theatre of Japan," *New York Times*, 27 January 1952.

11. Joshua Logan, "Mr. Logan Seconds Mr. Green," *New York Times*, 27 January 1952.

12. Klein, *Cold War Orientalism*, 117.

13. James Michener, "One More Vote for Kabuki Theatre," *New York Times*, 14 December 1952.

14. John W. Dower, *Embracing Defeat: Japan in the Wake of World War II* (New York: W. W. Norton, 1999), 207.

15. Shiro Okamoto, *The Man Who Saved* Kabuki: *Faubion Bowers and Theatre Censorship in Occupied Japan,* trans. and adapted by Samuel L. Leiter (Honolulu: University of Hawai'i Press, 2001).

16. Brandon, "Myth and Reality."

17. Dower, *Embracing Defeat,* 207.

18. Faubion Bowers, *Japanese Theatre* (New York: Hill and Wang, 1952), ix.

19. Joshua Logan, "Foreword," in Faubion Bowers, *Japanese Theatre* (New York: Hill and Wang, 1952), v–vii.

20. As Naoko Shibusawa has pointed out, in *The Chrysanthemum and the Sword* Ruth Benedict "depicted [the Japanese] as having a flawed culture that needed reforming in order to be more mature and masculine," with Benedict suggesting that character traits such as "extreme 'mood swings' had caused the Japanese to wage war in Asia." Naoko Shibusawa, *America's Geisha Ally: Reimagining the Japanese Enemy* (Cambridge: Harvard University Press, 2006), 61.

21. Bowers, *Japanese Theatre,* ix, xiv.

22. Paul Green, "From the River Bottoms Outside Kyoto" (review of Faubion Bowers, *Japanese Theatre*), *New York Times,* 12 October 1952. By 1969, as Clive Barnes wrote, kabuki was being lauded as "an early manifestation of what we now call 'total theater'." Clive Barnes, "Theater: Far from Remote Kabuki," *New York Times,* 11 September 1969.

23. Emerson R. Harris, "The Theater of Japan" (review of Faubion Bowers, *Japanese Theatre*), *Nation,* 22 November 1952.

24. Although the earphone translation was provided by Donald Richie for the Grand Kabuki visit in 1960, Bowers subsequently became the voice of kabuki for American audiences, which for decades experienced productions with the aid of his earphone translations and commentaries.

25. Harris, "The Theater of Japan," 471. Perhaps by way of explaining why he did not include citations, in the preface to *Japanese Theatre* Bowers wrote, "The written sources for much of the information in this book are manuscripts and now out-of-print books in Japanese." He also noted that he had been "somewhat arbitrary about dates" and had "selected middle dates in some instances, somewhere between the extremes of differences in opinion." Bowers, *Japanese Theatre,* xix.

26. Quoted in Brandon, "Myth and Reality," 18.

27. "Letter from Tokyo," published in the 14 March 1953 issue of the *New Yorker* is another example of the view that kabuki was being threatened, and that Americans could make a difference. The author is Harold Strauss, who was editor in chief of Alfred A. Knopf, the US publisher of writers such as Yasunari Kawabata and Yukio Mishima. Strauss wrote that on visiting Japan "after an absence of six years," he found "hardly an aspect of daily life that fails to bear witness to the profound cultural changes rocking Japan. . . . [Change] threatens traditional

dancing and theatre. . . . [Younger Japanese today] have concluded that because Japan lost the war, all things Japanese are bad. It is hard to find . . . one who really knows much about the Kabuki theatre, charcoal-ink painting, or any of the other traditional Japanese arts." His Japan, like that of Bowers, was in part an invented one. Ignoring earthquakes and typhoons, he wrote in the same article, "Nature is mild in Japan, and to live close to it, with the utmost simplicity, is an ancient ideal." Strauss devoted a large portion of the *New Yorker* piece to kabuki and "the ancient spirit" of the art form. Harold Strauss, "Letter from Tokyo," *New Yorker,* 14 March 1953.

28. John Martin, "Century Yields to Kabuki Troupe: Japanese Dancers in Ancient Drama-Music Presentation Impressive in Opening," *New York Times,* 19 February 1954.

29. Louis Calta, "Logan Would Back Japanese Company: Author Is Negotiating to Bring Kabuki Theatre Unit Here for Limited Engagement," *New York Times,* 4 June 1953.

30. Harlow Robinson, *The Last Impresario: The Life, Times, and Legacy of Sol Hurok* (New York: Viking Penguin, 1994), 399.

31. Robinson, *The Last Impresario,* 382.

32. Eric C. Rath, "Dance in Theatre: Japan," in *Encyclopedia of Asian Theatre,* ed. Samuel L. Leiter, vol. 1 (Westport, CT: Greenwood Press, 2007), 149.

33. Kevin J. Wetmore Jr., "1954: Selling *Kabuki* to the West," *Asian Theatre Journal* 26, no. 1 (2009): 81.

34. Tsurunosuke later became Tomijuro Nakamura V—and was designated a living national treasure. His biological father was Tomijuro Nakamura IV.

35. "A Gift of Our Ancestors," *Look,* 18 May 1954.

36. "Dancers of Japan," *New York Times,* 24 January 1954.

37. As discussed in chapter 4, a production of Puccini's *Madama Butterfly* presented jointly by the New York City Opera and the Fujiwara Opera of Japan in 1952 counts as the first major Japan-related presentation to take place in New York in the postwar period.

38. Shibusawa, *America's Geisha Ally,* 26.

39. "Kabuki Troupe Due at Century Feb. 16.," *New York Times,* 13 January 1954.

40. John Martin, "The Dance: Kabuki—a Glimpse of Japan's Classic Theatre in Its Choreographic Aspects," *New York Times,* 14 February 1954.

41. Joseph L. Anderson, *Enter a Samurai: Kawakami Otojirō and Japanese Theatre in the West,* vol. 1 (Tucson: Wheatmark, 2011), viii.

42. Ayako Kano, *Acting Like a Woman in Modern Japan: Theater, Gender, and Nationalism* (New York: Palgrave, 2001), 87. There was also Hanako, who was particularly well known in Europe as an actress, dancer, and model for Auguste Rodin. Faubion Bowers once commented, "It seemed a pity to me that geishas and their husbands appeared here and abroad to bring our first tastes of *kabuki* outside Japan." Faubion Bowers, "The Past within the Present: The Grand Kabuki Ventures into the New World," *Dance,* June 1960.

43. Martin, "The Dance: Kabuki."

44. Faubion Bowers, "Concerning Kabuki," *Saturday Review*, 27 February 1954.

45. Donald Richie, "Letter from Japan," *Nation*, 30 August 1958. Richie arrived in Japan in 1947 as a reporter for the US military newspaper *Stars and Stripes*. Having written many books and magazine articles on Japanese culture—especially film—he is prominent among those who constructed the image of Japan for Americans in the postwar period and the decades since then.

46. During the final discussion at an academic conference on the Occupation held at Old Dominion University in 1984, Faubion Bowers, who was a discussant for a presentation titled "Shingeki under the Occupation" and a panelist for one titled "Literature and the Arts," told conference participants, according to the published transcript:

> A lot of people here have talked about how bad things were before the Occupation. I am one of the few people in this group who knew Japan before the war. I was there in 1940 and 1941 and things were not so bad. To me it is irrelevant; it's like a man who buries his wife and you say, "But after all, isn't this better, he isn't mean to her anymore." So if things were terrible then—which I doubt that they were—that has no relevance to what happened afterward, I think.

John Dower responded, "I think that Mr. Bowers' statement is really off the mark," noting that "presurrender Japan was a repressive, imperialistic, militaristic society." Quoted in Thomas W. Burkman, ed., *The Occupation of Japan: Arts and Culture—The Proceedings of the Sixth Symposium Sponsored by The MacArthur Memorial, Old Dominion University, The General Douglas MacArthur Foundation, 18–19 October 1984* (Norfolk: General Douglas MacArthur Foundation, 1988), 241, 243.

47. John Martin, "Century Yields to Kabuki Troupe: Japanese Dancers in Ancient Drama-Music Presentation Impressive in Opening," *New York Times*, 19 February 1954.

48. John Martin, "The Dance: Japanese—The Azuma Kabuki Style Makes Alien Conquest," *New York Times*, 28 February 1954.

49. On 22 March several Azuma performers were escorted to the White House by the Japanese ambassador to meet President Eisenhower—another indication of the perceived significance of the troupe's visit. See "President Meets Kabuki Troupe," *New York Times*, 23 March 1954.

50. "Song-Dance-Skill," *Newsweek*, 1 March 1954.

51. Irving Kolodin, "Music to My Ears: Azuma Kabuki Dancers, Operatic Affairs, Etc.," *Saturday Review*, 6 March 1954.

52. Winthrop Sargeant, "Musical Events: Bartok and Kabuki," *New Yorker*, 6 March 1954.

53. B. H. Haggin, "Music," *Nation*, 13 March 1954.

54. B. H. Haggin, "Records," *Nation*, 19 June 1954.

55. Samuel L. Leiter, "When *Theatre Arts* Looked Eastward: Japan's Recep-

tion in America's Leading Theatre Periodical (1916–64)," in *Japanese Theatre and the International Stage,* ed. Stanca Scholz-Cionca and Samuel L. Leiter (Boston: Brill, 2001), 59.

56. As Leiter has pointed out, although *Theatre Arts* was enthusiastic about kabuki prior to 1960 (part of the magazine's postwar "love affair with the Japanese stage"), "it almost entirely ignored the 1960 visit. This suggests the confused policies that soon led to the magazine's downfall." Leiter, "When *Theatre Arts* Looked Eastward," 62.

57. Hisanaga Shimadzu, "An Appreciation," *Theatre Arts,* March 1954.

58. Paul Green, "East Meets West," *Theatre Arts,* March 1954.

59. Faubion Bowers, "Backstage at the Kabuki," *Theatre Arts,* March 1954.

60. James Michener, "Kabuki Is a Must for America," *Theatre Arts,* March 1954. In addition to the pieces by Consul General Shimadzu, Paul Green, Faubion Bowers, and James Michener, there were several other articles, including one on the aesthetics of Japanese theater by historian Sir George Sansom, one on film by Donald Richie, and a brief compilation of reminiscences on opera, ballet, and Western-style music in Japan by several artists (including Beate Gordon's father, Leo Sirota, a concert pianist who spent many years in Japan).

61. "Russia Invites Kabuki Troupe," *New York Times,* 2 February 1955.

62. "Japan: Invitation to Dance," *Newsweek,* 14 February 1955.

63. "Japanese Troupe Here: Kabuki Dancers and Musicians to Open Run Tonight," *New York Times,* 26 December 1955.

64. John Martin, "Dance: Azuma Kabuki Troupe Scores," *New York Times,* 27 December 1955.

65. John Martin, "The Dance: Kabuki Style," *New York Times,* 8 January 1956.

66. "Kabuki Dancers to Open Dec. 26: Japanese Troupe to Present New Acts and Stars in Its Return Engagement Here," *New York Times,* 6 December 1955.

67. Faubion Bowers, "The East on Stage" (review of A. C. Scott, *The Kabuki Theatre of Japan*), *New York Times,* 1 January 1956.

68. "Japanese Dancers to Perform Here," *New York Times,* 18 March 1959.

69. John Martin, "Gagaku in Debut Outside of Japan: Musicians and Dancers of Imperial Household Give City Center Performance," *New York Times,* 27 May 1959.

70. "Oddest and Oldest," *Newsweek,* 8 June 1959. The tour in fact included six cities: New York, Boston, Washington, DC, Seattle, San Francisco, and Los Angeles. See also "Dancers to the Emperor," *Time,* 8 June 1959.

71. *Takarazuka Dance Theatre,* program booklet, 1959, unpaginated.

72. "Special Report: Takarazuka—It's All Girls and It's All Japanese," *Newsweek,* 23 March 1953.

73. "Music: Honorable Rockettes," *Time,* 3 January 1955.

74. Robert Trumbull, "Japan's 'Living Dolls,'" *New York Times,* 23 August 1959.

75. John Martin, "Dance: Japanese—All-Girl Spectacle from Takarazuka Designed to Entertain the Tourist," *New York Times,* 13 September 1959. As Mar-

tin himself wrote about the Takarazuka in 1939, "[T]he aroma of honky-tonk is virtually the same the world over. . . . Occasionally they present brief bits of traditional native movement, but more frequently they are imitating their sisters of the West, strutting like Broadway chorus girls." He said he wanted to rush home and read about Japanese theatre in order to remind himself "of some of the true glories of Japan's theatre and dance arts." John Martin, "The Dance: Cherry Blossom Ballet," *New York Times,* 22 May 1939.

76. John Martin, "Dance: Japanese Girls—Takarazuka Company Bows at the 'Met,'" *New York Times,* 17 September 1959.

77. "Ziegfeld in a Kimono," *Time,* 28 September 1959.

78. Martin, "Dance: Japanese Girls."

79. "1,000 Years from B'way," *New York Times,* 3 May 1959.

80. "U.S. to See Kabuki by Japanese Troupe," *New York Times,* 16 January 1960.

81. "U.S. To See Kabuki"; "Japanese Opera Set: Kabuki Troupe Will Perform Traditional Works in U.S.," *New York Times,* 21 February 1960.

82. Several years earlier Logan had been in active negotiations with the Shochiku corporation to include footage of kabuki in the film *Sayonara.* In the end the negotiations with Shochiku and others fell through—though Logan was able to patch together his own kabuki, bunraku, and Takarazuka theater scenes. Logan cast Ricardo Montalban in the role of a kabuki actor named Nakamura. For a lively account of the filming of *Sayonara,* including a chronicle of Logan's failed negotiations, see Truman Capote, "Profiles: The Duke in His Domain," *New Yorker,* 9 November 1957.

83. Donald Richie and Miyoko Watanabe, trans., *Six Kabuki Plays* (Tokyo: Hokuseido Press, 1963), 103.

84. Richie and Watanabe, *Six Kabuki Plays,* contains all of the translations (except the one for *The Subscription List*) prepared for the earphone-guide service offered to audiences during the 1960 US tour. The least popular piece was *The Miracles of Tsubosaka Temple.* It was "included by Shochiku only because it had been a success when the Kabuki toured Russia in 1928. Shochiku apparently thought that what the Russians had presumably liked thirty years ago the Americans would now" (106).

85. "That Glitter in Curtain for Kabuki Is Gold Foil," *New York Times,* 18 May 1960.

86. Donald Keene, "Classic Spectacular from Japan: New Yorkers Are About to Witness Kabuki, the Dramatic Excitement That Has Fascinated Japanese Audiences for Over 350 Years," *New York Times,* 22 May 1960.

87. Brooks Atkinson, "Theatre: Grand Kabuki—Japanese Troupe Is at the City Center," *New York Times,* 3 June 1960.

88. Brooks Atkinson, "Visit by Kabuki: City Center Is Host to Troupe of Japanese," *New York Times,* 12 June 1960. Until relatively recently, articles on Japanese performing arts (and other aspects of Japanese culture) in publications such as

the *New York Times* often contained mechanical errors. Names and titles were frequently "misspelled"—in the sense that the romanization that was used did not reflect the pronunciation of the word. *Kinjincho* was used twice in Atkinson's essay, instead of *Kanjincho*—in Japanese, *Kanjinchō*.

89. Brooks Atkinson, "Theatre: Superb Clown—Kabuki's Kanzaburo Stars as a Drunk," *New York Times*, 17 June 1960.

90. Henry Hewes, "Broadway Postscript: The Song-Dance Tricksters," *Saturday Review*, 18 June 1960.

91. "New Show in Manhattan," *Time*, 13 June 1960.

92. "Import from Japan: Enchanting, Exciting," *Newsweek*, 13 June 1960.

93. Louis Calta, "Japanese Troupe Ends 3-Week Run: Grand Kabuki Completes Its Successful Engagement at Center, Heads for Coast," *New York Times*, 23 June 1960.

94. Faubion Bowers, "Kabuki in America," *Nation*, 9 July 1960.

95. Faubion Bowers, "Even Garbo Wasn't Allowed Backstage," *New York Times*, 7 September 1969.

96. Bowers, "Kabuki in America."

97. Faubion Bowers, "The Past within the Present: The Grand Kabuki Ventures into the New World," *Dance*, June 1960.

98. Quoted in Brandon, "Myth and Reality," 77.

99. Brandon, "Myth and Reality," 79, 81.

100. Gay Talese, "Japanese Enjoy Bit of Tokyo Here," *New York Times*, 7 January 1964.

101. Louis Calta, "Japanese Actors Perform Kyogen: Manzo Nomura and 2 Sons Show Ancient Art Here," *New York Times*, 6 February 1964.

102. Richard Shepard, "Japanese Troupe Stresses Comedy: Nomura Shows New Face of His Nation's Theater," *New York Times*, 7 March 1968.

103. See John Nathan, "Soap Opera, Japanese Style," *New York Times*, 19 December 1965.

104. John Nathan, "The World's Most Expressive Puppets," *New York Times*, 13 March 1966.

105. Clive Barnes, "Theater: Bunraku Puppets Appear at City Center—3 Classic Plays Given by Japanese Troupe," *New York Times*, 16 March 1966.

106. Clive Barnes, "Theater: Bunraku Drama of Revenge," *New York Times*, 18 March 1966.

107. *Japan Society Forum Newsletter*, 1 October 1966.

108. Emerson Chapin, "Noh Troupe Gives 2-Play Program: Touring Japanese Company Performs at Columbia," *New York Times*, 16 October 1966.

109. Leiter, "When *Theatre Arts* Looked Eastward," 60.

110. Leonard Cabell Pronko, *Theater East and West: Perspectives toward a Total Theater* (Berkeley: University of California Press, 1967), vii, 4.

111. Clive Barnes, "Theater: Far from Remote Kabuki," *New York Times*, 11 September 1969.

112. Harold Clurman, "Theatre," *Nation,* 29 September 1969.

113. Brendan Gill, "The Theatre: The Tightening of the Strings," *New Yorker,* 20 September 1969.

114. Anna Kisselgoff, "The Dance: Odori Festival of Japan," *New York Times,* 16 May 1976.

115. Quoted in David Oyama, "Can Our Theater Learn from Kabuki?," *New York Times,* 4 February 1979.

116. See Masao Miyoshi, *Off Center: Power and Culture Relations between Japan and the United States* (Cambridge: Harvard University Press, 1991), 66.

117. Jennifer Dunning, "Grand Kabuki to Tour U.S.," *New York Times,* 4 February 1982; Jennifer Dunning, "How Art and Tradition Cast the Spell of Kabuki," *New York Times,* 27 June 1982.

118. Steve Lohr, "The New Face of Kabuki," *New York Times,* 30 May 1982.

119. Jennifer Dunning, "Theater: Grand Kabuki Opens 2-Week Season," *New York Times,* 30 June 1982.

120. Mel Gussow, "Stage: Bunraku Puppets Appear at Japan House," *New York Times,* 15 March 1983.

121. Jack Anderson, "Dance: Japan's Kyogen," *New York Times,* 12 July 1984.

122. See Jennifer Dunning, "Dance: Noh Theater," *New York Times,* 1 September 1982.

123. Mel Gussow, "Art of Kabuki Makeup: The Actor's the Canvas," *New York Times,* 28 February 1985.

124. Bernard Holland, "From Kabuki to Mozart, Summer Offers Diversity at Lincoln Center," *New York Times,* 8 July 1985.

125. Anna Kisselgoff, "Stage: Kabuki, at the Met," *New York Times,* 10 July 1985.

126. Margaret Croyden, "'New Look' Kabuki," *New York Times,* 19 July 1987.

127. Howard Kissel, "The Whole Kit and Kabuki," *Daily News,* 8 September 1989.

128. Drew Fetherston, "Kabuki, Classical and Innovative," *New York Newsday,* 8 September 1989.

129. Jack Anderson, "Kabuki's Whirl of Illusions and Disguises," *New York Times,* 8 September 1989.

130. Faubion Bowers, "From Japan, Dazzle Aplenty," *New York Times,* 22 October 1989.

131. Jennifer Robertson, *Takarazuka: Sexual Politics and Popular Culture in Modern Japan* (Berkeley: University of California Press, 1998), 120.

132. Bowers, "From Japan, Dazzle Aplenty."

133. Stephen Holden, "Japan's Answer to the Ziegfeld Follies," *New York Times,* 27 October 1989.

134. Jack Anderson, "Anthropomorphic Acrobats from Japan," *New York Times,* 15 September 1989.

135. Mel Gussow, "Temple of Dendur as Setting for Noh," *New York Times,* 24 April 1993.

136. "Protecting Its Fannie: How Mortgage Giant Primed the Bubble, Covered Its Assets," http://www.pbs.org/newshour/bb/business/july-dec11/making sense_07-1.html (accessed 26 March 2012).

137. Eric Alterman, *Kabuki Democracy: The System vs. Barack Obama* (New York: Nation Books, 2011), 7.

138. Tyler Kepner, "Kabuki Auction: Bidding Intrigue behind the Scenes," *New York Times*, 5 November 2006.

139. David W. Chen, "The Social Security Debate Plays San Diego," *New York Times*, 7 September 2001.

140. Jack Hitt, "American Kabuki: The Ritual of Scandal," *New York Times*, 18 July 2004.

141. Patrick Healy, "Political Memo: A Hopeful Ponders Where to Plant Her Flag," *New York Times*, 10 January 2007.

142. Helen Schulman, *This Beautiful Life: A Novel* (New York: HarperCollins, 2011), 91.

143. Heather Havrilesky, "Riff: 'A Joyful Kabuki Mask to Obscure the Anguish of Marital Bliss Gone Sour,'" *New York Times*, 10 July 2011.

Chapter 2

1. Steven D. Lavine and Ivan Karp, "Introduction: Museums and Multiculturalism," in *Exhibiting Cultures: The Poetics and Politics of Museum Display*, ed. Ivan Karp and Steven D. Lavine (Washington, DC: Smithsonian Institution Press, 1991), 2.

2. *Japan Society: Performing Arts, Fall 2009 Season* (New York: Japan Society, 2009), inside front cover.

3. post theater, http://www.posttheater.com/aboutus.htm (accessed 8 March 2012).

4. Six years later Motoatsu Sakurai, formerly ambassador and consul general at the consulate general of Japan in New York, became the first president of the society born and educated in Japan.

5. Ivan Karp, "Culture and Representation," in *Exhibiting Cultures: The Poetics and Politics of Museum Display*, ed. Ivan Karp and Steven D. Lavine (Washington, DC: Smithsonian Institution Press, 1991), 15.

6. Quoted in "Japan Society Election: John D. Rockefeller 3d Heads Internation Friendship Unit," *New York Times*, 26 March 1952.

7. John Ensor Harr and Peter J. Johnson, *The Rockefeller Conscience: An American Family in Public and in Private* (New York: Charles Scribner's Sons, 1991), 86.

8. "Japan Society: About," http://www.japansociety.org/about (accessed 8 March 2012). The society previously noted on its website that it is "North America's single major producer of high-quality content on Japan for an English-speaking audience" (accessed 5 May 2009). On the cover of its pamphlets and other printed material the organization has also described itself as "America's Leading

Resource on Japan" and "New York's Leading Cultural and Intellectual Resource on Japan." The playbill distributed to audiences attending the January 2007 Japanese Contemporary Dance Showcase presented at the Joyce Theater "in association with Japan Society" noted that Japan Society "presents performers whose artistry strongly communicates an expression of Japanese tradition, art forms, or style. They include Japanese artists whose careers have developed internationally, American artists whose works are inspired by Japan, and Japanese-American artists whose work uniquely expresses their heritage. From its traditional noh & kyogen programs with master performers to the annual Contemporary Japanese Dance Showcase, Japan Society has established an inimitable niche in the performing arts in the U.S." *Playbill: Joyce Theater, Fall Season 2006* (New York: Joyce Theater, 2007), 27–28.

9. The name Japan House is no longer used. The organization now refers to both itself and its building as Japan Society. In 2011 the Japan Society structure (specifically, the elegantly designed facade on 47th Street) was accorded landmark status by the New York City Landmarks Preservation Commission.

10. Lynn Szwaja and Tomás Ybarra-Frausto, "Foreword," in *Museum Frictions: Public Cultures/Global Transformations,* ed. Ivan Karp, Corinne A. Kratz, Lynn Szwaja, and Tomás Ybarra-Frausto, with Gustavo Buntinx, Barbara Kirshenblatt-Gimblett, and Ciraj Rassool (Durham: Duke University Press, 2006), xi.

11. Michael Auslin, "Japan Society: Brief History," http://www.japansociety.org/brief_history (accessed 8 March 2012).

12. Among the founding members were Lindsay Russell, an international customs lawyer with clients in Japan who was Japan Society president from 1910 until 1919, and Jacob H. Schiff, an international banker with Kuhn, Loeb and Company.

13. Edwin O. Reischauer, *Japan Society, 1907–1982: 75 Years of Partnership across the Pacific* (New York: Japan Society, 1982), 16.

14. Lindsay Russell, quoted in Reischauer, *Japan Society,* 14.

15. "The Japan Society," editorial, *New York Times,* 21 May 1907.

16. Reischauer, *Japan Society,* 14–15.

17. Christopher Benfey, *The Great Wave: Gilded Age Misfits, Japanese Eccentrics, and the Opening of Old Japan* (New York: Random House, 2003), xi.

18. "Japan Society Born at Kuroki's Party: Organization Intended to Promote Good Feeling between the Two Nations," *New York Times,* 20 May 1907.

19. Reischauer, *Japan Society,* 30.

20. Reischauer, *Japan Society,* 60.

21. See Reischauer, *Japan Society,* 93, 97–98.

22. Ephemeral New York, http://ephemeralnewyork.wordpress.com/2010/03/31/the-stunning-roof-garden-of-the-hotel-astor/ (accessed 8 March 2012).

23. Unfortunately, there is no record of the identity of the performers or the titles of the pieces they presented.

24. Reischauer, *Japan Society,* 22.

25. "Schiff Hopes Japan Will Aid in China," *New York Times,* 16 March 1912.

26. H. D. Harootunian, "America's Japan/Japan's Japan," in *Japan in the World,* ed. Masao Miyoshi and H. D. Harootunian (Durham: Duke University Press, 1993), 216.

27. Dower goes on to add, "In a relationship of such glaring inequality and disparity of power, however, this was easier said than done. The two-way street amounted to a multilane highway on the U.S. side and [a] single lane on the other (accommodating, initially, mostly Japanese 'cultural' products of a traditional, aesthetic sort)." John W. Dower, "Foreword," in Takeshi Matsuda, *Soft Power and Its Perils: U.S. Cultural Policy in Early Postwar Japan and Permanent Dependency* (Washington, DC: Woodrow Wilson Center Press; Stanford: Stanford University Press, 2007), xiv.

28. See, for example, Martin Arnold, "John D. Rockefeller 3d Asserts U.S. Stifles Initiative of Asians," *New York Times,* 18 May 1966.

29. See Barbara E. Thornbury, "The View from Japan: The Traditional Performing Arts as Cultural Ambassadors Abroad," in *Japanese Theatre and the International Stage,* ed. Stanca Scholz-Cionca and Samuel L. Leiter (Boston: Brill, 2001), 213–27.

30. John Rockwell, "The Perils of Being a Purist," *New York Times,* 14 July 1991.

31. Beate Sirota Gordon, *The Only Woman in the Room: A Memoir* (New York: Kodansha International, 1997), 147. A *Times* editorial published early in 1955 called for more funding to bring Japanese graduate students to the United States, noting that only forty-six were currently enrolled in programs—down from a previous high of three hundred. "[H]igh resolves [to promote democracy through academic exchange] and appropriations have both fallen," the newspaper reported. "Japanese Students," *New York Times,* editorial, 20 February 1955.

32. Reischauer, *Japan Society,* 69.

33. Reproduced in Reischauer, *Japan Society,* 66.

34. A photoessay published in the *Times* toward the end of 1962 identified the kimono-clad Hanayagi as a "kabuki dancer," noting, "Artists studying here introduce Japanese culture in school assemblies. . . . Last year, specialists in flower arrangement, the tea ceremony and Japanese music and drama—all students here—demonstrated their arts at 75 school assemblies in the city and nearby suburbs." "Gentlewomen from Japan," *New York Times,* 4 November 1962.

35. I asked Beate Gordon if she was ever told to—or not to—present certain performers. She said no, adding that administrators at Japan Society and Asia Society trusted her judgment and were satisfied as long as audiences turned out and presentations garnered press coverage and reviews—conditions under which presenters typically work. Beate Gordon, interview with the author, 18 November 2004.

36. Thomas R. H. Havens, *Radicals and Realists in the Japanese Nonverbal Arts:*

The Avant-Garde Rejection of Modernism (Honolulu: University of Hawai'i Press, 2006), 120, 121.

37. "Rockefeller 3d Gift Will Provide a Site for Japan Society," *New York Times,* 11 May 1967. The $1.25 million cost of buying and clearing the land was donated by Rockefeller; the additional $3.5 million needed to build the structure was covered by donations from entities that included the Japan Business Federation (Keidanren) and the Japanese government. "An Authentic Bit of Japan Rises to House Society on East 47th St.," *New York Times,* 9 September 1971.

38. "Work on New Home for Japan Society Begun Near the U.N.," *New York Times,* 17 September 1969; "Japanese Center Here to Blend Styles," *New York Times,* 28 September 1969.

39. Even after Japan House was built, the society continued—as it does today—to arrange presentations on occasion at other venues in New York where the seating capacity might be greater or the facilities deemed better for certain performances. Off-site sponsored or co-sponsored events also help cultivate more widespread recognition and new audiences for society programs.

40. Reischauer, *Japan Society,* 94. The guest list at the opening ceremonies reflected the stature of the organization and the political and economic influence of the individuals associated with it—as well as the growing economic strength of Japan. The US ambassador to Japan and the Japanese ambassador to the United States were present, along with Prince Hitachi, a son of the emperor, who called for "'closer people-to-people contact' between the two countries." Making direct reference to the trade friction developing between the United States and Japan at the time, Rockefeller observed that there was "'perhaps less genuine mutual understanding' between the United States and Japan than between any other two big democracies in the world." "Japan House Here Opens with a Call for More Contact," *New York Times,* 14 September 1971.

41. Anna Kisselgoff, "Dance: Japanese Mime," *New York Times,* 4 December 1971.

42. Press coverage included Anna Kisselgoff, "Asian Dance: Is It 'Ethnic' or Classical?," *New York Times,* 13 March 1977, which refers to the "admirable" program run by Beate Gordon; and Jennifer Dunning, "Asia Society's Pursuit of Authenticity," *New York Times,* 25 March 1979, which praises Gordon's performing arts program for increasing the number of opportunities available to people in New York to get "a thought-provoking look at the dance and society of another culture."

43. Quoted in Eleanor Blau, "Asia Society Impresario Helps Tradition Survive," *New York Times,* 30 June 1991.

44. Dunning, "Asia Society's Pursuit of Authenticity."

45. Quoted in Erika Duncan, "A Link to Pre-war Japan Builds Bridges in the Arts," *New York Times,* 4 August 1996.

46. Quoted in William Harris, "Giant Themes, Minute Movements: Eiko and Koma Celebrate 20 Years in America," *Japan Society Newsletter,* November 1995.

47. Quoted in Harris, "Giant Themes."

48. Quoted in Harris, "Giant Themes."

49. Kenneth A. Grossberg, ed., *Japan Today* (Philadelphia: Institute for the Study of Human Issues, 1981), 1.

50. Richard F. Shepard, "7 U.S. Cities to See Show of Japanese Art, Culture," *New York Times,* 27 March 1979.

51. Quoted in David Oyama, "A Feast of the Arts from Japan," *New York Times,* 15 April 1979.

52. Mel Gussow, "Greek Tragedy: A Japanese 'Bacchae,'" *New York Times,* 3 June 1982.

53. Roger Pulvers, "Roll Over Cocteau: A Look at Contemporary Japanese Theater," *Japan Society Newsletter,* March 1982.

54. Clyde Haberman, "Presenting Kabuki for the Common Man," *New York Times,* 15 November 1987.

55. The festival was conceived and organized by Martin E. Segal, former chairman of Lincoln Center for the Performing Arts, as a New York showcase of performing arts and film from around the world. Although Segal intended to create a biennial event, there was just one more festival, which took place in 1991.

56. Mel Gussow, "Man and the Elements in a Mystical Drama," *New York Times,* 21 June 1988.

57. Japan Society has also on occasion mounted large-scale, thematically based season-long programs comprising performing arts events, gallery exhibitions, and film showings. In the mid-1980s, for example, there was Paris in Japan, and in the late 1990s there was Japanese Theater in the World, which is discussed later in this chapter.

58. *Japan Society: Performing Arts, 2008–09 Season* (New York: Japan Society, 2008), inside front cover.

59. E. Taylor Atkins, *Blue Nippon: Authenticating Jazz in Japan* (Durham: Duke University Press, 2001), 11, 29.

60. In 2012 the event was temporarily suspended and replaced with two concurrent productions that were part of the Public Theater's annual New York-wide Under the Radar festival—"a festival tracking new theater from around the world." "Under the Radar," http://www.undertheradarfestival.com/index.php?s=1 (accessed 25 April 2012). The productions were chelfitsch Theatre Company's *Hot Pepper, Air Conditioner, and the Farewell Speech* (*Hotto peppā, kūrā, soshite owakare no aisatsu*), written and directed by Toshiki Okada; and Tokyo Metropolitan Theatre/Soho Theatre, London/NODA MAP's *The Bee* (*THE BEE*), written by Hideki Noda and Colin Teevan and directed by Hideki Noda.

61. See, for example, *Japan Society Calendar of Events: January/February 2000* (New York: Japan Society, 2000).

62. *Japan Society: Performing Arts, Fall/Winter 2004–2005* (New York: Japan Society, 2004), 13.

63. Anna Kisselgoff, "Japanese Parables on Alienation in an Industrial Society," *New York Times,* 13 January 2004.

64. *Events at Japan Society: January/February 2003* (New York: Japan Society, 2003), 3.

65. *Japan Society Calendar of Events: January/February 2008* (New York: Japan Society, 2008), 6.

66. Claudia La Rocco, "Japan and Its Neighbors Scrutinized in Mirrors," *New York Times,* 14 January 2008.

67. A more recent contemporary-drama initiative is the series of professionally staged readings of plays in translation that the society launched in 2008.

68. Pamela Renner, "Showing the Quiet Profundity of Ordinary Life," *New York Times,* 22 October 2000.

69. Quoted in Renner, "Showing the Quiet Profundity."

70. Quoted in Carol Martin, "The Magic of Ancient Japan Onstage," *New York Times,* 23 March 2003.

71. The reviews include Jason Zinoman, "'Enjoy': 'Like, We Are a Lost Generation, You Know,'" *New York Times,* 13 April 2010; Jacob Gallagher-Ross, "*Five Days in March* Tracks Tokyo Hipsters in Time of War," *Village Voice,* 11 May 2010; and Jason Zinoman, "Strangers Find Solace from Riots against the U.S.," *New York Times,* 12 May 2010. Another factor that may explain why a play at Japan Society may not be accorded a published review is the short length of time plays run there—often not more than a single weekend.

72. "Presenter Interview: New Developments in the Japan Society, a Promoter of Exchange between Japan and the U.S. for 100 Years," Japan Foundation, Performing Arts Network Japan, 13 October 2007, http://performingarts.jp/E/pre_interview/0709/1.html (accessed 29 February 2012).

73. Sean Tomizawa, "Seeding Japanese Culture One Commission at a Time," http://japansocietyny.blogspot.com/2012/04/seeding-japanese-culture-one-commission.html (accessed 8 May 2012).

74. Anne Midgette, "A Japanese Heart Beating in a New American Work," *New York Times,* 11 June 2003.

75. Claudia La Rocco, "Hello Creepy: A Spooky Side to Japan's Cute Culture," *New York Times,* 13 January 2010.

76. Jon Pareles, "New Voices from Japan: Improvised Sounds at the Japan Society," *New York Times,* 15 May 2006.

77. Stanca Scholz-Cionca and Samuel L. Leiter, "Preface," in *Japanese Theatre and the International Stage,* ed. Stanca Scholz-Cionca and Samuel L. Leiter (Boston: Brill, 2001), ix. Among the array of Japanese Theater in the World events at Japan Society were the first "back-to-back" productions of the noh play *Sumidagawa* and Benjamin Britten's *Curlew River,* an adaptation of *Sumidagawa* set in medieval England. There were also Daisan Erotica's *A Man Called Macbeth (Makubesu to iu na no otoko),* written and directed by troupe founder and head Takeshi Kawamura; a recital by butoh dancer Masaki Iwana; presentations by the Awaji Puppet Theatre and the Nomura Kyogen Theatre; and a series titled Japanese Theater on Film.

78. Stanca Scholz-Cionca and Samuel L. Leiter, eds., *Japanese Theatre and the*

International Stage (Boston: Brill, 2001); Benito Ortolani and Samuel L. Leiter, eds., *Zeami and the Nō Theatre in the World* (New York: Center for Advanced Studies in Theatre Arts, Graduate School and University Center of the City University of New York, 1998).

79. Quoted in John Rockwell, "5 Poems in Movement by an Artist in Between Countries," *New York Times,* 7 November 2005.

80. *Japan Society: Performing Arts, Spring 2008 Season* (New York: Japan Society, 2008), 1.

81. Yoko Shioya, *New York City Is Turning Japanese: A City-Wide Celebration Commemorating Japan Society's Centennial* (New York: Japan Society, 2007), 1.

82. See Claudia La Rocco, "That Solo, That Look, and That Handstand," *New York Times,* 6 October 2007.

83. See Rachel Saltz, "'Drum of the Waves of Horikawa': Adultery, Blood, Guts, and Samurai," *New York Times,* 1 November 2007.

84. See Roslyn Sulcas, "Pappa Tarahumara: A Seascape Dotted by Chaotic Bursts," *New York Times,* 30 November 2007.

85. Patrick Lonergan, *Theatre and Globalization: Irish Drama in the Celtic Tiger Era* (New York: Palgrave Macmillan, 2009), 128.

86. Karp, "Culture and Representation," 15.

87. Fred Myers, "The Complicity of Cultural Production: The Contingencies of Performance in Globalizing Museum Practices," in *Museum Frictions: Public Cultures/Global Transformations,* ed. Ivan Karp, Corinne A. Kratz, Lynn Szwaja, and Tomás Ybarra-Frausto, with Gustavo Buntinx, Barbara Kirshenblatt-Gimblett, and Ciraj Rassool (Durham: Duke University Press, 2006), 532.

Chapter 3

1. James Traub, "Where It's At: Is Bohemia a Mentality, a Relic, or an Economic 'Cultural District'?," *New York Times,* 10 September 2006.

2. Yasunari Takahashi, "Alternative Japanese Drama: A Brief Overview," in *Alternative Japanese Drama: Ten Plays,* ed. Robert T. Rolf and John K. Gillespie (Honolulu: University of Hawai'i Press, 1992), 7. The remarkable activity in theater in Japan at the time was part of what E. Taylor Atkins has succinctly characterized as a broad "neonationalist cultural efflorescence inspired by student-led protests against U.S. hegemony in East Asia and facilitated by Japan's rise to economic prominence." E. Taylor Atkins, *Blue Nippon: Authenticating Jazz in Japan* (Durham: Duke University Press, 2001), 13.

3. Steven Clark, "Terayama in Amsterdam and the Internationalization of Experimental Theatre," in *Modern Japanese Theatre and Performance,* ed. David Jortner, Keiko McDonald, and Kevin J. Wetmore Jr. (New York: Lexington Books, 2006), 109.

4. Takayuki Tatsumi, *Full Metal Apache: Transactions between Cyberpunk Japan and Avant-Pop America* (Durham: Duke University Press, 2006), 137–38.

5. Carol Fisher Sorgenfrei, *Unspeakable Acts: The Avant-Garde Theatre of Tera-*

yama Shūji and Postwar Japan (Honolulu: University of Hawai'i Press, 2005), 88–89.

6. Akihiko Senda, "Japanese Theater in Transformation, 1960–1970," trans. Mari Boyd, in *Half a Century of Japanese Theater VI: 1960s, Part 1,* ed. Japan Playwrights Association (Tokyo: Kinokuniya, 2004), 2.

7. Anna Kisselgoff, "Dai Rakuda Kan's Theater of Raw Images," *New York Times,* 19 April 1987.

8. Ellen Stewart, quoted in Jennifer Dunning, "Dance and Stage Troupes Doing the Unexpected," *New York Times,* 7 March 1986.

9. Stephen J. Bottoms, *Playing Underground: A Critical History of the 1960s Off-Off-Broadway Movement* (Ann Arbor: University of Michigan Press, 2004), 87.

10. Josh Greenfeld, "Their Hearts Belong to La MaMa," *New York Times,* 9 July 1967.

11. Bottoms, *Playing Underground,* 272–73.

12. Stewart had also been awarded a Ford Foundation grant the previous year. See Cindy Rosenthal, "Ellen Stewart: La MaMa of Us All," *TDR: The Drama Review* 50, no. 2 (2006): 20. Many other grants have followed, including (in 1985) a MacArthur Foundation "genius" award.

13. Rosenthal, "Ellen Stewart," 14–15.

14. Mel Gussow, "In Search of Adventure Off Broadway," *New York Times,* 21 May 1982.

15. T. E. Kalem, "Theater: Arigato!," *Time,* 3 August 1970.

16. After opening at the Public Theater in 1967, *Hair* moved to Broadway in April 1968 to begin what would turn into a four-year run. The director was Tom O'Horgan, hired because of the reputation he had built at La MaMa. *Hair,* as Sally Banes has noted, "brought 'hippie' culture to the mainstream." Sally Banes, *Greenwich Village, 1963: Avant-Garde Performance and the Effervescent Body* (Durham: Duke University Press, 1993), 219.

17. Clive Barnes, "Theater: Oriental Rock—Tokyo Kid Brothers Play at La MaMa," *New York Times,* 27 June 1970.

18. Walter Kerr, "A Love Letter from Tokyo," *New York Times,* 16 August 1970.

19. Kalem, "Theater: Arigato!"

20. Clive Barnes, "Stage: The Tokyo Kid Brothers Again—'Coney Island Play' Also Includes Americans," *New York Times,* 31 October 1970.

21. Mel Gussow, "Stage: 'City,' by Tokyo Kid Brothers—a Motorcycle Musical Given at La MaMa," *New York Times,* 9 August 1974.

22. Henry Scott Stokes, "Samurai Musical Opens at La MaMa Tomorrow," *New York Times,* 6 November 1981.

23. Mel Gussow, "Stage: 'Japanesque' Samurai Musical," *New York Times,* 15 November 1981.

24. Elenore Lester, "'There Will Be No Audience,'" *New York Times,* 5 July 1970.

25. Mel Gussow, "Theater: Japanese View—Shuji Terayama's Play Now at La MaMa," *New York Times,* 15 July 1970.

26. Takashi Oka, "Tokyo: Kabuki, Rock, and the Twain," *New York Times,* 10 August 1970.

27. Clark, "Terayama in Amsterdam," 109.

28. Mel Gussow, "Stage: 'Little Elephant Is Dead,' a Japanese Play," *New York Times,* 16 May 1979.

29. Kobo Abe, *Woman in the Dunes,* trans. E. Dale Saunders (New York: Alfred A. Knopf, 1964). Abe's US reputation was enhanced by the critical success, which included Oscar nominations and a prize at the Cannes Film Festival, of Hiroshi Teshigahara's film *Woman in the Dunes* (1964).

30. Kobo Abe, *Friends,* trans. Donald Keene (New York: Grove Press, 1969).

31. Quoted in Nancy K. Shields, *Fake Fish: The Theater of Kobo Abe* (New York: Weatherhill, 1996), 173.

32. Shields, *Fake Fish,* 172.

33. Sorgenfrei, *Unspeakable Acts,* 141.

34. John Corry, "Stage: 'Directions to Servants' of Shuji Terayama at La MaMa," *New York Times,* 21 June 1980. Just before its run at La MaMa, *Directions to Servants* was presented at the Spoleto Festival USA in Charleston, South Carolina. For a detailed description of the production at Spoleto and La MaMa, see Maria Myers, "Terayama's *Directions to Servants,*" *TDR: The Drama Review* 25, no. 1 (1981): 79–94. Not all critics were as positive in their response as Corry. As Sorgenfrei has noted, a *Village Voice* critic referred to the play as "garbage." Sorgenfrei, *Unspeakable Acts,* 18.

35. See Janet Maslin, "Screen: Hide and Seek," *New York Times,* 24 June 1980.

36. Jennifer Dunning, "Modern Dance: On the Beach and under the Bridge," *New York Times,* 31 July 1981.

37. Jennifer Dunning, "The Dance: Kazuo Ohno," *New York Times,* 31 July 1981.

38. Gwin Chin, "Japanese Dancers in America: What Draws Them?," *New York Times,* 2 December 1979.

39. Anna Kisselgoff, "Dance That Startles and Challenges Is Coming from Abroad," *New York Times,* 13 October 1985.

40. Bonnie Sue Stein, "Butoh: 'Twenty Years Ago We Were Crazy, Dirty, and Mad,'" *TDR: The Drama Review* 30, no. 2 (1986): 107–26.

41. Jason Zinoman, "His Mission: Seeking Out Next Wave's Next Identity," *New York Times,* 3 July 2005.

42. Patricia Madsen, "*The Man from the East* by Stomu Yamash'ta," *Educational Theatre Journal* 25, no. 2 (1973): 241. The work was originally written and composed under the title *The Man from the East,* which is also the name of the soundtrack from the show that Yamashita released for sale.

43. Terry Trucco, "Dancers Who Probe the Dark Corners of the Mind," *New York Times,* 28 October 1984.

44. Anna Kisselgoff, "Dance That Startles."

45. Anna Kisselgoff, "New Choreographers Stretch the Very Definition of Dance," *New York Times,* 1 December 1985.

46. Anna Kisselgoff, "The Dance: Kazuo Ohno's 'Dead Sea,'" *New York Times,* 21 November 1985.

47. Takashi Oka, "Japanese Takes on Quixote Challenge," *New York Times,* 18 February 1970.

48. Quoted in Oka, "Japanese Takes on Quixote Challenge."

49. Steven C. Ridgely, *Japanese Counterculture: The Antiestablishment Art of Terayama Shūji* (Minneapolis: University of Minnesota Press, 2010), ix.

Chapter 4

1. Quoted in Matthias Kriesberg, "Japan's New Generation of Composers," *New York Times,* 6 February 2000.

2. Leslie Rubinstein, "Oriental Musicians Come of Age," *New York Times,* 23 November 1980.

3. Thomas R. H. Havens, *Radicals and Realists in the Japanese Nonverbal Arts: The Avant-Garde Rejection of Modernism* (Honolulu: University of Hawai'i Press, 2006), 3.

4. Havens, *Radicals and Realists,* 2.

5. Yoshio Sugimoto, *An Introduction to Japanese Society,* 3d ed. (New York: Cambridge University Press, 2010), 18.

6. Naoyuki Miura, "Artistic Director's Notes: Why Music From Japan for 25 Years?" *Music From Japan Newsletter* 5 (2001): 6.

7. Kriesberg, "Japan's New Generation of Composers."

8. M. J. Heale, "Anatomy of a Scare: Yellow Peril Politics in America, 1980–1993," *Journal of American Studies* 43, no. 1 (2009): 22.

9. Howard Taubman, "Japanese Impresario: Once a Tenor, Fujiwara Now Spreads Opera Gospel Where It Is Still Exotic," *New York Times,* 5 October 1952.

10. Howard Taubman, "Japanese Singers in Opera Cast Here: Members of Fujiwara Troupe Join in 'Madame Butterfly' at the City Center," *New York Times,* 10 October 1952.

11. John Briggs, "Cio-Cio-san from Japan: Soprano Accustomed to Mixing Languages but Insists on Authentic Acting Style," *New York Times,* 13 September 1953.

12. "City Center Stages a Bi-lingual Opera: Members of Fujiwara Troupe Take Leading Japanese Roles in 'Madame Butterfly,'" *New York Times,* 28 October 1953.

13. H. C. S. [Harold C. Schonberg], "Japanese Troupe Sings 'Butterfly,'" *New York Times,* 19 October 1956.

14. Donal Henahan, "Met Opera: Vintage '58 'Butterfly,'" *New York Times,* 30 September 1981.

15. "'Met' Is Going Native in Restaging 'Butterfly,'" *New York Times,* 28 June 1957.

16. John Briggs, "No Fireflies for 'Butterfly': They Do Not Fly during Cherry Blossom Season Says Opera Director," *New York Times,* 16 February 1958.

17. Howard Taubman, "Opera: Happy 'Butterfly,'" *New York Times,* 20 February 1958.

18. Eric Salzman, "Kenji Kobayashi in Debut Recital: Japanese Violinist Displays Great Skill at Town Hall," *New York Times,* 25 April 1961.

19. Harold Schonberg, "Music: Japanese Philharmonic Arrives—Group, Although Young, Is Cosmopolitan," *New York Times,* 12 October 1964.

20. Ross Parmenter, "Kimio Eto Offers Music on the Koto: Japanese Works Presented at Philharmonic Hall," *New York Times,* 5 November 1962.

21. Richard F. Shepard, "Philharmonic in Japan," *New York Times,* 2 February 1962.

22. Havens, *Radicals and Realists,* 171.

23. "Instrumentalists: Eto and the Koto," *Time,* 8 January 1965.

24. See, for example, Allen Hughes, "Koto: Reiko Kamata," *New York Times,* 26 April 1981.

25. Ondeko-za made a brief appearance in 1977 at the Brooklyn Academy of Music. See *New York Amsterdam News,* 19 November 1977.

26. Allen Hughes, "The Fierce Dedication of the 'Demon' Drummers," *New York Times,* 30 April 1978.

27. John Rockwell, "Ondeko-Za at the Beacon," *New York Times,* 3 May 1978.

28. Miura, "Artistic Director's Notes."

29. John Rockwell, "Music: Focus on Japan—Brooklyn Philharmonia Gets Around to Takemitsu in 'Modern' Series," *New York Times,* 27 March 1975.

30. Donal Henahan, "4 New Works from Japan Are Played," *New York Times,* 6 November 1975.

31. John Rockwell, "Musical Meeting of East and West," *New York Times,* 17 December 1976.

32. Raymond Ericson, "Concert: Japanese Music," *New York Times,* 3 November 1979.

33. Harold C. Schonberg, "Championing Japanese Music," *New York Times,* 21 February 1982.

34. Allen Hughes, "Concert: 'Music From Japan' Performed at Carnegie Hall," *New York Times,* 26 February 1982.

35. Allen Hughes, "Concert: Schuller Conducts New Japanese Music," *New York Times,* 24 February 1983.

36. Hughes, "Concert: Schuller Conducts New Japanese Music."

37. Henry Scott Stokes, "'Music From Japan' at Carnegie Hall," *New York Times,* 23 February 1983.

38. John Rockwell, "Concert: Music From Japan Series at Asia Society," *New York Times,* 4 December 1983.

39. Allen Hughes, "Concert: The Drum in Japanese Music," *New York Times,* 26 February 1984.

40. Tim Page, "Music: Miyata Plays the Sho," *New York Times,* 23 February 1987.

41. Bernard Holland, "Ritual and Technology," *New York Times,* 28 March 1990.

42. Quoted in Junichi Aoyagi, "New Yorkers Hear the Sounds of Japan: Annual Music Festival Features Dual Theme of Tradition and Innovation," *Nikkei Weekly*, 14 March 1994.

43. Aoyagi, "New Yorkers Hear the Sounds of Japan."

44. Christopher Keene, who was general director of the New York City Opera, translated Claus H. Henneberg's original German libretto into English. Keene was to have conducted the work, but he died shortly before the production opened. Joseph Colaneri took over as conductor.

45. Quoted in Lindsley Cameron, "The Happening of an Opera Waiting to Happen," *New York Times*, 15 October 1995.

46. Bernard Holland, "Resurrecting a Daydream of the Exotic East," *New York Times*, 21 October 1995.

47. Naoyuki Miura, "A Greeting from the Artistic Director," *Music From Japan Newsletter* 1 (1996): 6.

48. Allan Kozinn, "Today's Japanese Melodies as Heard in Japan," *New York Times*, 22 January 1998.

49. Matthias Kriesberg, "A Composer Beats the West at Its Own Game," *New York Times*, 1 February 2004.

50. Jon Pareles, "The Songs of a Culture Almost Lost," *New York Times*, 11 February 2004.

51. Music From Japan is not literally a one-person operation. Since the beginning, Naoyuki Miura's wife, Mari Ono, has been executive director.

52. Allan Kozinn, "Music From Japan: Interplay of Antiquity with Some Modernity," *New York Times*, 21 February 2010.

53. Kriesberg, "Japan's New Generation of Composers."

54. Kozinn, "Music From Japan."

55. Quoted in Kriesberg, "Japan's New Generation of Composers."

56. Kriesberg, "Japan's New Generation of Composers."

57. Jeremy Eichler, "New Interest in Ancient Sounds," *New York Times*, 15 September 2004.

58. Miura, "Artistic Director's Notes." Music From Japan has received a measure of recognition in Japan for its contributions to cultural exchange with the United States. See Kotoko Fukunaka, *Ongaku, michi e no tabi: "Myūjikku furomu japan ongakusai" kuronikuru* [Into the unknown with music: A chronicle of the "Music From Japan" concert series] (Kawasaki: Kozuikikaku, 2011).

Chapter 5

1. Nigel Redden, quoted in Matthew Gurewitsch, "Serving Two Cities, Staying True to Each," *New York Times*, 8 February 2009.

2. Patrick Lonergan, *Theatre and Globalization: Irish Drama in the Celtic Tiger Era* (New York: Palgrave Macmillan, 2009), 72.

3. Quoted in Gurewitsch, "Serving Two Cities."

4. Nigel Redden, "About Lincoln Center Festival: Note from the Director,"

http://www.lincolncenterfestival.org/index.php/2012-about (accessed 16 March 2012).

5. The heading is a quote from Allan Kozinn, "Lincoln Center Plans an 'Intense' Festival," *New York Times,* 15 November 1995.

6. *Lincoln Center for the Performing Arts, 2003–2004* (New York: Lincoln Center for the Performing Arts, 2003), unpaginated. The booklet also noted that "some 5,000 performances and events" would be offered that season.

7. "About Lincoln Center: Overview," http://about.lincolncenter.org/about/about-overview (accessed 18 April 2012).

8. Howard Taubman, "New Cultural Vista for the City: The Lincoln Square Project Promises Rich Creative Fulfillment for the Performing Arts," *New York Times,* 22 April 1956.

9. Seymour Peck, "A Rockefeller Enters 'Show Biz,'" *New York Times,* 18 November 1956.

10. Kozinn, "Lincoln Center Plans an 'Intense' Festival."

11. "Lincoln Center's Welcome Festival," *New York Times,* 29 November 1995.

12. Quoted in Susan Elliott, "A Transforming Event for Lincoln Center," *Atlanta Journal-Constitution,* 22 July 2001.

13. Aki Takahashi, the widely lauded pianist from Japan, was among those performing with Tan Dun's group.

14. Jon Pareles, "Japan's Sounds and Rituals, Bridging the Centuries," *New York Times,* 29 July 1996.

15. Barbara Kirshenblatt-Gimblett, "Intangible Heritage as Metacultural Production," *Museum* 56, nos. 1–2 (2004): 57.

16. Ben Brantley, "Genuinely Ugly Americans, as Viewed by the Japanese," *New York Times,* 11 July 2002.

17. Jesse Green, "Broadway's Fondest, Furthest Fan Comes Home," *New York Times,* 28 November 2004.

18. Amon Miyamoto, "Notes on the Program," *Stagebill: Lincoln Center Presents Lincoln Center Festival 2002* (New York: Lincoln Center for the Performing Arts, 2002), 20C.

19. Linda Winer, "Japanese See Us Seeing Them: Tokyo Troupe Mirrors 'Pacific Overtures,'" *Newsday,* 12 July 2002.

20. Green, "Broadway's Fondest, Furthest Fan."

21. Winer, "Japanese See Us Seeing Them."

22. Quoted in Patricia O'Haire, "Remade in Japan," *Daily News,* 8 July 2002. The production Miyamoto saw on television in Japan was "videotaped from the stage of the Winter Garden Theater," the *Times* reported in 1976. It was "the first telecast of an American stage musical in that country." "'Pacific Overtures' Taped for Japan," *New York Times,* 12 June 1976.

23. Brantley, "Genuinely Ugly Americans."

24. Anna Kisselgoff, "The Rarely Seen Side of a Brilliant Choreographer," *New York Times,* 8 July 2004.

25. Anna Kisselgoff, "A Japanese Dancer in Impressive Debut," *New York Times,* 7 April 1970.

26. Kisselgoff, "Rarely Seen Side."

27. Todd Zaun, "Tokyo Tales Onstage, Not Lost in Translation," *New York Times,* 19 July 2004.

28. Marigold Hughes, "The 'Elephant Vanished,' But Found Its Way Back," *Daily Yomiuri,* 24 June 2004.

29. "About Complicité," http://www.complicte.org/about/ (accessed 9 February 2005).

30. Quoted in John O'Mahony, "Simon McBurney: Anarchy in the UK," *Guardian,* 1 January 2005.

31. Ulf Hannerz, *Transnational Connections: Culture, People, Places* (New York: Routledge, 1996), 136.

32. Zaun, "Tokyo Tales Onstage."

33. Ben Brantley, "Sifting Through the Splinters of a Fragmented World," *New York Times,* 23 July 2004.

34. Quoted in Akihiko Senda, "Contemporary Theater," in Ronald Cavaye, Paul Griffith, and Akihiko Senda, *A Guide to the Japanese Stage: From Traditional to Cutting Edge* (New York: Kodansha International, 2004), 241.

35. Senda, "Contemporary Theater," 241.

36. For photos of the interior and exterior of the tent-theater, see Elaine Louie, "Currents: Kabuki, under a Big Top," *New York Times,* 15 July 2004.

37. Ben Brantley, "The Stuff of Nightmares in a Kabuki Carnival Maze," *New York Times,* 20 July 2004.

38. John K. Gillespie, "Ninagawa Yukio," in *Encyclopedia of Asian Theatre,* ed. Samuel L. Leiter, vol. 1 (Westport, CT: Greenwood Press, 2007), 465.

39. Ben Brantley, "A Cycle of Destruction, from Love to Despair," *New York Times,* 30 July 2005.

40. Kazuko Matsuoka, "Notes on the Program," in *Playbill: Lincoln Center Presents Lincoln Center Festival 2005* (New York: Lincoln Center for the Performing Arts, 2005), unpaginated.

41. Yukio Ninagawa, "Director's Note," in *Playbill: Lincoln Center Presents Lincoln Center Festival 2005* (New York: Lincoln Center for the Performing Arts, 2005), unpaginated.

42. Brantley, "A Cycle of Destruction."

43. Anna Kisselgoff, "Reconciling the Contradictions of Japan," *New York Times,* 9 November 1992.

44. John Rockwell, "A Rare Visitor Enchants His Audience with Images," *New York Times,* 24 July 2006.

45. *Lincoln Center Festival 2006* (New York: Lincoln Center for the Performing Arts, 2006), 2.

46. Charles Isherwood, "A Multifaceted New View of a Tradition Built on Dreams," *New York Times,* 29 July 2006.

47. Charles Isherwood, "Guilty Pleasures of Comic Kabuki," *New York Times,* 19 July 2007.

48. Ben Brantley, "'Musashi': Turning Swords into Slapsticks," *New York Times,* 9 July 2010.

49. Tadazumi Imamura, "Introduction to *Yabuhara, the Blind Master Minstrel,*" trans. Marguerite Wells, in *Half a Century of Japanese Theater VI: 1960s, Part 1,* ed. Japan Playwrights Association (Tokyo: Kinokuniya, 2004), 63.

50. Brantley, "'Musashi': Turning Swords into Slapsticks."

51. Gia Kourlas, "Pursuing Harmony, with Just a Bare Bulb Illuminating the Way," *New York Times,* 12 July 2010.

52. "Lincoln Center Festival 2011," http://lincolncenterfestival.org/2011/pdfs/LincolnCenterFestival2011_Brochure.pdf (accessed 18 April 2012). The material on *Temple of the Golden Pavilion* is on page 17 of the brochure.

53. Nigel Redden, "Lincoln Center Festival 2011: Temple of the Golden Pavilion," http://lincolncenterfestival.org/2011/index.php/lcf-2011-temple-of-the-golden-pavilion (accessed 18 April 2012).

54. Neil Genzlinger, "Pyrotechnics Aplenty in a Tale of Madness," *New York Times,* 22 July 2011.

55. "Lincoln Center Festival 2011."

56. Amon Miyamoto, "Program Notes: *Temple of the Golden Pavilion,*" http://www.lincolncenterfestival.org/index.php/lcf-2011-temple-of-the-golden-pavilion (accessed 23 July 2011).

57. John Rockwell, "A Country's Most Authentic Art Is Often Its Best Ambassador," *New York Times,* 19 December 2003.

Chapter 6

1. Brooks Atkinson, "Theatre: Grand Kabuki—Japanese Troupe Is at the City Center," *New York Times,* 3 June 1960.

2. Nancy K. Shields, *Fake Fish: The Theater of Kobo Abe* (New York: Weatherhill, 1996), 166.

3. Mel Gussow, "Stage: 'Little Elephant Is Dead,' a Japanese Play," *New York Times,* 16 May 1979.

4. Shields, *Fake Fish,* 166.

5. Henry Scott-Stokes, "Japan's Kafka Goes on the Road," *New York Times,* 29 April 1979.

6. It was a particularly interesting critique given that the production was part of the 1979 Japan Today festival, as previously mentioned in this study.

7. Susan Bassnett-McGuire, *Translation Studies* (New York: Routledge, 1991), xvi.

8. Jean Graham-Jones, "Editorial Comment: The Stakes of Theatrical Translation," *Theatre Journal* 59, no. 3 (2007): ix–x.

9. Scholars and critics in Japan often use the term *hon'yakugeki* (trans-

lated drama) in contrast to *sosakugeki* (literally "created drama"—referring to work originally written and produced in Japan). See, for example, the chapter "Hon'yakugeki no genzai" [Translated drama today], in Kojin Nishido, *Engeki wa kanō ka: 1995nen igo no gekiteki sōzōryoku* [Is drama possible? The dramatic imagination after 1995] (Tokyo: Bansei Shobo, 2008). The reference to 1995 in Nishido's title signifies the earthquake in Kobe and the sarin gas attack in the Tokyo subway system that occurred within weeks of each other early that year. Nishido begins the chapter on translated drama with the observation that in Japan the most critically acclaimed play of 2006 was a Japanese-language production of Edward Albee's *Who's Afraid of Virginia Woolf?* directed by Keralino Sandorovich (208).

10. "About Playco," http://www.playco.org/about.html (accessed 1 March 2012).

11. Numerous published translations already reflect long-standing interest in, and especially the history of, university-based projects focusing on English-language productions of classical works of kabuki, noh, and kyogen. A notable example is *Kabuki Plays on Stage*, edited by James R. Brandon and Samuel L. Leiter, a four-volume set published in 2002–3 by the University of Hawai'i Press.

12. *Half a Century of Japanese Theater*—a ten-volume collection of translated plays originally written and produced in Japan from the 1950s through the 1990s—was edited by the Japan Playwrights Association and published between 1999 and 2008 by Kinokuniya. The project was underwritten by the Japanese government's Agency for Culture Affairs, the Japan Foundation, and the Saison Foundation. As noted on the flyleaf of the volumes, "The threefold aim of the Japan Playwrights Association in publishing this series is to offer performable English translations of modern Japanese plays, to encourage the production of such plays by foreign theatrical companies, and to extend possibilities for further international exchange in theater." Other recent anthologies of translations or studies that feature them include M. Cody Poulton, *A Beggar's Art: Scripting Modernity in Japanese Drama, 1900–1930* (Honolulu: University of Hawai'i Press, 2010); Laurence Kominz, ed., *Mishima on Stage:* The Black Lizard *and Other Plays* (Ann Arbor: Center for Japanese Studies, University of Michigan, 2007); Mari Boyd, *The Aesthetics of Quietude: Ōta Shōgo and the Theatre of Divestiture* (Tokyo: Sophia University Press, 2006); Carol Fisher Sorgenfrei, *Unspeakable Acts: The Avant-Garde Theatre of Terayama Shūji and Postwar Japan* (Honolulu: University of Hawai'i Press, 2005); Hiroaki Sato, trans., My Friend Hitler *and Other Plays of Yukio Mishima* (New York: Columbia University Press, 2002); and Robert T. Rolf and John K. Gillespie, eds., *Alternative Japanese Drama: Ten Plays* (Honolulu: University of Hawai'i Press, 1992). In addition, *Asian Theatre Journal* is an important resource for plays in translation. Examples of work that has appeared include Ai Nagai's *The Three Hagi Sisters* (*Hagi-ke no san shimai*), trans. Loren Edelson (21, no. 1 [2004]); Koharu Kisaragi's *MORAL,* trans. Keiko Tsuneda, Colleen Lanki, and Lei Sadakari (21, no. 2 [2004]); Yukio Mishima's *Primary Colors* (*Sangenshoku*), trans. Christopher L. Pearce (23, no. 2 [2006]); and Toshiko Tamura's

Slave (*Dorei*), trans. Anne Sokolsky and Tim Yamamura (27, no. 2 [2010]). A new volume—M. Cody Poulton, J. Thomas Rimer, and Mitsuya Mori, eds., *The Columbia Anthology of Modern Japanese Drama*—is forthcoming from Columbia University Press. In 2006 Kevin J. Wetmore Jr. published a comprehensive bibliography of modern Japanese plays translated into English, "Modern Japanese Drama in English," *Asian Theatre Journal* 23, no. 1 (2006): 179–205.

13. A fourth play, Akio Miyazawa's *At the Entrance to New Town* (*Nyūtaun iriguchi*) was also read, but there were enough funds to stage only the three other works.

14. Graham-Jones, "Editorial Comment," x.

15. Tom Sellar, "Meanwhile, in the Rest of the World . . . ," *Village Voice*, 15 May 2007.

16. Brian Powell, review of J. Thomas Rimer, *Toward a Modern Japanese Theatre: Kishida Kunio, Monumenta Nipponica* 30, no. 1 (1975): 98. As theatre critic Yoichi Uchida has written, the "traditional performing arts and *shingeki* (the new theater) comprise the theatrical arts [in Japan]." Yoichi Uchida, "The 1980s in the Context of Japanese Theater History," trans. Mari Boyd, in *Half a Century of Japanese Theater III: 1980s, Part 1*, ed. Japan Playwrights Association (Tokyo: Kinokuniya, 2001), 1.

17. M. Cody Poulton, "Foreign or Domestic Drama? Osanai Kaoru and Modern Japanese Theatre," in *Text and Presentation, 2006*, ed. Stratos E. Constantinidis, Comparative Drama Conference Series, no. 3 (Jefferson, NC: McFarland, 2007), 169.

18. Poulton, "Foreign or Domestic Drama?," 167.

19. Thomas R. H. Havens, *Artist and Patron in Postwar Japan: Dance, Music, Theater, and the Visual Arts, 1955–1980* (Princeton: Princeton University Press, 1982), 145.

20. Poulton, "Foreign or Domestic Drama?," 169.

21. Poulton, "Foreign or Domestic Drama?," 178.

22. Poulton, "Foreign or Domestic Drama?," 178.

23. Yasunari Takahashi, "Introduction: Suzuki's Work in the Context of Japanese Theatre," in Ian Carruthers and Yasunari Takahashi, *The Theatre of Suzuki Tadashi* (Cambridge: Cambridge University Press, 2004), 2.

24. Technologies of access (supertitles and so on) are called into play, of course, when companies from abroad visit Japan—as well as in the case of works of opera performed in a language other than Japanese.

25. In the 1920s Osanai traveled abroad to see the work of, and consult with, directors such as Max Reinhardt and Konstantin Stanislavski. See M. Cody Poulton, "The Rhetoric of the Real" in *Modern Japanese Theatre and Performance*, ed. David Jortner, Keiko McDonald, and Kevin J. Wetmore Jr. (New York: Lexington Books, 2006), 28. Tamiya Kuriyama has directed numerous plays in translation. See Akihiko Senda, "Contemporary Theater," in Ronald Cavaye, Paul Griffith,

and Akihiko Senda, *A Guide to the Japanese Stage: From Traditional to Cutting Edge* (New York: Kodansha International, 2004), 238. Also, the example of Juro Kara, who emerged in the late 1960s as a leader of Japan's avant-garde movement, should be noted. The first production of his Situation Theatre (Jokyo Gekijo) was a translation of Jean-Paul Sartre's *La Putain Respecteuse* (*The Respectful Prostitute*). The name Situation Theatre was translated from *Un Théâtre de Situations,* the title of a book by Sartre. See David G. Goodman, "*Angura:* Japan's Nostalgic Avant-Garde," in *Not the Other Avant-Garde: The Transnational Foundations of Avant-Garde Performance,* ed. James M. Harding and John Rouse (Ann Arbor: University of Michigan Press, 2006), 259. Although the underground "little theater" movement is basically defined as a rebellion against *shingeki,* Akihiko Senda has pointed out that Minoru Betsuyaku, "the major playwright of the theater of the absurd in Japan[,] . . . was strongly influenced by Beckett's *Waiting for Godot,* which was first performed in Japan by the Literary Theater company [Bungaku-za, a major *shingeki* company] in 1960." Akihiko Senda, "Japanese Theater in Transformation, 1960–1970," trans. Mari Boyd, in *Half a Century of Japanese Theater VI: 1960s, Part 1,* ed. Japan Playwrights Association (Tokyo: Kinokuniya, 2004), 5.

26. Senda, "Japanese Theater in Transformation," 3.

27. Recent studies of theater that address periods of Japan's isolationism include James R. Brandon, *Kabuki's Forgotten War, 1931–1945* (Honolulu: University of Hawai'i Press, 2009); and Brian Powell, *Japan's Modern Theatre: A Century of Change and Continuity* (London: Japan Library, Routledge Curzon, 2002).

28. Edwin Gentzler and Maria Tymoczko, "Introduction," in *Translation and Power,* ed. Maria Tymoczko and Edwin Gentzler (Boston: University of Massachusetts Press, 2002), xxi.

29. Poulton, "Foreign or Domestic Drama?," 169.

30. Takahashi, "Introduction," 5. As previously mentioned, in 1982 Suzuki's Japanese-language *The Trojan Women* was presented at Japan Society, while *The Bacchae* was performed at La MaMa with a cast of American actors (speaking in English) and Japanese actors (speaking in Japanese).

31. Karen Kelsky, *Women on the Verge: Japanese Women, Western Dreams* (Durham: Duke University Press, 2001).

32. Havens, *Artist and Patron,* 148. The leading commercial producer of translated Broadway musicals in Japan is Shiki. It offers a full schedule of original and translated plays and musicals in its eight company-owned theaters—four in Tokyo and one each in Hokkaido, Nagoya, Kyoto, and Osaka—and public and private theaters around Japan.

33. Havens uses *shingeki* as a blanket term for these companies. Havens, *Artist and Patron,* 146. Hironori Terasaki divides theater in Japan into "commercial theatre (*shōgyō engeki*) and art theatre (*shingeki*)." Hironori Terasaki, "Trends in the Japanese Theatrical World," *Asian Theatre Journal* 1, no. 1 (1984): 105.

34. Gentzler and Tymoczko, "Introduction," xv.

35. Its bilingual website is "designed to promote the works of living French-language playwrights." "What is Entr-Actes?," http://entractes.sacd.fr/en/index.php (accessed 1 March 2012).

36. The article, by Jane Gardner, was published in Theatre Ontario's February–March 2007 newsletter. "Mining Canadian Theatre for a Japanese Audience," http://www.theatreontario.org/content/news26-5.htm (accessed 26 March 2009).

37. "*Cleanskins,*" http://www.nntt.jac.go.jp/english/season/s330e/s330e.html (accessed 1 March 2012).

38. Marvin Carlson, *Speaking in Tongues: Language at Play in the Theatre* (Ann Arbor: University of Michigan Press, 2006), 17.

39. Emerson Chapin, "Noh Drama Group May Tour U.S.: Japanese Hoping to Spread Interest in Ancient Theater," *New York Times,* 19 April 1964.

40. Carlson, *Speaking in Tongues,* 17.

41. Louis Calta, "Running Comment on Kabuki Slated," *New York Times,* 11 May 1960.

42. Margo Jefferson, "Strange Languages Convey More Than Mere Words," *New York Times,* 22 January 2005.

43. Brooks Atkinson, "Theatre: More Kabuki—'Chushingura' Heads City Center Bill," *New York Times,* 10 June 1960.

44. Ben Brantley, "The Stuff of Nightmares in a Kabuki Carnival Maze," *New York Times,* 20 July 2004.

45. Quoted in Matthew Gurewitsch, "Feel Free to Shout at the Visitors from Japan," *New York Times,* 15 July 2007.

46. Quoted in Charles Isherwood, "Guilty Pleasures of Comic Kabuki," *New York Times,* 19 July 2007.

47. Lawrence Venuti, *The Translator's Invisibility: A History of Translation* (New York: Routledge, 1995), 8.

48. Faubion Bowers, "Without Them, It's All Greek (or French, or Japanese)," *New York Times,* 30 August 1970.

49. Clive Barnes, "Theater: Far from Remote Kabuki," *New York Times,* 11 September 1969.

50. Bowers, "Without Them, It's All Greek."

51. The English- and Japanese-language earphone-guide system has developed into what is for many an indispensable part of the kabuki theatergoing experience in Japan. The high quality of the system is the product of the guides' thorough knowledge of all aspects of kabuki, the pleasing style of the presentation (sometimes the work of trained actors), and the ease of use and reliability of the technology.

52. Bowers, "Without Them, It's All Greek." Although "the knowledgeable Japanese spectator" is how Bowers generally characterized kabuki audiences, a few years earlier actor Danzo Ichikawa VIII was quoted as saying that in Japan "[m]ost of today's [kabuki] audiences come in tour groups as curiosity-seekers,

and fewer than a hundred in a full house really understand what is happening on the stage." Quoted in "Kabuki Actor Ending 82-Year Career," *New York Times,* 1 May 1966.

53. Bowers, "Without Them, It's All Greek."

54. Gentzler and Tymoczko, "Introduction," xxv.

55. Anna Kisselgoff, "Kabuki Arrives—and It's Grand," *New York Times,* 1 September 1977.

56. Richard Eder, "Grand Kabuki Does Theater and Dance," *New York Times,* 8 February 1979.

57. Anna Kisselgoff, "Stage: Kabuki, at the Met," *New York Times,* 10 July 1985.

58. Although unrelated to kabuki, perhaps the greatest praise came from Mel Gussow in 1990 when he wrote that Bowers delivered the lines of *Macbeth* (using the Shakespearian original)—on the occasion of a Japanese-language production of the play directed by Yukio Ninagawa at the Brooklyn Academy of Music—with "the diction of a trained actor." Mel Gussow, "Universality of 'Macbeth' in Japanese," *New York Times,* 22 October 1990.

59. Carlson, *Speaking in Tongues,* 53.

60. Bowers, "Without Them, It's All Greek."

61. John Martin, "The Dance: Kabuki: A Glimpse of Japan's Classic Theatre in Its Choreographic Aspects," *New York Times,* 14 February 1954.

62. John Martin, "Dance: Gagaku: Delicate Enchantments of Performers from Japanese Imperial Household," *New York Times,* 31 May 1959.

63. John Martin, "Gagaku in Debut Outside of Japan: Musicians and Dancers of Imperial Household Give City Center Performance," *New York Times,* 27 May 1959.

64. John Martin, "Ballet: Second Category—Another Gagaku-Style Program Offered by Japanese Troupe at City Center," *New York Times,* 29 May 1959.

65. John Martin, "Dance: Gagaku."

66. "Dancers to the Emperor," *Time,* 8 June 1959.

67. Robert Garfias, *Gagaku: The Music and Dances of the Japanese Imperial Household,* ed. Lincoln Kirstein (New York: Theatre Arts Books, 1959), unpaginated.

68. Clive Barnes, "Stage: Power of Kabuki—Drama and Dance Offer Theatrical Treats," *New York Times,* 18 September 1969.

69. Jennifer Dunning, "Dance: Noh Theater," *New York Times,* 1 September 1982.

70. Jack Anderson, "Sitting Back and Enjoying What Can't Be Understood," *New York Times,* 1 March 1993. Anderson identified Chuma, a longtime resident of New York, as "Japanese-born."

71. Mel Gussow, "Theater: 'Shingyo' Follows Death of Soul in Space," *New York Times,* 30 September 1975.

72. John Corry, "Stage: 'Directions to Servants' of Shuji Terayama at La Mama," *New York Times,* 21 June 1980.

73. Jennifer Dunning, "Theater: Grand Kabuki Opens 2-Week Season," *New York Times,* 30 June 1982.

74. D. J. R. Bruckner, "Potpourri of Galileo, Tom Sawyer, and Samurai," *New York Times,* 9 July 1988.

75. Jefferson, "Strange Languages."

76. Lincoln Kirstein, "Foreword," in Robert Garfias, *Gagaku: The Music and Dances of the Japanese Imperial Household,* ed. Lincoln Kirstein (New York: Theatre Arts Books, 1959), unpaginated.

77. Naoki Sakai, "Modernity and Its Critique: The Problem of Universalism and Particularism," in *Postmodernism and Japan,* ed. Masao Miyoshi and H. D. Harootunian (Durham: Duke University Press, 1989), 104.

78. Sakai, "Modernity and Its Critique," 105.

79. Anna Kisselgoff, "Dance: Japanese Mime," *New York Times,* 4 December 1971.

80. Jack Anderson, "Dance: Japan's Kyogen," *New York Times,* 12 July 1984. Universality has been invoked on the performers' side as well. Visiting the United States in 1964, kyogen actor Manzo Nomura "has not encountered any difficulty in communication. 'Movement is universal,' he said. For the first few minutes of a performance, he said, there usually are a few nervous giggles. But when the audience discovers the broadness of the comedy, it responds quickly." Louis Calta, "Japanese Actors Perform Kyogen: Manzo Nomura and 2 Sons Show Ancient Art Here," *New York Times,* 6 February 1964.

81. John Martin, "Century Yields to Kabuki Troupe: Japanese Dancers in Ancient Drama-Music Presentation Impressive in Opening," *New York Times,* 19 February 1954.

82. Mel Gussow, "Theater: All-Male, Japanese 'Medea,'" *New York Times,* 5 September 1986.

83. Mel Gussow, "Universality of 'Macbeth' in Japanese," *New York Times,* 22 October 1990.

84. Jon Pareles, "New Voices from Japan: Improvised Sounds at the Japan Society," *New York Times,* 15 May 2006.

85. Anthony Tommasini, "Created on the Computer, but Pristine It Is Not: 'Onkyo Marathon,' Japan Society," *New York Times,* 4 April 2005.

86. B. H. Haggin, "Music," *Nation,* 13 March 1954.

87. William Malm, "Japanese Ensemble Gives New Life to an Old Tradition," *New York Times,* 4 May 1986.

88. John Rockwell, "Opening the Ears to the Exciting Soundscape of World Music," *New York Times,* 10 September 2004.

89. John Rockwell, "Music: Shamisen Solo and Hayashi Ensemble," *New York Times,* 20 September 1981.

90. Bernard Holland, "Crossing Cultures and Blending Textures: Music From Japan, the Asia Society," *New York Times,* 27 February 1995.

91. Tetsuo Kishi and Graham Bradshaw, *Shakespeare in Japan* (New York: Continuum, 2005), 84.

92. Clive Barnes, "Theater: Bunraku Puppets Appear at City Center—3 Classic Plays Given by Japanese Troupe," *New York Times,* 16 March 1966.

93. Clive Barnes, "The Theater: An Avant-Garde Japanese Musical," *New York Times,* 24 October 1973.

94. Don McDonagh, "Japanese Dances Vividly Performed," *New York Times,* 10 November 1967.

95. Harold Clurman, "Theatre," *Nation,* 29 September 1969.

96. John Rockwell, "Campora Sings with City Opera," *New York Times,* 23 October 1973. This was the incorrect title of a review of a performance by the Shingon Buddhist Monks at the Brooklyn Academy of Music.

97. "Samurai Saga," *Time,* 19 September 1969.

98. Anna Kisselgoff, "Dance: Festival Enjoys Visit of Japan's Moderns," *New York Times,* 10 July 1982.

99. Anna Kisselgoff, "Turn (Biff!) and Spin (Shazam!)," *New York Times,* 10 February 2000.

100. John Rockwell, "The Enigmas, the Oddities: What to Make of Dance from Japan," *New York Times,* 20 January 2006.

101. J. Thomas Rimer, "Metamorphosis from a Distance," *Theatre Journal* 59, no. 3 (2007): 367.

102. Anita Gates, "Returning to New York to Retell an Ancient Tale," *New York Times,* 25 October 2008.

Chapter 7

1. Yoshio Sugimoto, *An Introduction to Japanese Society,* 3d ed. (New York: Cambridge University Press, 2010), 16.

2. Stephen Greenblatt, "Cultural Mobility: An Introduction," in Stephen Greenblatt, with Ines G. Županov, Reinhard Meyer-Kalkus, Heike Paul, Pál Nyíri, and Friederike Pannewick, *Cultural Mobility: A Manifesto* (New York: Cambridge University Press, 2010), 1–3.

3. As noted in the "Introduction," Zorn's concerts may have been the most visible expression on the part of the New York performing arts community of goodwill and generosity toward Japan immediately following the March 2011 catastrophes there, but it is important to point out that many other organizations and individuals associated with the theater, dance, and music worlds also held fund-raisers. A noteworthy example is "SHINSAI: Theatres for Japan," a project that came to fruition in March 2012. (*Shinsai* means "earthquake" in Japanese.) The idea of New York–based actor James Yaegashi, who is from the affected area in northeastern Japan, the fund-raiser took root first in New York and soon came to include scores of artists and dozens of theaters around the United States and

in several other countries. See "SHINSAI: Theaters for Japan," http://www.tcg.org/shinsai/ (accessed 6 April 2012).

4. Carnegie Hall Festivals, *JapanNYC: Music and Arts from Today's Japan—Over 65 Events Citywide on Sale Now* (New York: Carnegie Hall, 2010), 8.

5. Carnegie Hall Festivals, *JapanNYC,* inside front cover.

6. David Novak, *Japanoise: Music at the Edge of Circulation* (Durham: Duke University Press, forthcoming).

7. James R. Oestreich, "Carnegie Unveils Music Education Program," *New York Times,* 25 March 2011. Prior festivals have focused on Berlin, African Americans, Leonard Bernstein, and China. See Daniel J. Wakin, "Ozawa and James Taylor to Headline Carnegie Season," *New York Times,* 27 January 2010.

8. Winner of prestigious competitions for student conductors in the 1950s, Ozawa was invited by Leonard Bernstein to become an assistant conductor of the New York Philharmonic while still in his mid-twenties. He has conducted and served as music director of orchestras around the world, including the Boston Symphony Orchestra, with which he was associated for almost thirty years.

9. Carnegie Hall Festivals, *JapanNYC,* 3.

10. Allan Kozinn, "Calligraphy Made of Sound," *New York Times,* 24 March 2011.

11. Carnegie Hall Festivals, *JapanNYC,* 17.

12. Carnegie Hall Festivals, *JapanNYC,* 18.

13. James R. Oestreich, "In Japan, a Frail Ozawa Conducts Only One Tchaikovsky Movement," *New York Times,* 6 September 2010.

14. James R. Oestreich, "Japanese Musicians Still Turn to the West," *New York Times,* 12 September 2010.

15. James R. Oestreich, "Ozawa's Illness Shadows Festival He Inspired," *New York Times,* 10 December 2010.

16. Anthony Tommasini, "Leader and Players, Deeply Bound," *New York Times,* 16 December 2010.

17. Carnegie Hall Festivals, *JapanNYC,* 19.

18. Roslyn Sulcas, "Poetry of Stillness, in a Moment Stretched to Infinity," *New York Times,* 30 March 2011.

19. Carnegie Hall Festivals, *JapanNYC,* 23.

20. "National Endowment for the Arts Jazz Masters," http://www.nea.gov/honors/jazz/jmCMS/master.php?id=2007_01&type=bio (accessed 3 May 2012).

21. Ben Ratliff, "Remembering Hiroshima, in a Farewell Performance," *New York Times,* 21 October 2003.

22. Leslie Rubinstein, "Oriental Musicians Come of Age," *New York Times,* 23 November 1980.

23. Shawn Bender, "Drumming from Screen to Stage: Ondekoza's *Ōdaiko* and the Reimaging of Japanese Taiko," *Journal of Asian Studies* 69, no. 3 (2010): 843.

24. Zachary Woolfe, "Strum, Pluck, Rescue, Rebuild," *New York Times,* 11 April 2011.

25. Ellie M. Hisama, "John Zorn and the Postmodern Condition," in *Locating East Asia in Western Art Music,* ed. Yayoi Uno Everett and Frederick Lau (Middletown, CT: Wesleyan University Press, 2004), 72.

26. Hisama, "John Zorn," 76.

27. Elliot Levin, "X Japan Enthralls the Roseland Ballroom," *New York Examiner,* 11 October 2010 (http://www.examiner.com/hard-rock-music-in-new-york/x-japan-enthralls-the-roseland-ballroom [accessed 9 April 2012]).

28. Roslyn Sulcas, "From Japan, a Reminder That We Are Dust, and to Dust We Return," *New York Times,* 6 October 2010.

29. Steve Smith, Vivien Schweitzer, and Allan Kozinn, "Music in Review: Music From Japan," *New York Times,* 16 February 2011.

30. Edward Rothstein, "A Violinist Tests Limits in Music of Her Times," *New York Times,* 21 April 1994.

31. "Mari Kimura: Biography," http://www.marikimura.com/Site_2/biography.html (accessed 9 April 2012). See also Matthew Gurewitsch, "For a Violinist, Success Means a New Low Point, *New York Times,* 13 May 2011.

32. Quoted in Rothstein, "A Violinist Tests Limits."

33. Mari Kimura, "Curator's Note," in program booklet for Music From Japan, Festival 2009, Merkin Concert Hall at Kaufman Center, New York.

34. Deborah Wong, *Speak it Louder: Asian Americans Making Music* (New York: Routledge, 2004), 215.

35. Midori Yoshimoto, *Into Performance: Japanese Women Artists in New York* (New Brunswick, NJ: Rutgers University Press, 2005), 4.

36. John Martin, "Century Yields to Kabuki Troupe: Japanese Dancers in Ancient Drama-Music Presentation Impressive in Opening," *New York Times,* 19 February 1954.

37. John S. Wilson, "Music: Undampened Jazz," *New York Times,* 6 July 1956.

38. "Music: Jazz Import," *Time,* 26 August 1957.

39. Allen Hughes, "Koto: Reiko Kamata," *New York Times,* 26 April 1981.

40. Harold Schonberg, "Championing Japanese Music," *New York Times,* 21 February 1982.

41. Harold Schonberg, "Music: Japanese Philharmonic Arrives: Group, Although Young, Is Cosmopolitan," *New York Times,* 12 October 1964.

42. Steven C. Ridgely, *Japanese Counterculture: The Antiestablishment Art of Terayama Shūji* (Minneapolis: University of Minnesota Press, 2010), ix–x.

43. Anna Kisselgoff, "Dance Review: Japanese Women Wear Red and Vent in Controlled Mayhem," *New York Times,* 10 January 2005.

44. Novak, *Japanoise,* forthcoming.

45. Phillip Vannini and J. Patrick Williams, "Authenticity in Culture, Self, and Society," in *Authenticity in Culture, Self, and Society,* ed. Phillip Vannini and J. Patrick Williams (Burlington, VT: Ashgate, 2009), 5.

46. Mansai Nomura, "Foreword," in Ronald Cavaye, Paul Griffith, and Akihiko Senda, *A Guide to the Japanese Stage: From Traditional to Cutting Edge* (New York: Kodansha International, 2004), 17.

47. The profile of Stewart on the Praemium Imperiale website notes that she has "long been a champion of Asian performing artists." It specifically refers to the invitations she extended to Shuji Terayama and Yutaka Higashi to present their work at La MaMa starting in 1970. "Praemium Imperiale: Ellen Stewart," http://www.praemiumimperiale.org/en/laureate/theatrefilm/item/40-stewart (accessed 9 April 2012).

Select Bibliography

The following list is limited mostly to scholarly works. The endnotes provide full information on all works cited in the text.

Anderson, Joseph L. *Enter a Samurai: Kawakami Otojirō and Japanese Theatre in the West*, vol. 1. Tucson: Wheatmark, 2011.

Atkins, E. Taylor. *Blue Nippon: Authenticating Jazz in Japan*. Durham: Duke University Press, 2001.

Banes, Sally. *Greenwich Village, 1963: Avant-Garde Performance and the Effervescent Body*. Durham: Duke University Press, 1993.

Banes, Sally. "Introduction." In *Reinventing Dance in the 1960s: Everything Was Possible*, edited by Sally Banes, xiii–xvi. Madison: University of Wisconsin Press, 2003.

Bassnett-McGuire, Susan. *Translation Studies*. New York: Routledge, 1991.

Bender, Shawn. "Drumming from Screen to Stage: Ondekoza's *Ōdaiko* and the Reimaging of Japanese Taiko." *Journal of Asian Studies* 69, no. 3 (2010): 843–67.

Bender, Shawn. *Taiko Boom: Japanese Drumming in Place and Motion*. Berkeley: University of California Press, 2012.

Benfey, Christopher. *The Great Wave: Gilded Age Misfits, Japanese Eccentrics, and the Opening of Old Japan*. New York: Random House, 2003.

Blumner, Holly A., Julie A. Iezzi, Alice E. Luhrmann, and Kathy Welch, eds. *101 Years of Kabuki in Hawai'i*. Honolulu: Department of Theatre and Dance, University of Hawai'i at Manoa, 1995.

Bottoms, Stephen J. *Playing Underground: A Critical History of the 1960s Off-Off-Broadway Movement*. Ann Arbor: University of Michigan Press, 2004.

Bourdieu, Pierre. *Distinction: A Social Critique of the Judgement of Taste*, translated by Richard Nice. Cambridge: Harvard University Press, 1984.

Bowers, Faubion. *Japanese Theatre*. New York: Hill and Wang, 1952.

Boyd, Mari. *The Aesthetics of Quietude: Ōta Shōgo and the Theatre of Divestiture*. Tokyo: Sophia University Press, 2006.

Brandon, James R. *Kabuki's Forgotten War, 1931–1945*. Honolulu: University of Hawai'i Press, 2009.

Brandon, James R. "Myth and Reality: A Story of *Kabuki* during American Censorship, 1945–1949." *Asian Theatre Journal* 23, no. 1 (2006): 1–110.

Burkman, Thomas W., ed. *The Occupation of Japan: Arts and Culture—The Proceedings of the Sixth Symposium Sponsored by The MacArthur Memorial, Old Dominion University, The General Douglas MacArthur Foundation, 18–19 October 1984*. Norfolk: General Douglas MacArthur Foundation, 1988.

Carlson, Marvin. *Speaking in Tongues: Language at Play in the Theatre.* Ann Arbor: University of Michigan Press, 2006.

Cavaye, Ronald, Paul Griffith, and Akihiko Senda. *A Guide to the Japanese Stage: From Traditional to Cutting Edge.* New York: Kodansha International, 2004.

Chuh, Kandice, and Karen Shimakawa. "Introduction: Mapping Studies in the Asian Diaspora." In *Orientations: Mapping Studies in the Asian Diaspora,* edited by Kandice Chuh and Karen Shimakawa, 1–21. Durham: Duke University Press, 2001.

Clark, Steven. "Terayama in Amsterdam and the Internationalization of Experimental Theatre." In *Modern Japanese Theatre and Performance,* edited by David Jortner, Keiko McDonald, and Kevin J. Wetmore Jr., 109–21. New York: Lexington Books, 2006.

Dower, John W. *Embracing Defeat: Japan in the Wake of World War II.* New York: W. W. Norton, 1999.

Dower, John W. "Foreword." In Takeshi Matsuda, *Soft Power and Its Perils: U.S. Cultural Policy in Early Postwar Japan and Permanent Dependency,* xiii–xvi. Washington, DC: Woodrow Wilson Center Press; Stanford: Stanford University Press, 2007.

Everett, Yayoi Uno. "Intercultural Synthesis in Postwar Western Art Music: Historical Contexts, Perspectives, and Taxonomy." In *Locating East Asia in Western Art Music,* edited by Yayoi Uno Everett and Frederick Lau, 1–21. Middletown, CT: Wesleyan University Press, 2004.

Fujita, Yuiko. *Cultural Migrants from Japan: Youth, Media, and Migration in New York and London.* New York: Lexington Books, 2009.

Fukunaka, Kotoko. *Ongaku, michi e no tabi: "Myūjikku furomu japan ongakusai" kuronikuru* [Into the unknown with music: A chronicle of the "Music From Japan concert series"]. Kawasaki: Kozuikikaku, 2011.

Garfias, Robert. *Gagaku: The Music and Dances of the Japanese Imperial Household,* edited by Lincoln Kirstein. New York: Theatre Arts Books, 1959.

Gentzler, Edwin, and Maria Tymoczko. "Introduction." In *Translation and Power,* edited by Maria Tymoczko and Edwin Gentzler, xi–xxviii. Boston: University of Massachusetts Press, 2002.

Gillespie, John K. "Ninagawa Yukio." In *Encyclopedia of Asian Theatre,* edited by Samuel L. Leiter, vol. 1, 464–65. Westport, CT: Greenwood Press, 2007.

Goodman, David G. "*Angura:* Japan's Nostalgic Avant-Garde." In *Not the Other Avant-Garde: The Transnational Foundations of Avant-Garde Performance,* edited by James M. Harding and John Rouse, 250–64. Ann Arbor: University of Michigan Press, 2006.

Gordon, Beate Sirota. *The Only Woman in the Room: A Memoir.* New York: Kodansha International, 1997.

Goto, Shizuo. "Bunraku." *Gekkan bunkazai* [Cultural treasures monthly] 275 (1986): 14–20.

Graham-Jones, Jean. "Editorial Comment: The Stakes of Theatrical Translation." *Theatre Journal* 59, no. 3 (2007): ix–xiii.

Greenblatt, Stephen. "Cultural Mobility: An Introduction." In Stephen Greenblatt, with Ines G. Županov, Reinhard Meyer-Kalkus, Heike Paul, Pál Nyíri, and Friederike Pannewick, *Cultural Mobility: A Manifesto,* 1–23. New York: Cambridge University Press, 2010.

Grossberg, Kenneth A., ed. *Japan Today.* Philadelphia: Institute for the Study of Human Issues, 1981.

Hannerz, Ulf. *Transnational Connections: Culture, People, Places.* New York: Routledge, 1996.

Harootunian, H. D. "America's Japan/Japan's Japan." In *Japan in the World,* edited by Masao Miyoshi and H. D. Harootunian, 196–221. Durham: Duke University Press, 1993.

Harr, John Ensor, and Peter J. Johnson. *The Rockefeller Conscience: An American Family in Public and in Private.* New York: Charles Scribner's Sons, 1991.

Havens, Thomas R. H. *Artist and Patron in Postwar Japan: Dance, Music, Theater, and the Visual Arts, 1955–1980.* Princeton: Princeton University Press, 1982.

Havens, Thomas R. H. *Radicals and Realists in the Japanese Nonverbal Arts: The Avant-Garde Rejection of Modernism.* Honolulu: University of Hawai'i Press, 2006.

Heale, M. J. "Anatomy of a Scare: Yellow Peril Politics in America, 1980–1993." *Journal of American Studies* 43, no. 1 (2009): 19–47.

Hisama, Ellie M. "John Zorn and the Postmodern Condition." In *Locating East Asia in Western Art Music,* edited by Yayoi Uno Everett and Frederick Lau, 72–84. Middletown, CT: Wesleyan University Press, 2004.

Homberger, Eric. *New York City: A Cultural and Literary Companion.* Oxford: Signal Books, 2002.

Ichikawa, Ichiro. "Kabuki no kaigai kōen are kore" [Some thoughts on kabuki productions abroad]. *Gekkan bunkazai* [Cultural treasures monthly] 275 (1986): 12.

Imamura, Tadazumi. "Introduction to *Yabuhara, the Blind Master Minstrel,*" translated by Marguerite Wells. In *Half a Century of Japanese Theater VI: 1960s, Part 1,* edited by Japan Playwrights Association, 63–67. Tokyo: Kinokuniya, 2004.

Ivy, Marilyn. *Discourses of the Vanishing: Modernity, Phantasm, Japan.* Chicago: University of Chicago Press, 1995.

Kano, Ayako. *Acting Like a Woman in Modern Japan: Theater, Gender, and Nationalism.* New York: Palgrave, 2001.

Karp, Ivan. "Culture and Representation." In *Exhibiting Cultures: The Poetics and*

Politics of Museum Display, edited by Ivan Karp and Steven D. Lavine, 11–24. Washington, DC: Smithsonian Institution Press, 1991.

Kawatake, Toshio. "Kabuki no kaigai kōryū" [Overseas exchange of kabuki]. *Gekkan bunkazai* [Cultural treasures monthly] 201 (1980): 4–11.

Kawatake, Toshio. "Kaigai kōen sanjū-nen" [Thirty years of presentations abroad]. *Engekikai* [Drama world] 42, no. 9 (1984): 74–77.

Kearney, Amanda. "Intangible Cultural Heritage: Global Awareness and Local Interest." In *Intangible Heritage,* edited by Laurajane Smith and Natsuko Akagawa, 209–25. New York: Routledge, 2009.

Kelsky, Karen. *Women on the Verge: Japanese Women, Western Dreams.* Durham: Duke University Press, 2001.

Kirshenblatt-Gimblett, Barbara. "Intangible Heritage as Metacultural Production" *Museum* 56, nos. 1–2 (2004): 52–65.

Kirstein, Lincoln. "Foreword." In Robert Garfias, *Gagaku: The Music and Dances of the Japanese Imperial Household,* edited by Lincoln Kirstein, unpaginated. New York: Theatre Arts Books, 1959.

Kishi, Tetsuo, and Graham Bradshaw. *Shakespeare in Japan.* New York: Continuum, 2005.

Klein, Christina. *Cold War Orientalism: Asia in the Middlebrow Imagination, 1945–1961.* Berkeley: University of California Press, 2003.

Kodama, Makoto. "Nō." *Gekkan bunkazai* [Cultural treasures monthly] 275 (1986): 24–28.

Kominz, Laurence. "Introduction." In *Mishima on Stage:* The Black Lizard *and Other Plays,* edited by Laurence Kominz, 1–65. Ann Arbor: Center for Japanese Studies, University of Michigan, 2007.

Kominz, Laurence, ed. *Mishima on Stage:* The Black Lizard *and Other Plays.* Ann Arbor: Center for Japanese Studies, University of Michigan, 2007.

Kubo, Kazuaki. "Kokusai Kōryū Kikin ga okonatta dentō geinō no kaigai kōryū" [Overseas exchange of the traditional performing arts carried out by the Japan Foundation]. *Gekkan bunkazai* [Cultural treasures monthly] 275 (1986): 44–46.

Lavine, Steven D., and Ivan Karp. "Introduction: Museums and Multiculturalism." In *Exhibiting Cultures: The Poetics and Politics of Museum Display,* edited by Ivan Karp and Steven D. Lavine, 1–9. Washington, DC: Smithsonian Institution Press, 1991.

Leheny, David. "A Narrow Place to Cross Swords: Soft Power and the Politics of Japanese Popular Culture in East Asia." In *Beyond Japan: The Dynamics of East Asian Regionalism,* edited by Peter J. Katzenstein and Takashi Shiraishi, 211–33. Ithaca: Cornell University Press, 2006.

Leiter, Samuel L. "The Good Censors: Evading the Threat to Postwar *Kabuki.*" In *Rising from the Flames: The Rebirth of Theater in Occupied Japan, 1945–1952,* edited by Samuel L. Leiter, 89–107. New York: Lexington Books, 2009.

Leiter, Samuel L. "When *Theatre Arts* Looked Eastward: Japan's Reception in America's Leading Theatre Periodical (1916–64)." In *Japanese Theatre and the*

International Stage, edited by Stanca Scholz-Cionca and Samuel L. Leiter, 59–77. Boston: Brill, 2001.

Logan, Joshua. "Foreword." In Faubion Bowers, *Japanese Theatre,* v–vii. New York: Hill and Wang, 1952.

Logan, William S., and Laurajane Smith. "Series General Co-editors' Foreword." In *Intangible Heritage,* edited by Laurajane Smith and Natsuko Akagawa, xii–xiii. New York: Routledge, 2009.

Lonergan, Patrick. *Theatre and Globalization: Irish Drama in the Celtic Tiger Era.* New York: Palgrave Macmillan, 2009.

Madsen, Patricia. "*The Man from the East* by Stomu Yamash'ta." *Educational Theatre Journal* 25, no. 2 (1973): 241–42.

Marcus, Daniel. *Happy Days and Wonder Years: The Fifties and the Sixties in Contemporary Cultural Politics.* New Brunswick, NJ: Rutgers University Press, 2004.

Matsuda, Takeshi. *Soft Power and Its Perils: U.S. Cultural Policy in Early Postwar Japan and Permanent Dependency.* Washington, DC: Woodrow Wilson Center Press; Stanford: Stanford University Press, 2007.

Mayo, Marlene J. "To Be or Not to Be: Kabuki and Cultural Politics in Occupied Japan." In *War, Occupation, and Creativity: Japan and East Asia, 1920–1960,* edited by Marlene J. Mayo and J. Thomas Rimer, 269–309. Honolulu: University of Hawai'i Press, 2001.

McGray, Douglas. "Japan's Gross National Cool." *Foreign Policy* 130 (May–June 2002): 44–54.

Minor, William. *Jazz Journeys to Japan: The Heart Within.* Ann Arbor: University of Michigan Press, 2004.

Miura, Hiroko. *Nōgaku nyūmon (1): Hajimete no nō/kyōgen* [Introduction to noh (1): Seeing noh and kyogen for the first time]. Tokyo: Shogakkan, 1999.

Miyagawa, Chiori. "Artistic Statement: Chiori Miyagawa." In *Global Foreigners: An Anthology of Plays,* edited by Carol Martin and Saviana Stanescu, 262–63. New York: Seagull Books, 2006.

Miyagawa, Chiori, and Caridad Svich. "Communing with Culture: Chiori Miyagawa in Conversation with Caridad Svich." In *Trans-global Readings: Crossing Theatrical Boundaries,* edited by Caridad Svich, 104–9. New York: Manchester University Press, 2003.

Miyamoto, Amon. *Araibu: Boku ga ikiru imi o mitsukeru made* [Alive: Until I find the meaning of life]. Tokyo: Nihon Hoso Shuppan Kyokai, 2001.

Miyoshi, Masao. *Off Center: Power and Culture Relations between Japan and the United States.* Cambridge: Harvard University Press, 1991.

Miyoshi, Masao, and H. D. Harootunian. "Japan in the World." In *Japan in the World,* edited by Masao Miyoshi and H. D. Harootunian, 1–9. Durham: Duke University Press, 1993.

Moeller, Susan D. "Pictures of the Enemy: Fifty Years of Images of Japan in the American Press, 1941–1992." *Journal of American Culture* 19, no. 1 (1996): 29–42.

Mogi, Chikashi. "Kabuki." *Gekkan bunkazai* [Cultural treasures monthly] 275 (1986): 4–10.

Mogi, Chikashi, ed. *Kabuki kaigai kōen no kiroku* [A history of kabuki productions abroad]. Tokyo: Shochiku, 1992.

Munroe, Alexandra. "A Continent Away: Japanese Artists in New York City." *Winds,* August 1986: 43–51.

Myers, Fred. "The Complicity of Cultural Production: The Contingencies of Performance in Globalizing Museum Practices." In *Museum Frictions: Public Cultures/Global Transformations,* edited by Ivan Karp, Corinne A. Kratz, Lynn Szwaja, and Tomás Ybarra-Frausto, with Gustavo Buntinx, Barbara Kirshenblatt-Gimblett, and Ciraj Rassool, 504–35. Durham: Duke University Press, 2006.

Myers, Maria. "Terayama's *Directions to Servants.*" *TDR: The Drama Review* 25, no. 1 (1981): 79–94.

Nishi, Kazuyoshi, and Matsuda Tamotsu, eds. *Nōgaku kaigai kōen shiyō* [A history of noh productions abroad]. Tokyo: Kinseisha, 1988.

Nishido, Kojin. *Engeki wa kanō ka: 1995nen igo no gekiteki sōzōryoku* [Is drama possible? The dramatic imagination after 1995]. Tokyo: Bansei Shobo, 2008.

Nomura, Mansai. "Foreword." In Ronald Cavaye, Paul Griffith, and Akihiko Senda, *A Guide to the Japanese Stage: From Traditional to Cutting Edge,* 17–19. New York: Kodansha International, 2004.

Nomura, Mansai. *Mansai de gozaru* [I am Mansai]. Tokyo: Asahi Shinbunsha, 1999.

Nomura, Mansaku. "Kyōgen no kaigai kōryū" [Overseas exchange of kyogen]. *Gekkan bunkazai* [Cultural treasures monthly] 275 (1986): 30.

Nomura, Mansaku. *Tarōkaja o ikiru* [To live as Tarokaja]. Tokyo: Hakusuisha, 1984.

Norikoshi, Takao. *Hyper: Kontenporarī dansu tettei gaido* [Hyper: Contemporary dance perfect guidebook]. Tokyo: Sakuhinsha, 2003.

Novak, David. *Japanoise: Music at the Edge of Circulation.* Durham: Duke University Press, forthcoming.

Nye, Joseph S. *Bound to Lead: The Changing Nature of American Power.* New York: Basic Books, 1990.

Okamoto, Shiro. *The Man Who Saved* Kabuki: *Faubion Bowers and Theatre Censorship in Occupied Japan,* translated and adapted by Samuel L. Leiter. Honolulu: University of Hawai'i Press, 2001.

Ong, Aihwa. *Flexible Citizenship: The Cultural Logics of Transnationality.* Durham: Duke University Press, 1999.

Ortolani, Benito, and Samuel L. Leiter, eds. *Zeami and the Nō Theatre in the World.* New York: Center for Advanced Studies in Theatre Arts, Graduate School and University Center of the City University of New York, 1998.

Oshida, Yoshihisa. "Gagaku." *Gekkan bunkazai* [Cultural treasures monthly] 275 (1986): 32–39.

Poulton, M. Cody. *A Beggar's Art: Scripting Modernity in Japanese Drama, 1900–1930.* Honolulu: University of Hawai'i Press, 2010.

Poulton, M. Cody. "Foreign or Domestic Drama? Osanai Kaoru and Modern

Japanese Theatre." In *Text and Presentation, 2006,* edited by Stratos E. Constantinidis, Comparative Drama Conference Series, no. 3, 167–81. Jefferson, NC: McFarland, 2007.

Poulton, M. Cody. "The Rhetoric of the Real." In *Modern Japanese Theatre and Performance,* edited by David Jortner, Keiko McDonald, and Kevin J. Wetmore Jr., 17–31. New York: Lexington Books, 2006.

Powell, Brian. *Japan's Modern Theatre: A Century of Change and Continuity.* London: Japan Library, Routledge Curzon, 2002.

Powell, Brian. Review of J. Thomas Rimer, *Toward a Modern Japanese Theatre: Kishida Kunio. Monumenta Nipponica* 30, no. 1 (1975): 98–100.

Pratt, Mary Louise. *Imperial Eyes: Travel Writing and Transculturation.* New York: Routledge, 1992.

Pronko, Leonard Cabell. *Theater East and West: Perspectives toward a Total Theater.* Berkeley: University of California Press, 1967.

Rath, Eric C. "Dance in Theatre: Japan." In *Encyclopedia of Asian Theatre,* edited by Samuel L. Leiter, vol. 1, 148–49. Westport, CT: Greenwood Press, 2007.

Reischauer, Edwin O. *Japan Society, 1907–1982: 75 Years of Partnership across the Pacific.* New York: Japan Society, 1982.

Richie, Donald, and Miyoko Watanabe, trans. *Six Kabuki Plays.* Tokyo: Hokuseido Press, 1963.

Ridgely, Steven C. *Japanese Counterculture: The Antiestablishment Art of Terayama Shūji.* Minneapolis: University of Minnesota Press, 2010.

Rimer, J. Thomas. "Metamorphosis from a Distance." *Theatre Journal* 59, no. 3 (2007): 366–69.

Robertson, Jennifer. *Takarazuka: Sexual Politics and Popular Culture in Modern Japan.* Berkeley: University of California Press, 1998.

Robinson, Harlow. *The Last Impresario: The Life, Times, and Legacy of Sol Hurok.* New York: Viking Penguin, 1994.

Rodgers, Tara. *Pink Noises: Women on Electronic Music and Sound.* Durham: Duke University Press, 2010.

Rolf, Robert T., and John K. Gillespie, eds. *Alternative Japanese Drama: Ten Plays.* Honolulu: University of Hawai'i Press, 1992.

Rosenthal, Cindy. "Ellen Stewart: La MaMa of Us All," *TDR: The Drama Review* 50, no. 2 (2006): 12–51.

Sakai, Naoki. "Modernity and Its Critique: The Problem of Universalism and Particularism." In *Postmodernism and Japan,* edited by Masao Miyoshi and H. D. Harootunian, 93–122. Durham: Duke University Press, 1989.

Sassen, Saskia. "Analytic Borderlands: Race, Gender, and Representation in the New City." In *Re-presenting the City: Ethnicity, Capital, and Culture in the 21st-Century Metropolis,* edited by Anthony D. King, 183–202. New York: New York University Press, 1996.

Sato, Hiroaki, trans. My Friend Hitler *and Other Plays of Yukio Mishima.* New York: Columbia University Press, 2002.

Scholz-Cionca, Stanca, and Samuel L. Leiter. "Preface." In *Japanese Theatre and the International Stage,* edited by Stanca Scholz-Cionca and Samuel L. Leiter, ix–x. Boston: Brill, 2001.

Senda, Akihiko. "Contemporary Theater." In Ronald Cavaye, Paul Griffith, and Akihiko Senda, *A Guide to the Japanese Stage: From Traditional to Cutting Edge,* 207–58. New York: Kodansha International, 2004.

Senda, Akihiko. "Japanese Theater in Transformation, 1960–1970," translated by Mari Boyd. In *Half a Century of Japanese Theater VI: 1960s, Part 1,* edited by Japan Playwrights Association, 1–15. Tokyo: Kinokuniya, 2004.

Shibusawa, Naoko. *America's Geisha Ally: Reimagining the Japanese Enemy.* Cambridge: Harvard University Press, 2006.

Shields, Nancy K. *Fake Fish: The Theater of Kobo Abe.* New York: Weatherhill, 1996.

Shochiku Company, ed. *Grand Kabuki: Overseas Tours, 1928–1993.* Tokyo: Shochiku, 1994.

Smith, Laurajane. *Uses of Heritage.* New York: Routledge, 2006.

Sorgenfrei, Carol Fisher. *Unspeakable Acts: The Avant-Garde Theatre of Terayama Shūji and Postwar Japan.* Honolulu: University of Hawai'i Press, 2005.

Stein, Bonnie Sue. "Butoh: 'Twenty Years Ago We Were Crazy, Dirty, and Mad.'" *TDR: The Drama Review* 30, no. 2 (1986): 107–26.

Stevens, Carolyn S. *Japanese Popular Music: Culture, Authenticity, and Power.* New York: Routledge, 2008.

Sugimoto, Yoshio. *An Introduction to Japanese Society,* 3d ed. New York: Cambridge University Press, 2010.

Szwaja, Lynn, and Tomás Ybarra-Frausto. "Foreword." In *Museum Frictions: Public Cultures/Global Transformations,* edited by Ivan Karp, Corinne A. Kratz, Lynn Szwaja, and Tomás Ybarra-Frausto, with Gustavo Buntinx, Barbara Kirshenblatt-Gimblett, and Ciraj Rassool, xi–xiv. Durham: Duke University Press, 2006.

Takahashi, Yasunari. "Alternative Japanese Drama: A Brief Overview." In *Alternative Japanese Drama: Ten Plays,* edited by Robert T. Rolf and John K. Gillespie, 1–9. Honolulu: University of Hawai'i Press, 1992.

Takahashi, Yasunari. "Introduction: Suzuki's Work in the Context of Japanese Theatre." In Ian Carruthers and Yasunari Takahashi, *The Theatre of Suzuki Tadashi,* 1–5. Cambridge: Cambridge University Press, 2004.

Tatsumi, Takayuki. *Full Metal Apache: Transactions between Cyberpunk Japan and Avant-Pop America.* Durham: Duke University Press, 2006.

Terasaki, Hironori. "Trends in the Japanese Theatrical World." *Asian Theatre Journal* 1, no. 1 (1984): 104–8.

Thornbury, Barbara E. *The Folk Performing Arts: Traditional Culture in Contemporary Japan.* Albany: State University of New York Press, 1997.

Thornbury, Barbara E. "The View from Japan: The Traditional Performing Arts as Cultural Ambassadors Abroad." In *Japanese Theatre and the International Stage,* edited by Stanca Scholz-Cionca and Samuel L. Leiter, 213–27. Boston: Brill, 2001.

Uchida, Yoichi. "The 1980s in the Context of Japanese Theater History," translated by Mari Boyd. In *Half a Century of Japanese Theater III: 1980s, Part 1*, edited by Japan Playwrights Association, 1–13. Tokyo: Kinokuniya, 2001.

Uchino, Tadashi. *Crucible Bodies: Postwar Japanese Performance from Brecht to the New Millennium.* New York: Seagull Books, 2009.

Vannini, Phillip, and J. Patrick Williams. "Authenticity in Culture, Self, and Society." In *Authenticity in Culture, Self, and Society,* edited by Phillip Vannini and J. Patrick Williams, 1–18. Burlington, VT: Ashgate, 2009.

Venuti, Lawrence. *The Translator's Invisibility: A History of Translation.* New York: Routledge, 1995.

Wetmore, Kevin J., Jr. "Modern Japanese Drama in English." *Asian Theatre Journal* 23, no. 1 (2006): 179–205.

Wetmore, Kevin J., Jr. "1954: Selling *Kabuki* to the West." *Asian Theatre Journal* 26, no. 1 (2009): 78–93.

Wong, Deborah. *Speak It Louder: Asian Americans Making Music.* New York: Routledge, 2004.

Yoon, Paul J. "Asian Masculinities and Parodic Possibility in Odaiko Solos and Filmic Representations." *Asian Music* 40, no. 1 (2009): 100–130.

Yoon, Paul J. "'She's Really Become Japanese Now!' Taiko Drumming and Asian American Identifications." *American Music* 19, no. 4 (2001): 417–38.

Yoshida, Minosuke. "Bunraku kaigai kōen no zuisō" [Reflections on bunraku productions abroad]. *Gekkan bunkazai* [Cultural treasures monthly] 275 (1986): 21.

Yoshihara, Mari. *Musicians from a Different Shore: Asians and Asian Americans in Classical Music.* Philadelphia: Temple University Press, 2007.

Yoshimoto, Midori. *Into Performance: Japanese Women Artists in New York.* New Brunswick, NJ: Rutgers University Press, 2005.

Yoshinaga, Junichi. "Minzoku geinō" [Folk performing arts]. *Gekkan bunkazai* [Cultural treasures monthly] 275 (1986): 40–43.

Index